*Forest Hydrology*

# FOREST
# HYDROLOGY

Columbia University Press

# RICHARD LEE

*New York*

Richard Lee is professor of forestry at West Virginia University.

Library of Congress Cataloging in Publication Data

Lee, Richard, 1926–
Forest hydrology.

Includes bibliographies and index.
1. Hydrology, Forest.   I. Title.
GB842.L43     551.4′8′09152     79-19542
ISBN 0-231-04718-5

*Title page photograph by Laiying Chong.*

7     6     5     4     3     2

COLUMBIA UNIVERSITY PRESS
NEW YORK   GUILDFORD, SURREY

*To Rosita*

# THE CONTENTS

# PRELIMINARY REMARKS

Water husbandry is a major concern of the professional forester; most accredited forestry schools now offer at least one formal course in hydrology, forest influences, or watershed management. Some of the primary textbooks and reference sources that have been used in teaching these subjects are listed under Selected Readings at the end of chapter 1; in the author's judgment, no single volume has been adequate. More often than not professors must assign readings from various sources; this practice is at best an inconvenience, and it suggests a more profound liability.

As a science develops it is important to define its essential nature and scope, to give it recognizable form and substance, and to place it in proper perspective with regard to related disciplines. But forest hydrology has not been clearly delineated, and forest hydrologists are prone to accept their science as a spurious conglomerate of engineering hydrology, climatology, geomorphology, soil science, plant physiology, and forest ecology. This is unfortunate because forest hydrology has become a distinct discipline; it is not simply the sum of dependent parts.

This text is an attempt to define the essential and unique characteristics of forest hydrology for undergraduates and other aspirants. The treatment is general enough to be of interest to all students of the earth sciences. The text was written with the idea that all learning is self-learning and that, as student thought processes are stimulated beyond the memorization syndrome, the class meeting becomes a dialogue among interested minds.

Chapter 1 is an introduction to the substance, importance, history, and nature of hydrologic sciences, and chapter 2 is a review of pertinent water properties, hydrologic processes, and the characteristics of natural catchment areas; chapters 3 to 7 discuss the quantitative aspects of forest hydrology in terms of water movements and transient storages in the forest ecosystem. Chapter 8, Water Quality, was written by Dr. William E. Sharpe (water quality specialist) and Dr. David R. DeWalle (forest hydrologist) of the Institute for Research on Land and Water Resources at the Pennsylvania State University; Special Topics and Hydrologic Observations are treated in chapters 9 and 10. Distance, area, volume, and mass are expressed in metric units, with pressure in millibars, temperature in degrees Celsius, and energy in calories; symbols with explanatory notes are listed separately preceding chapter 1, and additional elaboration is provided in the text.

The subject matter of *Forest Hydrology* is equivalent to that presented by the author in an upper-level undergraduate course at West Virginia University over a period of more than ten years; the material has been revised frequently in response to research findings and student reactions. Manuscript revisions were based in part on penetrating reviews by R. E. Behling, P. E. Black, D. G. Boyer, R. E. Dils, C. L. Dodson, A. R. Eschner, G. E. Hart, R. H. Hawkins, H. W. Rauch, E. W. Repa, and S. J. Tajchman; Dr. Tajchman and Dr. Ralph D. Rush provided mathematical verifications at several critical points. Line drawings were drafted by Virginia Swecker, and the manuscript was typed and proofed with exceptional care by Rosa Lee.

# SYMBOL LIST

$A$     Area: $A_c$ catchment; $A_h$ horizontal; $A_s$ surface
Advected vapor: $A_i$ inflow; $A_o$ outflow
$a_i$     Cross-sectional area, stream segment $i$
$\alpha$     Precipitation fraction evaporated during storm
Streamflow recession constant
$B$     Conduction
$BI$     Biotic index
$\beta$     Bowen ratio
$C$     Canopy storage capacity
Cloud cover fraction
Coefficient: mass transport; runoff; weir
Consumptive use
Contour length
$C_d$     Rainfall catch deficiency
$c$     Specific heat
$\gamma$     Psychrometer constant
$D$     Diffusivity; water vapor in air
Distance, depth
Drainage density
Raindrop heat
$D_m$     Diffusivity for unsaturated flow
$d$     Characteristic dimension; diameter; distance
$\delta$     Boundary layer depth: $\delta_c$ convection; $\delta_v$ evaporation
$E$     Evaporation: $E_i$ intercepted water; $E_p$ potential;
       $E_t$ transpiration
$E_m$     Snowmelt energy: $E_c$ convective; $E_l$ longwave radiation;
       $E_r$ raindrop heat; $E_s$ shortwave radiation; $E_v$ vapor
       condensation
$E_n$     Net energy to heat water

| | |
|---|---|
| $e$ | Vapor pressure: $e_a$ ambient ($e_z$ at height $z$); $e_s$ saturation ($e_{sz}$ at height $z$, $e_w$ at $T_w$) |
| $\epsilon$ | Emissivity coefficient: $\epsilon_a$ atmosphere; $\epsilon_s$ surface |
| | Porosity: $\epsilon_a$ aquifer; $\epsilon_s$ soil |
| $F$ | Infiltration |
| $f$ | Infiltration rate: $f_o$ initial; $f_c$ constant |
| | Fraction of forest |
| $f(T)$ | Temperature function |
| $g$ | Acceleration of gravity |
| $H$ | Convection |
| | Total catchment relief |
| $h$ | Head of water; height |
| | Relative humidity ratio |
| | Heat transfer coefficient: $h_b$ conduction; $h_c$ convection |
| $I$ | Contour interval |
| | Interception: $I_c$ canopy; $I_f$ litter |
| | Local heat index |
| | Radiative index |
| | Raindrop inclination angle |
| $i$ | Rainfall intensity |
| JTU | Jackson turbidity unit |
| $K$ | Turbulent transfer coefficient: $K_h$ convection; $K_v$ evaporation |
| $KE$ | Kinetic energy |
| $k$ | Hydraulic conductivity: $k_s$ saturated; $k_u$ unsaturated |
| | Infiltration constant |
| | Thermal conductivity |
| $L$ | Latent heat: $L_f$ fusion; $L_s$ sublimation; $L_v$ vaporization |
| | Length: catchment; overland flow; stream |
| | Longwave radiation: $L_i$ incoming; $L_o$ outgoing |
| | Subsurface flow: $L_i$ inflow; $L_o$ outflow |
| $l$ | Stomatal length |
| $M$ | Mass: soil; $M_d$ dye; $M_w$ water |
| | Meltwater depth: by $M_b$ conduction; $M_c$ convection; $M_l$ longwave radiation; $M_r$ raindrop heat; $M_s$ shortwave radiation; $M_v$ vapor condensation |
| $m$ | Raindrop mass |

| | |
|---|---|
| $m$ | Volume fraction soil moisture |
| $\mu$ | Viscosity of water |
| $N$ | Number: storms; streams |
| $n$ | Number: stations in network; indicator species |
| | Persistence period of cutting effect |
| | Roughness coefficient |
| | Stomatal density |
| $P$ | Catchment perimeter |
| | Precipitation: $P_a$ from advected moisture; $P_e$ effective; $P_i$ isohyetal mean; $P_m$ minimum for tree growth; $P_n$ normal or net; $P_o$ observed; $P_s$ station; $P_t$ true or Thiessen mean |
| $p$ | Barometric pressure |
| | Probability of occurrence |
| $Q$ | Discharge: $Q_b$ base flow; $Q_c$ control catchment; $Q_d$ stormflow; $Q_i$ inflow or interflow; $Q_o$ outflow or initial flow; $Q_p$ peak; $Q_s$ channel precipitation; $Q_t$ test catchment or at time $t$ |
| $q$ | Flow rate, porous media or stream segment |
| | Probability of nonoccurrence |
| | Snowpack thermal quality |
| | Specific humidity |
| $R$ | Hydraulic radius |
| | Hydrologic response: $R_p$ to precipitation; $R_q$ discharge |
| | Net radiation |
| | Ratio: $R_a$ area; $R_b$ bifurcation; $R_l$ length; $R_r$ relief; $R_s$ gradient |
| $r$ | Albedo, shortwave reflectivity |
| | Correlation coefficient |
| | Radius, root or stem |
| | Resistance: $r_a$ air; $r_c$ canopy; $r_s$ stomatal |
| $rh$ | Relative humidity: $rh_s$ soil air |
| $\rho$ | Absolute humidity: $\rho_a$ ambient; $\rho_i$ inlet; $\rho_o$ outlet; $\rho_s$ saturation; $\rho_v$ vapor |
| | Density: $\rho_{da}$ dry air; $\rho_{ma}$ moist air; $\rho_p$ snowpack; $\rho_s$ soil; $\rho_w$ water |
| $\rho c$ | Thermal capacity |

$S$      Aquifer: $S_r$ specific retention; $S_y$ specific yield
        Shortwave radiation: $S_b$ direct; $S_d$ diffuse; $S_p$ potential; $S_r$ reflected; $S_t$ global
        Slope: land, stream, energy gradient
        Stemflow
        Storage: soil moisture; $S_a$ by atmospheric advection; $S_{ea}$ increase in precipitable water; $S_t$ depth at time $t$

$s$      Catchment order (trunk stream)
        Hydraulic gradient
        Slope: $s_d$ depletion curve; $s_r$ retention curve
        Standard deviation
        Stomatal radius
        Surface tension

$\sigma$      Stefan-Boltzmann constant

$T$      Temperature: $T_a$ air; $T_b$ biotemperature; $T_c$ canopy; $T_d$ dew-point; $T_m$ weighted mean; $T_n$ normal; $T_r$ raindrop; $T_s$ surface; $T_w$ wet-bulb
        Throughfall: $T_v$ volume

$t$      Time interval: $t_c$ time of concentration; $t_p$ rainfall period; $t_r$ recurrence interval

$u$      Stream or catchment order
        Windspeed

$V$      Stream velocity
        Vaporization rate
        Volume: $V_a$ aggregate solids (aquifer); $V_r$ water retained (aquifer); $V_s$ solids (soil); $V_y$ drainage (aquifer)

$v$      Terminal velocity (raindrops)
        Velocity: $v_i$ stream segment

$\phi$      Infiltration index
        Latitude

$W$      Infiltration index
        Stream width
        Water withdrawal

$w$      Mixing ratio

$X$      Horizontal distance: $X_p$ half distance between trees

$Y$      Sediment yield

$Z$      Elevation

$z$      Vertical distance; height; depth

$\psi$      Water potential: $\psi_g$ gravity; $\psi_h$ hydraulic; $\psi_l$ leaf; $\psi_p$ pressure; $\psi_s$ soil; $\psi_u$ total for unsaturated flow; $\psi_v$ vapor

*Forest Hydrology*

*Of all the direct influences of the forest
the influence upon the supply of water in
streams and upon the regularity of their
flow is the most important in human economy.*

RAPHAEL ZON

# 1 HYDROLOGIC PERSPECTIVE

## 1.1. Planetary View

The earth is a wet planet. Its mass, distance from the sun, and rotational and orbital movements ensure that global water will exist in three phases and move incessantly, dissolving, eroding, and redistributing earth materials in the process of converting and transferring solar energy. Quantification of these phenomena on a planetary scale provides perspective for the study of more localized hydrologic events.

### 1.1.a. Captive Water

The earth's water exists entirely within a thin layer, the hydrosphere, that extends about one-thousandth of a global diameter above and beneath the surface. The hydrosphere contains about $1.4(10^{18})$ metric tons of water which, in the liquid phase, would be sufficient to cover the sphere to a depth of 2.7 km. Estimates of the distribution of water among solid, liquid, and gaseous phases, and in other categories, are listed in table 1.1; almost 98% occurs in liquid form, and only 2.6% of the total is freshwater.

The earth's freshwater, about $3.6(10^{16})$ metric tons, occurs primarily in solid form (table 1.2). Polar ice and glaciers account for 77.2% of the total, 22.4% occurs as groundwater and soil moisture, leaving only 0.4% in lakes, rivers, and the atmosphere. Atmospheric water, which as a liquid would be sufficient to cover the earth to a depth of 2.55 cm (precipitable water), is held captive by the force of gravity; it is replenished continuously by evaporation

Table 1.1. The Earth's Water
(adapted from Baumgartner and
Reichel, 1975)

| Category | Volume[a] (km$^3$) | Percent |
|---|---|---|
| *Solid* | 2.782 (10$^7$) | 2.010 |
| *Liquid* | 1.356 (10$^9$) | 97.989 |
| Oceans | 1.348 (10$^9$) | 97.390 |
| Land: subsurface | 8.062 (10$^6$) | 0.583 |
| Land: surface | 2.250 (10$^5$) | 0.016 |
| *Gas* | 1.300 (10$^4$) | 0.001 |
| *Total, all forms* | 1.384 (10$^9$) | 100.000 |
| Saline water | 1.348 (10$^9$) | 97.398 |
| Freshwater | 3.602 (10$^7$) | 2.602 |

[a]Volume expressed as equivalent in the liquid phase.

Table 1.2. The Earth's Freshwater
(adapted from Baumgartner and Reichel, 1975)

| Category | Volume[a] (km$^3$) | Percent |
|---|---|---|
| *Solid* | 2.782 (10$^7$) | 77.23 |
| *Liquid* | 8.187 (10$^6$) | 22.73 |
| Groundwater | 7.996 (10$^6$) | 22.20 |
| Soil moisture | 6.123 (10$^4$) | 0.17 |
| Lakes | 1.261 (10$^5$) | 0.35 |
| Rivers, hydrated, organic | 3.602 (10$^3$) | 0.01 |
| *Gas* | 1.300 (10$^4$) | 0.04 |
| *Total, all phases* | 3.602 (10$^7$) | 100.00 |

[a]Volume expressed as equivalent in the liquid phase.

from the surface, and reduced by precipitation—which represents the only naturally renewable source of freshwater on earth.

### 1.1.b. Water Movement

With the exception of life-related phenomena, water is by far the most visible of moving entities on earth; consider, e.g., clouds, precipitation, streams, ocean waves, waterfalls, avalanches, and geysers. Water also moves along less obvious pathways in oceanic and atmospheric currents, and in water-bearing strata (aquifers) within the earth's crust. Perhaps even more obscure are the movements of water among topographic elements, or in ecosystems where flows are alternatively impeded, diverted, and facilitated under the influence of biological mechanisms.

Water movement on a global scale can be described in terms of the exchanges that occur among land, ocean, and atmosphere. Table 1.3 lists the estimated annual totals of water inflows (+) and outflows (-) averaged for all land areas, oceans, and the entire globe. Precipitation ($P$) always takes a positive sign, evaporation ($E$) a negative sign, and discharge ($Q$) is negative for land and positive for oceans; this means that

$$P + E + Q = 0 \qquad\qquad 1.1$$

for the static condition (i.e., constant storage) implied by the data of table 1.1.

Both precipitation and evaporation for the earth amount to about $5(10^5)$ km$^3$/yr, or enough to cover the global surface to a depth of 973 mm; it follows that it would take about 28 centuries

Table 1.3. **Mean Annual Water Balance Components for the Earth (after Baumgartner and Reichel, 1975)**

| Item | Land | Ocean | Earth |
|---|---|---|---|
| Area ($10^6$ km$^2$) | 148.9 | 361.1 | 510.0 |
| Volume[a] ($10^3$ km$^3$) | | | |
|    Precipitation | 111 | 385 | 496 |
|    Evaporation | -71 | -425 | -496 |
|    Discharge | -40 | 40 | 0 |
| Mean Depth[a] (mm) | | | |
|    Precipitation | 745 | 1066 | 973 |
|    Evaporation | -477 | -1177 | -973 |
|    Discharge | -269 | 111 | 0 |

[a]Volumes and depths are expressed as equivalents in the liquid phase.

to cycle all of the earth's water, $1.4(10^9)$ km$^3$, through the atmospheric distillation process. Precipitation volume over the oceans is 3.5 times as great as over land, and evaporation volume is 6.0 times as great. Over land, precipitation exceeds evaporation by $4(10^4)$ km$^3$/yr—the total discharge of the earth's rivers and streams—which must be equal to the net influx of water vapor from oceans to land in atmospheric currents.

### 1.1.c. Energy Relations

Water exchanges on the global scale among elements of land, ocean, and atmosphere can be described in terms of equivalent energy fluxes. Evaporation requires the absorption of energy, as measured by the latent heat of vaporization ($L_v = 590$ cal/g at mean surface temperature), which is released when condensation occurs. This means that as water is transferred in the vapor phase (e.g., in atmospheric currents from ocean to land) it carries with it an equivalent flux of energy in the form of latent heat.

Energy fluxes per unit of surface area (expressed in kly/yr, 1 ly = 1 cal/cm$^2$) associated with water flows for land, oceans, and the entire earth are given in table 1.4. As an average for the planet, 57.4 kly/yr are absorbed in surface evaporation and released in atmospheric condensation; this represents about 80% of available energy (i.e., net radiation; see section 2.2.c) at the surface. Over oceans the energy absorbed in evaporation ($L_v E$) is greater than that released in condensation ($L_v P$), so there is a net loss or cool-

Table 1.4. **Energy Equivalents of Water Balance Components**

| Item | Land | Ocean | Earth |
|------|------|-------|-------|
| $L_v P$ (kly/yr) | 44.0 | 62.9 | 57.4 |
| $L_v E$ (kly/yr) | −28.1 | −69.4 | −57.4 |
| Net (kly/yr) | 15.9 | −6.5 | 0.0 |
| $R$ (kly/yr) | 49 | 82 | 72 |
| $L_v E/R$ (%) | −57.3 | −84.6 | −79.7 |

NOTE: $L_v P$, latent heat of precipitation; $L_v E$, latent heat of evaporation; $R$, net radiation (after Budyko, 1974).

ing effect; over land there is a net warming effect equal to about one-third of net radiation.

## 1.2. Water's Importance

Water near the surface of the earth is at once vital and commonplace, unusual and ubiquitous, convenient and destructive. The properties of water (section 2.1) give rise to its overt manifestations as a building material of living cells, a nourishing and cleansing agent, a universal solvent with exceptional mobility, a transport medium, the "great distributor," an energy carrier and regulator, the "great moderator" of climate, and an erosive and destructive force. Water has been called the "mysterious and eternal elixir of life," the "miracle of nature" (King, 1961), and the "mirror of science" (Davis and Day, 1961).

### 1.2.a. Vital Need

Life began in water, and a prerequisite for its continuance is that water be available in liquid form. Water is the bearer of life; it is the primary constituent of protoplasm—the only form of matter in which the phenomena of life are manifested. But water is not only the stuff of life, it is the home of living things; about 90% of all earth organisms (measured in mass or numbers) are immersed in liquid water, and the remainder, immersed in an ocean of water vapor, can draw liquid water from the land surface and substrata.

Water, as a mobile solvent, is a carrier of nutrients and gases to the cells of living organisms. In plants it is indispensable as a reagent in photosynthesis and hydrolytic processes, and in the maintenance of cell turgor; in animals it also serves as a cleansing agent, removing impurities and the byproducts of metabolism. The absorption, storage, and release of water by organisms are effective thermal regulators, mitigating unfavorable extremes of body temperature.

Organisms require a continuing supply of water. Humans need about 1 kg/day $\cdot$ m$^2$ of body surface area, or 1 to 2 liters/day for the average adult, to maintain the normal functions and to offset evaporative losses; about 20% of this is supplied internally as a product of oxidation, but the remainder must be consumed (annual consumption for humans is 5 to 10 times body weight). A forest may transpire 200 to 1000 kg/yr · m$^2$ of land surface while producing 1 to 2 kg (dry matter)/yr · m$^2$; the ratio of transpiration to dry matter production (transpiration ratio) varies between about $10^2$ and $10^3$ depending on water availability, climate, and the characteristics of the forest.

Water is also vital as a moderator of global climate, as suggested in section 1.1. Atmospheric water vapor, and its condensed form (clouds), reflect and absorb part of incoming solar radiation over the bright (day) side of the earth, and provide a continuous stream of energy to the surface in the form of longwave radiation (see section 2.2.c); as a result the dark (night) side is insulated against rapid cooling. The net effects, favoring the existence and proliferation of life forms, are that surface temperature maxima are lower, minima are much higher, and the globe is considerably warmer than it would be in the absence of atmospheric water.

Water, by virtue of its high thermal capacity and latent heats (see section 2.1), is an energy regulator, storing surplusage and mitigating deficiency; temperature fluctuations are greater over land than over water, and maritime climates are temperate. Moving water is an energy carrier, tending to moderate and equalize temperatures in the biosphere. Ocean currents carry energy from tropical toward polar regions, but atmospheric fluxes are directed from areas of high to low evaporation with more direct effects on terrestrial climates.

### 1.2.b. Human Convenience

The uses of water have multiplied along with the growth of human knowledge and invention. In primitive cultures water could satisfy only a few vital needs, but in much of the contemporary world its use is attuned more to the demands of industry, mechanized agriculture, and human convenience. Modern societies frequently equate water "need" with "demand", and even the distinction between "need" and "convenience" is apt to be arbitrary.

Surface waters are used *in situ* for numerous purposes including recreation, fishing, navigation, power generation, and aesthetic appreciation. Water that is withdrawn from its natural course in streams, lakes, or the ground may be used and returned (nonconsumptive use), or lost (consumptive use) through evaporation, transpiration, or discharge to locations (e.g., oceans) where it is practically irretrievable. Most forms of nonconsumptive water use affect its quality to some extent; consumptive use diminishes the quantity available for withdrawal during a single liquid phase of the natural water cycle.

In practice water uses cannot be identified categorically as either consumptive or nonconsumptive; some evaporative loss is almost always inevitable, and coastal areas may discharge used water directly to the oceans. As an example, some major water-use categories in the United States are listed in table 1.5 along with per-capita withdrawals and consumptive use data. Current (1975) consumptive use per capita is about 2 $m^3$/day, or about 30% of the withdrawal rate, 6.4 $m^3$/day; the remainder, nonconsumptive use, is about 70%.

Table 1.5 shows that crop irrigation, cooling in steam electric generation plants, and manufacturing processes account for more than 90% of all withdrawals and consumptive use; domestic use (including household, garden-lawn irrigation, automobile and street cleaning, and fire fighting) and other uses (for mineral

**Table 1.5. Per Capita Withdrawal and Consumptive Use of Water in the United States (adapted from U.S. Forest Service, 1977)**

| Major use | Withdrawal ($W$) (liters/day) | (%) | Consumptive use ($C$) (liters/day) | (%) | $C/W$ (%) |
|---|---|---|---|---|---|
| Crop irrigation | 3219 | 50.6 | 1660 | 83.2 | 51.6 |
| Steam electric | 1643 | 25.8 | 33 | 1.6 | 2.0 |
| Manufacturing | 906 | 14.2 | 105 | 5.3 | 11.6 |
| Domestic use | 393 | 6.2 | 107 | 5.4 | 27.2 |
| Other uses | 206 | 3.2 | 89 | 4.5 | 43.2 |
| All uses | 6367 | 100.0 | 1994 | 100.0 | 31.3 |

processing, livestock, fish hatcheries, and public lands) account for less than 10% of the totals. Water demand already exceeds supply in some of the warmer and drier regions of the country, and demand is expected to increase by about 20% over the next quarter-century—largely as a result of increased manufacturing and steam electric usage. The imminence of widespread water shortages is a challenge that focuses attention on conservation measures and the possibilities for increasing the gross supply.

Vast quantities of subsurface water are extracted and used *in situ* by forest cover in the natural production of wood and other products; in fact, the water lost to evaporation and transpiration from forest land is more than three times the quantity extracted for uses specified in table 1.5. Forests cover about one-third of the conterminous United States, and are located at higher elevations where about half of total precipitation falls, and three-fourths of total streamflow is generated. Yet forests do not conserve water (see sections 1.3.c and 1.4.a), but rather use it luxuriously, and this is a matter of central concern in forest hydrology.

### 1.2.c. Destructive Force

The properties of water that make it vital and convenient are also frequently manifested as inconvenience, injury, and destruction; the "miracle of nature" may become a scourge, and the life-bearer a killer. In each of its phases, and as it undergoes phase changes, water demonstrates the ambivalence and impartiality of natural force, and also the meager ability of human understanding to cope with bothersome or deleterious natural phenomena. A cursory review of the problems that water creates or accentuates as it moves through the hydrosphere suggests the scope of related hydrologic concern.

Atmospheric water vapor retards essential drying (e.g., of crops, lumber, and forest roads), reduces the rate of snow ablation and the effectiveness of evaporative cooling, and encourages the proliferation of antagonistic life forms and the deterioration of commodities (wood, metal, and foodstuff). In a warm environment humidity increases organism heat stress, and in a cold environment is directly correlated with the frequency and severity of discomfort and illness. Water vapor is omnipresent, and its condensation near the surface causes nuisance, jeopardizes the purity of other liquids, reduces visibility, and endangers human life.

Water vapor condensation in the atmosphere is the major source of energy to power violent storms. The latent heat released in an average thunderstorm is equivalent to the kinetic energy of an atomic bomb, and that released in a hurricane may be ten thousand times as great. Whirling masses of air (vortices), violent winds, and associated electrical discharges kill humans, destroy homes and property, uproot trees, and ignite forest fires.

Nonvaporous water causes multifarious damage beginning with its arrival at the surface of the earth; hail damage is most dramatic perhaps, but it is relatively rare, as are glaze and freezing rain that can accumulate and effectively delimb a forest, break communication lines, or immobilize vehicular traffic. The kinetic energy of falling raindrops can dislodge soil particles, drastically reduce infiltration capacity, and initiate fluvial erosion, mud flows, and mass-wasting. Mineral and organic sediments that are carried to streams, or eroded from stream banks and beds, clog reservoirs, reduce water quality, and multiply damages caused by floods.

Water destroys as it moves; even the slight movement associated with expansion upon freezing can burst pipes, fragment road surfaces, heave seedlings from the ground, crack tree stems, and destroy living cells. Snow can be devastating as it moves rapidly in avalanches, or compacts and moves slowly in glaciers. Liquid water is especially destructive as it moves out of normal channels, inundating flood plains, ravaging croplands and cities, and exacting a heavy toll of human life.

## 1.3. Historical Perspective

Historical records show that the ancients knew much about the necessity, convenience, and destructive power of water. But knowledge, unlike mass and energy, always grows because it is provocative, ever stimulating new attempts toward understanding. An important branch of knowledge, born of ancient curiosity and centuries of observation and careful thought, has to do with the influences of forests on water movement through the biosphere.

## 1.3.a. Ancient Knowledge

The earliest civilizations apparently developed along the banks of rivers, principally the Yellow (Huang-Ho) in China, the Indus in India, the Tigris-Euphrates in Iraq, and the Nile in Egypt. "Gradually, they developed their water supply systems, constructed dams and levees, made channel improvements, and dug canals for drainage and irrigation" (Biswas, 1970). Concrete evidence exists that major engineering controls were in use more than 5000 years ago.

The abutments of one of the oldest dams in history are still in existence (south of Cairo, Egypt); its capacity was greater than $5(10^5)$ m$^3$ but it failed because no mortar was used in construction and there was no spillway. The ancient Egyptians, so dependent upon on the Nile for irrigation water, were also concerned with serious flooding and developed a warning system; measurements of river levels, using "nilometers," can be traced back to at least 3000 B.C. The flood of biblical fame, Noah's flood, is legendary, based on the simultaneous flooding of the Tigris and Euphrates Rivers (Kazmann, 1965).

In ancient times a learned person was supposedly knowledgeable in all fields; Thales (about 600 B.C.), who has been called "the ancient hydrologist," proclaimed that the earth floats on water, and that water is the material cause of all things. Plato, who was interested in knowledge for its own sake, imagined a great reservoir of subterranean water that explained the origin of rivers and springs; but Aristotle, his pupil, who was more concerned with observations than abstractions, wrote the first treatise on meteorology and suggested that condensation (subterranean or other), rainfall, or percolation were the explanation. Theophrastus (fourth century B.C.), who lived at about the time when Kantilya of India made the first recorded measurement of rainfall, is said to have written the first correct description of the hydrologic cycle.

The Romans (100 B.C.–200 A.D.) built remarkable aqueducts and sewer systems, but thought that flow rates were simply proportional to the cross-sectional area of a stream; Hero of Alexandria was apparently first to recognize the importance of stream velocity and slope. Vitruvius (first century B.C.) suggested rational methods of locating underground water, preferring mountainous regions where there is "no loss of water . . . due to evaporation" because "the presence of a forest makes it impossible for the sun's rays to reach the surface water," and "snow remains on the ground there much longer because of the dense forests" (Biswas, 1970). Apparently Vitruvius was one of the first forest hydrologists and, according to Chow (1964), the "theory of Vitruvius may be considered the forerunner of modern concepts of the hydrologic cycle."

In the western world all science was subordinate to theology from Roman times to the Renaissance; the universalist ideals of Hellenic philosophy combined with Roman autocracy to produce widespread intellectual stagnation under the auspices of Christianity. During this period the greatest achievement in hydrology was the quantitative measurement of precipitation in China and Korea. Problems of flooding and the need for rainfall during rice cultivation sparked the improvement of rain and snow gages, and the development of areal estimates of precipitation based on point measurements.

### 1.3.b. Scientific Development

Undoubtedly "the roots of modern hydrology lie deeply buried in antiquity" (Biswas, 1970), but its modern concepts were devised following the long era of religious suppression. Chow (1964) traced the progress of hydrologic advances through periods of observation (1400–1600), measurement (1600–1700), experimentation (1700–1800), modernization (1800–1900), empiricism (1900–1930), rationalization (1930–1950), and theorization (1950–to date). A brief review of some major accomplishments will serve as background for an historical discussion of forest influences (section 1.3.c).

Leonardo da Vinci (1452–1519), an Italian painter, sculptor, architect, musician, engineer, mathematician, and scientist, observed and wrote prolifically but made little impression on the world of hydrology until his notes were published, some three centuries later, by Giovanni Venturi. He (da Vinci) made original contributions in the field of open channel flow, and is credited with the first clear conception of the continuity principle. Bernard Palissy (1510–1590), another giant of the observational period, eschewed theoretical abstractions but achieved through observation a correct understanding of the origin of streams, the principles of artesian wells, water level fluctuations in wells and rivers, and the importance of forest cover in the prevention of soil erosion.

The seventeenth century is frequently called the "cradle of modern science"; in hydrology it was essentially a period of measurement, the beginning of quantitative hydrology. Pierre Perrault (1608–1680) measured the annual volume of flow in the headwaters of the Seine River and found it to be only one-sixth of rainfall, and Edme Mariotte (1620–1684) repeated the experiment for the entire basin above Paris with similar results, confirming that rainfall was more than adequate to account for the flow; Mariotte timed the movement of a wax ball float to determine streamflow velocity at the surface and, recognizing that surface velocity is greater than the mean, reduced it by one-third in calculations. Edmond Halley (1656–1742) initiated systematic measurements of evaporation and demonstrated that evaporative losses from lakes and seas are sufficient to counterbalance inflows from rivers and streams.

Other contributors to the period of measurement were Benedetto Castelli (1577–1644) who restated the continuity principle so convincingly that it was universally accepted, and built the first rain gage in Europe before mid-century, and Christopher Wren (1632–1723) and Robert Hooke (1635–1703) who pioneered in the construction of recording gages. Hooke also designed an early current meter, but his was preceded by that designed by an Italian physician, Santorio Santorio (1561-1630), in about 1610. Evangelista Torricelli (1608-1647) is credited with the first demonstration that the velocity of flow through a submerged orifice is proportional to the square root of depth, but Giovanni Guglielmini (1656-1710) carried out more precise experiments on the efflux principle and adapted it for practical applicability in analogous situations; the latter is also credited with the idea that streamflow velocity increases with stream cross-sectional area but decreases with the length of wetted perimeter.

The eighteenth century marked the beginning of modern hydrologic experimentation. Henry De Pitot's (1695-1771) invention, the Pitot tube, made it possible for the first time to measure accurately stream velocities at various depths; Daniel Bernoulli (1700-1782) investigated the dynamic relationship between velocity and pressure; Giovanni Venturi (1746-1822) laid the groundwork for a flow-measuring device that bears his name (the Venturi flume); and Paolo Frisi (1727-1784) compiled a comprehensive treatise on rivers and torrents. Antoine Chezy (1718-1798) and Pierre Du Buat (1738-1809) developed theoretical-empirical expressions for stream velocity based on channel configuration and slope; a form of the Chezy equation (equation 7.21) still appears in modern textbooks (the original was not published until a century after the author's death).

Evaporation measurements during the eighteenth century by John Dalton (1766-1844) and others led to a generalized theory of vapor pressure (Dalton's law of partial pressures) and to a method of estimating evaporation (Dalton's equation; equation 2.38) that appeared at the beginning of the ninteenth century, the period of modernization. Other major developments of this period include the investigation of rainfall-elevation relationships by John Miller (1790-1875); development and refinement of current meters by Reinhard Woltman (1757-1837), Theodore Ellis (1829-1883), and William Price (1853-1928); elaboration of flow velocity-resistance relationships by Emile Ganguillet (1818-1894) and William Kutter (1818-1888); improvement and further development of stream velocity equations by Robert Manning (1816-1897); and derivation of the "rational" formula for flood flows by Thomas Mulvaney (1822–1892). In the field of groundwater hydrology, William Smith (1769–1839) demonstrated the efficacy of geologic concepts in solving practical hydrologic problems and is credited with joining the two disciplines, and Henri Darcy (1803–1858) developed the theoretical basis for groundwater flow (Darcy's law).

The combined efforts of nineteenth century scientists, and the interest and participation of government agencies in routine data collections, provided a wealth of conceptual and empirical information for the twentieth century. Knowledge increases the thirst for it, and data collections were greatly accelerated during the first three decades, the period of empiricism; this led, predictably, to periods of rational analysis and theorization. Progress during the current century has been tremendous, but it is the subject matter of modern textbooks, and any attempt to personalize it would be difficult and perhaps unfair; moreover, the science has advanced to the point where specialization is a practical necessity.

### 1.3.c. Forest Influences

Many of the overt influences of forest cover on climate and water phenomena were undoubtedly appreciated by the ancients, much as they are today by the laity. The forest provides shade, moderates temperature extremes, and reduces incursions of wind, dust, and noise; it intercepts fractions of rain and snowfall, reduces surface runoff, increases relative humidity, and inhibits snowmelt, soil erosion, and surface drying. For these and other reasons the forest environment is frequently characterized as pleasant, peaceful, sublime, and salutary.

Much of the history of forestry is written in terms of human concern and speculation with regard to sylvan influences. Medieval and Renaissance governments established "protection forests" for the express purpose of controlling avalanches, mountain torrents, shifting sands, erosion, and siltation. Many of the early concepts were undoubtedly intuitive, or legendary in origin, and some, though demonstrably false, were still implicit in public policies and management activities during the early decades of the twentieth century (see section 1.4.a).

Published reports dealing specifically with vegetative influences on climate and hydrologic phenomena began to appear with greater frequency during the eighteenth and nineteenth centuries. The early writers were prone to emphasize an assumed "harmony" in nature, to adopt teleological explanations, and to proffer learned opinion as proof. According to Kittredge (1948), Noah Webster was convinced by 1799 that forest clearing by the American colonists had caused winds and winter weather to be more variable, autumn to encroach upon winter, spring upon summer, and snow to be less permanent; apparently these modifications were thought to extend even to areas not originally forested.

Interest in forest influences increased dramatically during the nineteenth century; in the United States deforestation accelerated rapidly, naturalists were alarmed, the Forest Service was created, and vast areas of the public domain "adjacent to the sources of the navigable waters and other streams" were set aside, ostensibly at least, to protect the streams. The first edition of *The Earth as Modified by Human Action* (Marsh, 1907) was published in 1863; a large section of the book was devoted to a summary of European experience and opinion on forest influences. *Forests and Moisture* (Brown, 1877) was apparently one of the first major works in English to deal exlusively with the topic.

By the end of the nineteenth century the idea that streamflow is regulated by forest cover had many proponents; it also had many opponents, and there was very little hard evidence to support either position. During the first decades of the current century, researches designed to resolve the issue were initiated on small catchment areas in both Switzerland and the United States; the results of these tests tended to confirm a forest influence, but raised important new questions with regard to experimental design, instrumental accuracy, the independent effects of other factors, and interactions among factors. Literally hundreds of similar experiments have since been conducted under a wide variety of conditions in many countries.

The scientific literature on forest influences was summarized by Zon (1927) in *Forests and Water in the Light of Scientific Investigation*; its bibliography listed upward of a thousand references to reports covering a period of more than 150 years. Zon's monograph was followed by an era of unparalleled research, conservation, and education; Kittredge's (1948) *Forest Influences* became a standard text and reference. The knowledge explosion of recent years has revealed serious inadequacies in these earlier works, but has also confirmed the correctness of Zon's observation:

> Of all the direct influences of the forest the influence upon the supply of water in streams and upon the regularity of their flow is the most important in human economy.

## 1.4. Modern Impetus

Much of the early impetus for public policy and governmental action in the area of forest conservation was based on popular concepts and forestry lore. By the middle of the current century, population growth, industrialization, urbanization, land disturbance, and the increased use of forested areas for recreation and other purposes had engendered widespread concern for environmental quality. Such concern, coupled with increasing awareness of forest influences in general, and the intimate association of forests and water in particular, led to renewed efforts in the search for knowledge and to the development of forest hydrology (the science) and forest watershed management (its vocational counterpart).

### 1.4.a. Forestry Lore
Natural phenomena are frequently mysterious and troubling, presenting an element of doubt to the human mind; but the perfect remedy for doubt is belief, so it is perhaps understandable that belief is often credulous, fixed by tradition, authority, intuition, or "self-evident" facts. Many of the early explanations of the forest's influence on hydrologic phenomena failed to survive the scrutiny of modern scientific research, yet have persisted as a kind of "common knowledge" that affects public decisions. The most persistent misconceptions are that forests increase local precipita-

tion, reduce the impact of raindrops under the canopy, prevent disastrous floods, and conserve water for streamflow during periods of drought; in other words forest cutting would supposedly decrease gross precipitation (even to the point of turning humid forest regions into deserts!), and cause the drying up of springs and streams.

Exaggerated and distorted claims for the forest influence on streamflow provided much of the impetus for early forestry development in the United States ("wood famine" prognostications were equally exaggerated and efficacious). The navigability of streams was a central issue because of its economic importance, and because river navigation was impeded during periods of low water stages. Foresters claimed erroneously that the mean low stages in rivers "depend upon the extent of forest cover on the watersheds" and that the "forest tends to equalize the flow throughout the year by making the low stages higher" (Zon, 1927), and used the argument repeatedly to support the establishment of national forest reserves in headwater areas; many of the early claims were tempered with time, but Kittredge (1948) also concluded that forests "prolong increased flow in low-water periods."

Many people still think that forested land, because it is forested, produces greater average streamflow; the fact is that forests use water extravagantly, and forested land almost always produces less streamflow volume than does land with other cover types. The misconception may have been perpetuated by Zon's (1927) argument that "forests are conservers of water for stream flow" and that they "save a greater amount of precipitation for stream flow than does any other vegetable cover similarly situated"; but Zon was referring to groundwater seepage, explicitly omitting surface runoff, and even in this reduced sense his argument is generally untenable. By mid-century it had been demonstrated that with deforestation "the annual flow is increased" (Kittredge, 1948), and this general rule has been confirmed in numerous subsequent experiments.

The notion that forests affect gross precipitation has persisted for centuries; the forest interior was known as a place of high relative humidity, and this suggested a greater probability for precipitation. The consensus of foresters was summarized by Zon (1927): "Forests increase both the abundance and frequency of local precipitation over the areas they occupy, the excess of precipitation, as compared with that over adjacent unforested areas, amounting in some cases to more than 25 per cent." Fortunately Zon's statement served well as a research hypothesis, and it was soon learned that forests enjoy greater total precipitation primarily because they occur more frequently at higher elevations, and that rainfall catch in forest openings is greater because gages are sheltered from air currents that reduce the catch; despite numerous clarifications (see section 3.3.a), this "precipitation-humidity fallacy" persists in various forms.

Other alleged influences of the forest on the storage and movement of water have also succumbed to careful inquiry. It is untrue that "by its foliage and branches it [the forest] breaks the force of the rain, so that water reaches the soil without violence" (Zon, 1927)—a tenet of modern forestry that is supposed to help explain the forest's resistance to soil erosion. Forests do not "increase underground storage of water" (in humid regions forest soils are usually drier in summer than those in deforested areas; see section 5.2.c); also, as was correctly foreseen (Zon, 1927) but poorly appreciated, "floods which are produced by exceptional meteorological conditions can not be prevented by forests."

### 1.4.b. Environmental Concern

Public concern for environmental quality is based on a complexity of material and psychological needs that expand with population pressure. The latter is not merely a matter of numbers, however, because urbanization and industrialization cause the pressure on forest and water resources to increase exponentially with population density. Areas of major concern are the effects of forest land use and management on the volume, quality, and timing of water yield to downstream areas, and on related local factors including erosion, forest site quality, and ecological stability.

The total volume of streamflow has always been a prime consideration in areas of climatological water shortage, but population increases and rising per-capita demand have extended the problem to more humid regions; overall consumptive use of water in the United States is increasing by more than a billion cubic meters each year. Forest cutting and cover-type manipulation have been used to increase streamflow, especially during the dry season, and hundreds of municipal watersheds have been set aside and managed primarily to secure a stable supply of high-quality water. Seasonal shortages have been mitigated to some extent by storage of water in reservoirs, but this has often led to other problems; reservoirs disrupt the normal streamflow regimen, alter aquatic habitat, and submerge valuable land.

The beneficial effects of forest cutting to increase water yield are frequently overshadowed by real or imaginary threats of increased flooding and water quality deterioration; public concern, and public awareness of the genuine physical and economic issues involved, have been instrumental in the evolution of modern environmental forestry. When small forested watersheds are clearcut and logged without proper care, and without concern for long-term values, the downstream costs in terms of sedimentation, pollution, and increased flood damages may far exceed the value of timber and additional water that is produced. Proper management practices can usually reduce the adverse effects to an acceptable level, but such practices are costly, especially in areas of rugged terrain or where approved logging must be timed to coincide with clement weather and favorable watershed conditions.

The forest has long been recognized as a source of high-quality water, not only because it inhibits erosion but also because forest land is relatively little used by humans; the situation is changing, however, as expanding populations find manifold reasons for intruding into the farthermost reaches of the pristine forest environment. Forest land is used more and more intensively for the production of timber and as rangeland for domestic livestock, and is otherwise disturbed by the extraction of minerals which exposes unweathered rock to the eroding influence of running water and changes the chemical composition of streams. A mobile population demands roads, hiking trails, and recreational facilities, and its incursion into heretofore untrampled areas is a two-edged sword, mitigating the stresses of modern existence while adulterating a prized natural resource.

The practice of forest management for water yield improvement and streamflow regulation causes additional concern with regard to local site quality, thermal pollution, and stream ecology. Timber harvesting entails watershed nutrient losses as wood is removed, slash is burned, organic material undergoes more rapid decomposition, soils are more thoroughly leached, and dissolved solids are discharged into streams. Soil and organic sediments may destroy streambed microorganisms that constitute the base of the food chain and, unless a buffer strip is left to shade cove areas, maximum water temperatures may exceed optimum or lethal levels for major aquatic organisms, upset the ecological balance, and modify species composition.

### 1.4.c. Knowledge Growth

Societal awareness of environmental problems and ecosystem limitations has been a major force behind the modern search for understanding in forest hydrology. Research programs sponsored by governments and private agencies in many countries have expanded continuously during recent decades in a synergistic search for new knowledge. Institutions of higher learning have also contributed significantly in the research effort, in the academic education of scientists, and in the training of practitioners for forest-water resources management and planning.

University coursework in hydrology, initiated during the first decade of the twentieth century in the United States (Chow, 1964), has grown and diversified tremendously, especially since mid-century. The forestry schools, which had traditionally introduced the subject of forest-water relationships in courses dealing with forest protection, soils, physiology, silvics, and silviculture, began offering specific studies of forest influences, forest hydrology, and watershed management. With the advent of a "multiple-use" concept in forestry, and the recognition of water husbandry as a major goal along with timber, wildlife, forage management, and recreational development, the profession became specialized and forestry curricula were expanded; most of the accredited forest schools now offer some form of hydrologic studies, and separate curricula in forest-water resources have existed for more than two decades.

Research in forest hydrology and related topics has produced a vast and ever-increasing body of knowledge. Contemporary research results are published in academic and government experiment station reports, symposium transactions, and various journals including those of forestry, hydrology, and meteorology. Numerous books that elaborate salient aspects of forest-water relationships have appeared since 1950; a partial list is given in Selected Readings at the end of this chapter.

## 1.5. Hydrologic Sciences

"Hydrology" is a general term for the science that deals with the earth's single abundant liquid; it is truly an "earth" science because earth is the only planet in the solar system with significant components of all three phases of matter, and the only place where liquid water is common. Hydrology has numerous branches; specialization, a natural result of knowledge growth and a necessary basis for its further expansion, is a characteristic of all modern sciences. Forest hydrology is a distinct area of specialization that recognizes the singular importance of forest cover influences on hydrologic phenomena and related environmental qualities.

### 1.5.a. General Definition

To the generalist, or etymologist, hydrology is simply "the science of water"; but this definition often appears too vague, and it is widely eschewed by specialists who hold parochial views. More elaborate definitions can be obtained from unabridged dictionaries or modern textbooks; according to Chow (1964), the U.S. Federal Council for Science and Technology decided that:

> Hydrology is the science that treats of the waters of the Earth, their occurrence, circulation, and distribution, their chemical and physical properties, and their reaction with their environment, including their reaction to living things.

More succinctly hydrology is the "science of water and water-related phenomena"—which pinpoints the inadequacy of general definitions; more helpful forms of definition apply to individual scientific specialties where perspective is the key.

### 1.5.b. Scientific Specialization

Natural phenomena become more intelligible when they are studied in parts or for particular purposes; this is, of course, the basis for traditional categorizations of scientific disciplines. With the rapid expansion of knowledge in recent times this has led to the development of numerous subdivisions within disciplines (e.g., nuclear physics, geophysics, atmospheric physics, etc.), and to multidisciplinary fields that obscure traditional demarcation lines (e.g., physical chemistry, biophysics, and biochemistry). In hydrology this natural progression, and the ubiquity of hydrologic phenomena, are responsible for the birth of distinct areas of specialization.

Water phenomena in the atmosphere (hydrometeors) are the subject matter of *hydrometeorology*, those in the ground of *hydrogeology*, in the oceans of *oceanography*, and in freshwater bodies of *limnology*; *hydrometry* is the science of water measurement, and *hydrography* deals with the charting of the earth's waters, especially for navigational purposes. Hydrology has become a broad and diverse field, sometimes including aspects of agronomy, ecology, geomorphology, glaciology, and plant physiology; the physicist or microclimatologist may be concerned primarily with water and energy relations, and the chemist or bacteriologist with water quality. Other well-established terms include *agricultural*, *urban*, and *wildland hydrology* (with reference to particular land segments), *engineering hydrology* (a branch of civil engineering that emphasizes hydraulics and open-channel flow), *medical hydrology* (water therapy), and in a more general sense, *scientific* and *applied hydrology*; *forest hydrology* is given more definite meaning in the section that follows.

### 1.5.c. Forest Hydrology

Forest hydrology is clearly an interdisciplinary science, the union of forestry and hydrology; it is rooted in the ancient concern for forests and waters, and has evolved through various stages to become a major area of scientific specialization. As in any hydrologic science the focus is on water, but the operational sphere is forest land. Forests cover about 4 billion hectares (or one-fourth) of the land area of the earth, and are restricted to regions of relatively high precipitation where they yield an inproportionate share of high-quality streamflow.

During the first part of the twentieth century, the growing body of knowledge concerning forests and water was included under the general heading of *forest influences* (section 1.3.c); but by mid-century Kittredge (1948) had suggested that "the important phases of forest influences concerned with water, such as precipitation, soil water, stream flow, and floods, might appropriately be called 'forest hydrology'." Since very few foresters were grounded in the principles of hydrology at that time, professionals were apparently reluctant to adopt the new terminology; instead they opted for the utilitarian term, *watershed management*, with its multiple-use connotations. *Forest watershed management* is now used extensively to denote operational activities based on a knowledge of forest hydrology, the science.

*Forest hydrology* is the science of water-related phenomena that are influenced by forest cover. Its principles have been given piecemeal by various authors, and in more comprehensive form by some of those listed under Selected Readings at the end of this chapter. The purpose of the remaining chapters is to elaborate the essential principles, nature, and scope of forest hydrology, and to give it recognizable form and substance as a distinct science.

## LITERATURE CITED

Baumgartner, A. and E. Reichel. 1975. *The World Water Balance*. Munich: R. Oldenbourg.

Biswas, A. K. 1970. *History of Hydrology*. New York: American Elsevier.

Brown, J. C. 1877. *Forests and Moisture; or Effects of Forests on Humidity of Climate*. London: Simpkin, Marshall.

Budyko, M. I. 1974. *Climate and Life*. New York: Academic Press.

Chow, V. T. 1964. Hydrology and its development. In V. T. Chow, ed., *Handbook of Applied Hydrology*. New York: McGraw-Hill.

Davis, K. S. and J. A. Day. 1961. *Water the Mirror of Science.* Garden City, N.Y.: Doubleday.

Kazmann, R. G. 1965. *Modern Hydrology.* New York: Harper & Row.

King, T. 1961. *Water the Miracle of Nature.* New York: Crowell-Collier.

Kittredge, J. 1948. *Forest Influences.* New York: McGraw-Hill.

Marsh, G. P. 1907. *The Earth as Modified by Human Action.* New York: Scribner's.

U.S. Forest Service. 1977. *The Nation's Renewable Resources—An Assessment, 1975.* Forest Resource Report No. 21. Washington, D.C.: U.S. Government Printing Office.

Zon, R. 1927. *Forests and Water in the Light of Scientific Investigation.* Washington, D.C.: U.S. Government Printing Office.

## SELECTED READINGS

Anderson, H. W., M. D. Hoover, and K. G. Reinhart. 1976. *Forests and Water: Effects of Forest Management on Floods, Sedimentation, and Water Supply.* General Technical Report PSW-18, Washington, D.C.: U.S.D.A., Forest Service.

Colman, E. A. 1953. *Vegetation and Watershed Management.* New York; Ronald Press.

Geiger, R. 1965. *The Climate near the Ground.* Cambridge, Mass.: Harvard University Press.

Hewlett, J. D. and W. L. Nutter. 1969. *An Outline of Forest Hydrology.* Athens, Georgia: University of Georgia Press.

Kramer, P. J. 1969. *Plant and Soil Water Relationships: A Modern Synthesis.* New York: McGraw-Hill.

Miller, D. H. 1977. *Water at the Surface of the Earth.* New York: Academic Press.

Penman, H. L. 1963. *Vegetation and Hydrology.* Technical Communication No. 53. Farnham Royal, England: Commonwealth Agricultural Bureaux.

Satterlund, D. R. 1972. *Wildland Watershed Management.* New York: Ronald Press.

Slatyer, R. O. 1967. *Plant-Water Relationships.* New York: Academic Press.

Sopper, W. E. and H. W. Lull, eds. 1967. *International Symposium on Forest Hydrology.* New York: Pergamon Press.

# 2 HYDROLOGIC ENTITIES

## 2.1. Water Properties

Water ($H_2O$) is a common substance with uncommon properties (rare forms, composed of uncommon isotopes of hydrogen and oxygen, will not be considered). The molecular structure of water accounts for its versatility as a solvent, its mobility in mineral and organic bodies, its unique thermal properties, and its existence in all three phases at common earth temperatures. At standard atmospheric pressure (1013 mb), solid, liquid, and gaseous water are in equilibrium at 0°C where the partial pressure of water vapor is 6.1 mb; a review of some physical properties of the three phases is basic to an understanding of hydrologic processes.

### 2.1.a. Solid Water

More than three-fourths of the earth's freshwater is stored in solid form (table 1.2); ice and snow cover are perennial in polar regions and at higher latitudes and elevations where the mean temperature is lower than about -10°C. In temperate regions, where it is not uncommon for 10 to 20% of annual precipitation to occur as snow, liquid water in soils and surface water bodies may freeze temporarily during colder periods and exert profound effects on water flows. Water in solid form is relatively impermeable and immobile; it can effectively block liquid water pathways in soils and modify the timing of streamflow.

The physical characteristics of solid water are useful in explaining its overt behavior; some temperature-dependent properties are listed in table 2.1. Ice is a true solid in that it exhibits both rigidity

Table 2.1. Some properties of Solid Water at Standard Pressure

| Temperature (°C) | Density (g/cm³) | Specific heat (cal/g·°C) | Thermal capacity (cal/cm³·°C) | Thermal conductivity (cal/cm·min·°C) | Latent heat | |
|---|---|---|---|---|---|---|
| | | | | | Fusion (cal/g) | Sublimation (cal/g) |
| *Ice* | | | | | | |
| 0 | 0.9167 | 0.503 | 0.461 | 0.321 | 79.7 | 677.0 |
| −10 | 0.9187 | 0.485 | 0.446 | 0.332 | 74.5 | 677.5 |
| −20 | 0.9203 | 0.468 | 0.431 | 0.349 | 69.0 | 677.9 |
| −30 | 0.9216 | 0.450 | 0.415 | 0.365 | 63.0 | 678.0 |
| −40 | 0.9228 | 0.433 | 0.400 | 0.381 | 56.3 | 678.0 |
| *Snow* (approximate) | | | | | | |
| 0 | 0.1 | 0.50 | 0.05 | 0.01 | 80 | 677 |
| | 0.3 | 0.50 | 0.15 | 0.04 | 80 | 677 |
| | 0.5 | 0.50 | 0.25 | 0.09 | 80 | 677 |
| | 0.7 | 0.50 | 0.35 | 0.18 | 80 | 677 |
| −40 | 0.1 | 0.43 | 0.04 | 0.01 | 56 | 678 |
| | 0.3 | 0.43 | 0.13 | 0.04 | 56 | 678 |
| | 0.5 | 0.43 | 0.22 | 0.10 | 56 | 678 |
| | 0.7 | 0.43 | 0.30 | 0.21 | 56 | 678 |

and a fixed molecular (crystalline) structure; but unlike most other substances it occupies a greater volume in the solid phase (it expands upon freezing). Its density is only about 92% of that of liquid water, so ice floats on liquid water and is readily melted (not tied up in stream bottoms, for example, as it would be if water were not unusual).

The *specific heat* of ice is a measure of the energy required to heat a unit mass, and its *thermal capacity* is a measure of that required to heat a unit volume; these values are about half, or less, of those for liquid water (see table 2.3), and they decrease slightly with temperature. The *thermal conductivity* of ice is a measure of its efficiency as a heat transfer medium; in this respect solid ice is about four times as efficient as liquid water. The energy per unit mass that is released in freezing, or absorbed in melting, is the *latent heat of fusion*, and the corresponding term for direct solid ⇆ vapor transformations is the *latent heat of sublimation*; the latent heats of water are higher (usually much higher) than those of any other common substance.

Snow that has accumulated at the surface is a mixture of ice crystals and air, and may contain significant quantities of liquid water at 0°C; the approximate bulk properties of a snowpack are also given in table 2.1. The bulk density of new snow is usually between 0.1 and 0.2 g/cm$^3$, but after aging it may range from 0.2 to 0.6 g/cm$^3$; at constant temperature, the thermal capacity of snow increases linearly with density increases. A low-density snowpack is a poor conductor; it can insulate the soil against rapid temperature changes, prevent deep freezing, and maintain a more permeable substratum for liquid water infiltration.

The radiative properties of water are important in energy budgeting for hydrologic purposes (see sections 2.2.c and 6.1.c); some typical values are given in table 2.2. The *albedo* (or *shortwave reflectivity coefficient*) of a surface is the fraction of incoming solar radiation that it reflects, and the *emissivity coefficient* of a surface is a measure of its efficiency in emitting *longwave* radiation (i.e., invisible radiation emitted at earth temperatures). Snow usually reflects about one-half to three-fourths of incident solar radiation, depending on surface conditions and other factors

Table 2.2. Some Typical Radiative Properties of Water Surfaces

| Surface | Description; conditions | Shortwave reflectivity coefficient |
|---------|-------------------------|-----------------------------------|
| Clouds | low overcast: 100 m thick | 0.40 |
|  | 200 m thick | 0.50 |
|  | 500 m thick | 0.70 |
| Liquid | clear sky; solar altitude: 60° | 0.05 |
|  | 30° | 0.10 |
|  | 20° | 0.15 |
|  | 10° | 0.35 |
|  | 5° | 0.60 |
|  | high sun: smooth surface | 0.05 |
|  | wavy surface | 0.10 |
|  | cloudy sky; high sun: smooth surface | 0.05 |
|  | low sun: smooth surface | 0.10 |
| Solid | fresh snow: low density | 0.85 |
|  | high density | 0.65 |
|  | old snow: clean | 0.55 |
|  | dirty | 0.45 |
|  | glacier ice: clean | 0.35 |
|  | dirty | 0.25 |

| Surface | Description; conditions | Longwave emissivity coefficient |
|---------|-------------------------|--------------------------------|
| Atmosphere | dense clouds (condensed vapor) | 0.99 |
| Liquid | normal to surface | 0.99 |
|  | mean | 0.95 |
| Solid | at freezing point | 0.97 |

(albedoes are greater for clean low-density snow, and at high latitudes or low sun angles); snow and ice are highly efficient radiators (and absorbers) of longwave radiation.

## 2.1.b. Liquid Water

Water in the liquid phase is said to have a "broken down" ice structure because it retains some crystalline properties; one evidence of this is that its density increases slightly between the freezing point and 4°C where it attains a maximum (table 2.3). The density, which varies by only about 1% through the common range of temperatures, is used as a measure of the relative densities (specific gravity) of other materials, and was the original basis for metric standards of mass and volume. Water density changes with temperature are responsible for the thermal stratification of lakes and ponds, and for autumn and spring turnovers: at temperatures greater than 4°C autumnal cooling of surface layers is retarded as the *cooled* water sinks, and at temperatures less than 4°C the rate of vernal warming is retarded as the *warmed* water sinks.

The specific heat of liquid water is much higher than that of most other substances; this property is used to define a heat energy unit, the calorie (i.e., the energy required to raise the temperature of 1 g of water from 14.5 to 15.5°C). Both the specific heat ($\simeq 1$ cal/g) and thermal capacity ($\simeq 1$ cal/cm$^3$) of liquid water vary insignificantly with temperature over the common range, and are not listed in table 2.3. The high thermal capacity ensures that temperatures of water, moist soils, and other bodies of high water content will fluctuate slowly compared with those of dry materials.

Molecular attractions (cohesion forces) in liquid water, which are stronger near the freezing point, are responsible for its high tensile strength and for manifestations of *surface tension* and *viscosity* (table 2.3). Surface tension acts as a thin skin that tends to give water droplets a spherical shape, and in combination with its wetting properties (adhesion forces) accounts for the rise of water in capillaries against the force of gravity. The viscosity of water is a measure of its internal resistance to flow, and is an important variable under conditions of laminar (streamline) flow at low velocities.

The single water molecule is composed of two atoms of hydrogen and one of oxygen, but the positively charged hydrogen protons are also attracted to the negatively charged oxygen electrons of neighboring molecules. Cohesive forces are a manifestation of this hydrogen bonding, and the latent heats of water are measures of the energy required to break the bonds. The *latent heat of vaporization* (table 2.3) decreases by about $\frac{5}{9}$ cal/g · °C as temperature

Table 2.3. Some Properties of Liquid Water at Standard Pressure

| Temperature (°C) | Density (g/cm³) | Surface tension (dyne/cm) | Viscosity (dynamic) (g/cm · min) | Thermal conductivity (cal/cm · min · °C) | Latent heat Freezing (cal/g) | Latent heat Vaporization (cal/g) |
|---|---|---|---|---|---|---|
| 0  | 0.9999 | 75.6 | 1.08 | 0.080 | 79.7 | 597.3 |
| 4  | 1.0000 | 75.0 | 0.94 | 0.082 | —    | 595.1 |
| 10 | 0.9997 | 74.2 | 0.78 | 0.084 | —    | 591.7 |
| 20 | 0.9982 | 72.7 | 0.60 | 0.086 | —    | 586.0 |
| 30 | 0.9957 | 71.1 | 0.48 | 0.089 | —    | 580.4 |
| 40 | 0.9923 | 69.5 | 0.39 | 0.091 | —    | 574.7 |
| 50 | 0.9881 | 67.9 | 0.33 | 0.092 | —    | 569.0 |

increases over the common range; but since the latent heat of freezing (or fusion) increases by the same amount, their sum, the latent heat of sublimation (table 2.1) is virtually constant.

The albedo of a liquid water surface is affected by its smoothness, and by cloudiness and solar altitude; specular (mirrorlike) reflectance is most pronounced under clear skies where the shortwave reflectivity coefficient decreases from about 0.60 at 5° solar altitude to 0.05 at 60° (table 2.2). Water may transmit a part of the visible portion of solar radiation (light) to depths greater than 100 m; about 5% is transmitted to this depth in pure water, but under natural conditions in clear lakes less than 1% is transmitted. Liquid water, even as thin films at the surface or as droplets in dense clouds, emits and absorbs longwave radiation with almost perfect efficiency.

## 2.1.c. *Water Vapor*

Water vapor constitutes only about 0.25% of the earth's total atmospheric mass; it is more plentiful in warmer regions and near the surface but rarely exceeds 2.5% of a moist air mass, or 25 g/kg of moist air. Momentary storage of water vapor in the atmosphere is only about 0.04% of the earth's total freshwater (table 1.2), but somewhat better perspective is achieved by recognizing that this quantity is more than ten times the amount of transient storage in all rivers and streams. The importance of water vapor is much greater than that suggested by these quantities alone, however, since it modifies the radiation balance, transports enormous amounts of latent energy, and is rapidly recycled: about 10% of atmospheric water vapor is precipitated each day and simultaneously replaced by evaporation (see section 1.1.b).

The vaporization of liquid and solid water requires from 569 to 678 cal/g to break molecular bonds (tables 2.1 and 2.3) and to expand the water to more than 1000 times its original volume. The molecular density of any gas at standard temperature and pressure is its molecular weight/22.4 liters, so for water vapor it must be 18.016 g/22.4 liters, or 804 g/m$^3$; the specific heat of water vapor varies from 0.44 to 0.46 cal/g · °C over the temperature range from -40 to 50°C. But under natural conditions water vapor invariably occurs in mixture with air, and its most useful hydrologic properties are those exhibited in the mixture and at equilibrium with its solid and liquid phases.

The molecular weight of air is 28.966 g, so its density at standard temperature and pressure must be 28.966 g/22.4 liters, or 1293 g/m$^3$; this means that air is more dense than water vapor, that a unit volume of dry air is heavier than moist air at the same pressure, and that the difference in density increases with moisture content. The densities of dry and saturated air at standard pressure are given in table 2.4 as a function of temperature. The density difference (dry minus saturated) is equal to the ratio of molecular weights of water vapor and air (i.e., 18.016/28.966, or 0.622) times the saturation density of water vapor.

The *saturation density* of water vapor is its maximum bulk density at a given temperature; at equilibrium with a liquid or solid water interface it is strictly a function of surface temperature. Table 2.4 gives the bulk saturation density of water vapor over ice and liquid water as a function of temperature (liquid water droplets occur in clouds down to -40°C). Saturation vapor densities are greater over liquid water than over ice and, as a rule of thumb that is more accurate near the freezing point, density doubles as temperature increases by 10°C increments.

*Saturation vapor pressure* is the partial pressure of water vapor in a saturated atmosphere; it is independent of atmospheric pressure (Dalton's law) and, as with saturation density, is strictly a function of temperature. Saturation vapor pressures over ice and liquid water are given in table 2.4; the partial pressure over liquid water $e_s$ (in mb) is given approximately by

$$\ln e_s = 21.382 - \frac{5347.5}{T} \tag{2.1}$$

where $T$ is the absolute temperature (Tabata, 1973). The ratio of vapor pressure to density is $T/217$.

Water vapor densities and pressures vary considerably near the surface, especially in the vertical dimension over water bodies, moist soils, and transpiring vegetation; consequently, water vapor is continually moving in the direction of lower density or pressure.

Table 2.4. Some Properties of Air and Water Vapor at Standard Pressure

| Temperature (°C) | Air density | | Saturation vapor density | | Saturation vapor pressure | | Diffusion coefficient in air (cm²/sec) |
|---|---|---|---|---|---|---|---|
| | Dry (kg/m³) | Saturated (kg/m³) | Over ice (g/m³) | Over liquid (g/m³) | Over ice (mb) | Over liquid (mb) | |
| -40 | 1.514 | 1.514 | 0.119 | 0.176 | 0.128 | 0.189 | 0.150 |
| -35 | 1.482 | 1.482 | 0.203 | 0.286 | 0.223 | 0.314 | |
| -30 | 1.452 | 1.452 | 0.339 | 0.453 | 0.380 | 0.509 | 0.165 |
| -25 | 1.422 | 1.422 | 0.552 | 0.705 | 0.632 | 0.807 | |
| -20 | 1.394 | 1.394 | 0.884 | 1.074 | 1.032 | 1.254 | 0.180 |
| -15 | 1.367 | 1.366 | 1.387 | 1.605 | 1.652 | 1.912 | |
| -10 | 1.341 | 1.340 | 2.139 | 2.358 | 2.597 | 2.863 | 0.195 |
| -5 | 1.316 | 1.314 | 3.246 | 3.407 | 4.015 | 4.215 | |
| 0 | 1.292 | 1.289 | 4.847 | 4.847 | 6.107 | 6.108 | 0.210 |
| 5 | 1.269 | 1.265 | — | 6.797 | — | 8.719 | |
| 10 | 1.247 | 1.241 | — | 9.399 | — | 12.272 | 0.225 |
| 15 | 1.225 | 1.217 | — | 12.83 | — | 17.044 | |
| 20 | 1.204 | 1.193 | — | 17.30 | — | 23.373 | 0.240 |
| 25 | 1.184 | 1.170 | — | 23.05 | — | 31.671 | |
| 30 | 1.164 | 1.146 | — | 30.38 | — | 42.430 | 0.255 |
| 35 | 1.145 | 1.121 | — | 39.63 | — | 56.236 | |
| 40 | 1.127 | 1.096 | — | 51.19 | — | 73.777 | 0.270 |
| 45 | 1.109 | 1.069 | — | 65.50 | — | 95.855 | |
| 50 | 1.092 | 1.041 | — | 83.06 | — | 123.40 | 0.285 |

The rate of this mass flow in the absence of wind (e.g., through leaf stomata or the thin boundary layer of virtually still air near a moist surface) is proportional to the vapor pressure or density gradient (rate of change with distance); the proportionality factor is the *diffusion coefficient* for water vapor in air (see section 6.1.a). The diffusion coefficient $D$ (in $cm^2$/sec) is a function of air temperature $T$ and pressure $p$, or

$$D = \frac{210 + 1.5T}{p} \tag{2.2}$$

for $T$ in °C and $p$ in mb; solutions to equation 2.2 for $p = 1000$ mb are given in table 2.4.

## 2.2. Hydrologic Processes

Forest hydrology is concerned with the mass movements and phase changes of water in a sylvan environment; in its most basic form it is the study of hydrologic processes. Water budgeting is a quantitative method of accounting for mass flows and transformations that are amenable to direct measurement; as such it is a natural outgrowth of the *hydrometric method*. Energy budgeting is a *physical method* of assessing mass transfers in terms of equivalent energy fluxes; it is especially applicable to hydrologic processes that involve changes in water phase.

### 2.2.a. Some Definitions

The *hydrologic cycle* is a general circulatory pattern that comprises a complicated array of water movements and transformations; as applied to any particular mass or molecule of water the pattern may be acyclic and the term a misnomer. In the most simplified "cycle" water flows from atmosphere to land to ocean to atmosphere as in figure 2.1 (based on table 1.3); note that if only average *net* flows are considered, flow rates are the same in all stages of the cycle. It is more precise etymologically, and more useful practically, to envision a *hydrologic sequence* of events in which

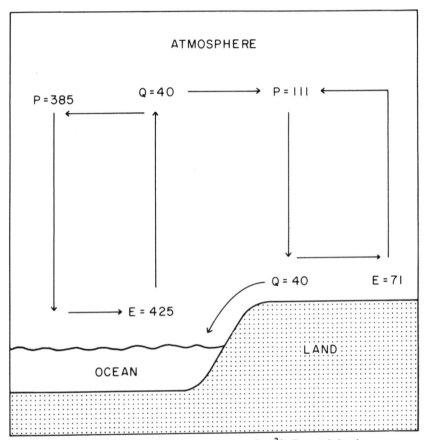

**Figure 2.1. Global water balance components (km$^3$); $P$, precipitation; $E$, evaporation; $Q$, discharge.**

the numerous individual processes can be interrelated and quantified.

The forest hydrologist is more concerned with the sequence of hydrologic events that is initiated as water vapor condenses in the atmosphere. *Condensation* is the process by which water vapor is transformed to liquid or ice with the release of energy (the latent heat of condensation or sublimation); it occurs predominately at higher levels in the atmosphere with the formation of clouds, but is also commonly exhibited at the surface in the form of dew and frost. Condensation, and the conditions under which it occurs, are discussed in greater detail in section 3.1.c; it is a prerequisite but not a sufficient condition for precipitation.

*Precipitation* (see sections 3.2 and 3.3) is the general term for atmospheric condensation products that reach the surface, e.g., rain, snow, hail, sleet, and glaze; *virga* is the meteorologist's name for precipitation that evaporates while falling. Liquid precipitation, primarily rainfall but also *occult precipitation* (i.e., fog droplets that are intercepted by a forest canopy), is usually of greatest immediate concern to the hydrologist since it moves rapidly through the forest and soil, initiating or modifying other hydrologic processes, and generating streamflow. Contrastingly, snowfall and other solid forms, which may lie immobile at the surface for weeks or months, are called *delayed precipitation*.

Precipitation over a forest is depleted before it contacts the mineral soil; the total depletion, which is subsequently evaporated, is called *interception* (section 4.1). *Canopy interception* is the fraction of precipitation that is held temporarily (prior to evaporation) by leaves, limbs, and stems; that which is eventually evaporated from dead organic material at the forest floor is called *litter interception*. Rain or snow that is initially held on the forest canopy or floor may subsequently be reduced by mechanical shaking (wind) or melting; total interception is that part of precipitation that does not reach the mineral soil (sublimation from the surface of a snowpack at the forest floor may be considered separately; see section 9.4).

Precipitation over a forest canopy may reach the forest floor by either of two pathways (sections 4.2 and 4.3); *throughfall* is the part that reaches the floor directly or by dripping from leaves and branches, and a less significant volume, *stemflow*, descends along the surfaces of tree stems. The total, throughfall plus stemflow, reduced only by litter interception (or snow sublimation), is the fraction of precipitation that reaches the mineral soil. *Net precipitation* is usually taken as the sum of throughfall and stemflow, and *effective precipitation* as the fraction that reaches the mineral soil; in an undisturbed forest the latter is usually equal to total infiltration.

*Infiltration* is the process whereby liquid water enters the mineral soil (the term is sometimes loosely applied to related subsurface flow in soil); for bare soil it is equal to the difference between precipitation and surface runoff volumes. *Percolation* is the movement of liquid water through porous soils and geologic strata; the movement is generally downward (as opposed, e.g., to upward movements by capillary flow), but is frequently more nearly horizontal than vertical (as in subsurface flow along hillsides or in tilted rock layers). Water held transiently in any space is called *storage*; one refers, for example, to interception, stream channel, and snowpack storages, but the term is applied most frequently to soil moisture and groundwater reserves.

*Evaporation* is the physical process by which liquid water is converted to vapor; it occurs when water is in contact with an unsaturated atmosphere at the same temperature. *Transpiration* is the evaporation of water from internal surfaces of living plant organs and its subsequent diffusion from the plant. Evaporation, transpiration, and sublimation are all vaporization processes but, since it is frequently difficult to identify each separately, total vaporization is called *evapotranspiration*.

*Runoff* is a general term for surface and subsurface discharges of water from a hydrologic system (e.g., a plot or catchment); in forest hydrology it is usually unrealistic to equate runoff with streamflow. Surface discharge includes *streamflow* or *stream discharge* (flow in channels) and *surface runoff* or *overland flow* (not restricted to channels); subsurface discharge may occur as *deep percolation* or *leakage* in rock strata, as *underflow* beneath streambeds, or as *interflow* in the upper horizons of a soil profile. *Direct runoff* or *stormflow* is the distinctive discharge increase or "quickflow" that results from specific rainfall events or snow melting, irrespective of its pathway; that part of total discharge not identified as direct runoff is called *base flow* or *groundwater flow*.

## 2.2.b. Water Budgeting

Water budgeting is a simple accounting procedure that is based on the mass conservation principle; it is used to isolate and estimate the most elusive flow parameters, or as an independent check on the accuracy of observational data. The central idea as applied to any hydrologic system is simply that the algebraic sum of all flow elements can be equated to zero when water additions and losses to flow are given opposite signs, for example, as in equation 1.1. In a more general form, the *storage equation*,

$$\text{Inflow} + \text{Outflow} + \text{Storage change} = 0 \qquad (2.3)$$

where the sum of inflow (+) and outflow (−) is equal to the storage change; as illustrated in figure 2.2, storage increase (−) in a system is a loss to the immediate flow cycle, and storage decrease (+) is an addition.

Equation 2.3 applies to any discrete hydrologic system (e.g., the atmosphere, total earth, land or water mass, river basin, or catchment area), and the terms of the equation represent mass or volumetric flow rates (mass/time, or volume/time) which, in hydrology, are frequently expressed as depth/time (for a given area) or total depth (for a given area and time interval); some common flow units and conversions are given in table A.1. *Inflow* to a terrestrial system may be predominately precipitation but it also includes any other surface or subsurface flows *into* the area, and *outflow* may consist entirely of stream discharge and vapor flow but usually includes other drainages *from* the system. Likewise, for particular purposes, it may be necessary to identify the components of storage (e.g., soil moisture, groundwater, or snowpack storages).

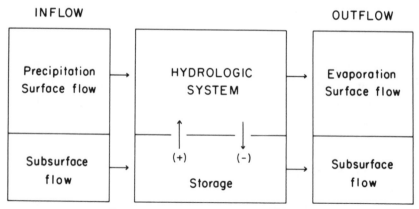

Figure 2.2. Storage equation elements.

Climatological (long-term average) water-budget equations for extensive hydrologic systems can be written in the fewest terms. For example, for the earth's atmosphere it is apparent that, since the storage change is zero,

$$P + E = 0 \qquad (2.4)$$

where outflow $P(-)$ and inflow $E(+)$ are average depths of precipitation and evaporation; the same equation applies to the total earth surface with inflow $P(+)$ and outflow $E(-)$. Obviously equation 2.4 can be written in terms of absolute quantities as

$$|P| = |E| \qquad (2.5)$$

which applies equally to both systems; in practice the sign convention is often tacitly ignored, positive and negative flow symbols are simply assembled on opposite sides of the equality sign, and

$$P = E \qquad (2.6)$$

is understood as an equality of absolute values.

Climatological water-budget equations for entire land and water masses, representing the data of table 1.3, are only slightly more complex. Expressing equation 1.1 in the form of 2.6, with inflows to the left of the equality sign, average flow volumes are given by

$$P + Q = E \qquad \text{(Oceans)} \qquad (2.7)$$
$$P = Q + E \qquad \text{(Land)} \qquad (2.8)$$

where $Q$ is the total liquid discharge from land to oceans ($Q$ is also equal to the net atmospheric vapor flow from oceans to land). Here it is also assumed that ocean and land storages are constant (storage change, equation 2.3, equal to zero).

The long-term average water budget for a river basin or small catchment is frequently written in the form of equation 2.8; the usual assumptions are that 1) precipitation is the only inflow (no subsurface leakage into the basin), 2) river or stream discharge is an adequate measure of liquid water outflow (underflow and deep percolation from the basin are negligible), and 3) basin storage is steady (subject only to random or seasonal fluctuations). None of these assumptions is rigorously or universally true, and they are especially suspect as applied to the small upland watersheds that are of primary concern in forest hydrology; nevertheless equation 2.8 has considerable practical value as an hypothesis or first approximation. In carefully chosen research areas, $E = P - Q$ (from equation 2.8) is still the most accurate estimate of total evaporation loss (see section 6.3); this is true despite the uncertainties involved in quantifying basin precipitation and stream discharge.

The short-term water budget for a basin or catchment must include a storage term; in the form of equations 2.6 through 2.8,

$$P = Q + E + S \qquad (2.9)$$

where $S$ is defined as a storage increase (representing a loss to the immediate flow cycle) and negative values are to the right of the equality sign. This means simply that if $P > (Q + E)$ water storage must increase; if $P < (Q + E)$

$$P + S = Q + E \qquad (2.10)$$

and water withdrawn from storage is an addition to the immediate flow cycle. Ordinarily the value of $Q$ is taken as the measured stream discharge, and equations 2.9 and 2.10 do not account for subsurface flows.

In controlled experiments on small plots where it is possible to measure subsurface flows, the water budget during periods of drying (storage decrease) is

$$P + Q_i + L_i + S = E + Q_o + L_o \qquad (2.11)$$

where $Q_i$ and $Q_o$ are surface inflow and outflow respectively, and $L_i$ and $L_o$ are the corresponding subsurface flows. Equation 2.11 is used most frequently to estimate total evaporation loss. When precipitation $P = 0$ during a drying period

$$S + (Q_i - Q_o) + (L_i - L_o) = E \qquad (2.12)$$

where $Q_i - Q_o$ and $L_i - L_o$ are net inflows; if under these conditions the soil surface is sealed to prevent direct evaporation, $E$ is a measure of plant transpiration.

## 2.2.c. Energy Budgeting

Energy budgeting is a simple accounting procedure that is based on the energy conservation principle; in hydrology it is used to quantify water phase changes in terms of equivalent energy flows. As in water budgeting the central idea is simply that the algebraic sum of all energy flows can be equated to zero when inputs and losses of energy from a surface element are given opposite signs. In general form the energy-budget equation is analogous to equation 2.3, and the sum of energy inflow (+) and outflow (−) is equal to a heat storage change (±).

Energy transfer in the forest occurs primarily as *radiation* (*R*), which does not require a transfer medium, *conduction* (*B*) in solids, *convection* (*H*) in moving fluids, and *latent heat exchange* ($L_v E$) associated with the vaporization of water. Observing the sign convention the energy-budget equation is

$$R + B + H + L_v E = 0 \qquad (2.13)$$

or, during periods of positive radiation (daytime) when, as a rule, $B, H$, and $L_v E$ are negative,

$$R = B + H + L_v E \qquad (2.14)$$

is understood as an equality of absolute values. Energy flow is measured as a rate or *flux* (energy/time, power), and the flux per unit area of surface, *flux density* (energy/area · time, power/area) is often expressed in $cal/cm^2$ · min, langley/min (1 ly = 1 $cal/cm^2$), or $watt/m^2$ (1 ly/min = 697 $watt/m^2$); some common energy units and conversions are given in table A.1.

*Radiant energy.* The ability to emit radiant energy is an intrinsic property of all matter, but the quality (wavelength spectrum) of emission is determined by body surface temperature. Solar radiation, emitted at sun surface temperature (about 6000°K), is called *shortwave radiation* (*S*) because it occurs primarily at wavelengths between 0.2 and 4.0 microns; bodies at common earth temperatures (about 300°K) emit *longwave radiation* (*L*) at wavelengths between about 4 and 100 microns. This means that *R* in equations 2.13 and 21.4 is a net flux (*net radiation*) that must be evaluated in terms of both *S* and *L*.

Radiation from the sun is partially reflected, absorbed, and scattered by the earth's atmosphere, a part arrives at the surface as *direct* or *beam radiation* ($S_b$), and another part as *diffuse radiation* ($S_d$) from the sky; $S_b$ is strongly affected by surface exposure (topographic slope and aspect) whereas $S_d$ is largely unaffected. The sum, $S_b + S_d$, called *global radiation*, is partially reflected at the surface, and the *reflected flux* ($S_r$) is equal to $rS_t$ where $r$ is the surface albedo, or shortwave reflectivity coefficient; some typical values of $r$ for common surfaces are given in table 2.5. Ordinarily only the total incoming flux $S_t$ (global radiation) is measured, and *net shortwave radiation* (i.e., the difference between incoming and outgoing fluxes) is estimated as

$$S = S_b + S_d - S_r = S_t (1 - r) \qquad (2.15)$$

where $S \geqslant 0$ (positive during the day and virtually zero at night).

Longwave radiation, sometimes referred to as "infrared" radiation (but not to be confused with shortwave radiation at wavelengths between 0.7 and 4.0 microns, which is also infrared), includes both the incoming *atmospheric* or *counter radiation* ($L_i$) that is emitted continuously by atmospheric gases (primarily water vapor and carbon dioxide), aerosols, and clouds, and outgoing *terrestrial* or *thermal radiation* ($L_o$) emitted by surface elements. In accordance with Stefan's law, the emitted flux densities are

$$L_i = \epsilon_a \sigma T_a^4 \qquad (2.16)$$

and

$$L_o = \epsilon_s \sigma T_s^4 \qquad (2.17)$$

where $\epsilon_a$ and $\epsilon_s$ are atmospheric and surface emissivity coefficients, $\sigma$ is the Stefan-Boltzmann constant [i.e., $81.7(10^{-12})$ly/min·°K⁴], $T_a$ (in °K) is air temperature near the surface (screen temperature), and $T_s$ is the absolute surface temperature; some typical values of $\epsilon_a$ and $\epsilon_s$ are given in table 2.6, and solutions to equations 2.16 and 2.17 for $\epsilon_a = \epsilon_s = 1$ (representing a *blackbody* that emits with perfect efficiency) are given in table A.2. The absolute value of $L_o$ is almost always greater than $L_i$ and, since according to Kirchhoff's law the longwave reflectivity of a surface is $1 - \epsilon_s$ so that the

Table 2.5.  Typical Shortwave Reflectivity Coefficients for Some Natural Surfaces

| Surface | Description; conditions | Reflectivity coefficient (albedo), % |
|---|---|---|
| *Water* (see table 2.2) | | |
| *Ground* | | |
| Sand | dry, light:  high sun | 35 |
| | low sun | 60 |
| | gray sand:  wet | 10 |
| | dry | 20 |
| | white sand:  wet | 25 |
| | dry | 35 |
| Rock | high sun:  sandstone spoil, dry | 20 |
| | black coal spoil, dry | 5 |
| Soil | dark, organic | 10 |
| | clay | 20 |
| | light sandy | 30 |
| *Vegetation* | | |
| Grass | typical fields | 20 |
| | dead grass:  wet | 20 |
| | dry | 30 |
| | dry steppe | 25 |
| | tundra, heather | 15 |
| Crops | cereals, tobacco | 25 |
| | cotton, potato, tomato | 20 |
| | sugar cane | 15 |
| Trees | rain forest | 15 |
| | eucalyptus | 20 |
| | red pine forest | 10 |
| | mixed hardwoods (in leaf) | 18 |

reflected flux density is $(1 - \epsilon_s)L_i$, the *net longwave radiation* at the surface given by

$$L = L_i - L_o - (1 - \epsilon_s)L_i$$
$$= \epsilon_s (L_i - \sigma T_s^4) \qquad (2.18)$$

is almost always negative, representing an effective outgoing flux, or loss of energy from the surface.

Table 2.6. Typical Longwave Emissivity Coefficients

| Surface | Description; conditions | | Emissivity coefficient |
|---|---|---|---|
| *Water* (see table 2.2) | | | |
| *Atmosphere* | | | |
| Clear sky[a] | screen temperature, °C: | 0 | 0.74 |
| | | ±10 | 0.76 |
| | | ±20 | 0.81 |
| | | ±30 | 0.87 |
| | | ±40 | 0.92 |
| Partly cloudy[b] | | | $\epsilon'_a$ |
| Deep overcast | at cloud base temperature | | 1.00 |
| *Ground* | | | |
| Sand | dry | | 0.95 |
| | wet | | 0.98 |
| Peat | dry | | 0.97 |
| | wet | | 0.98 |
| Rock | light sandstone | | 0.98 |
| | black coal spoil | | 0.99 |
| | limestone, gravel | | 0.92 |
| *Vegatation* | | | |
| Grass | typical fields | | 0.95 |
| | grass lawn | | 0.97 |
| Leaves | corn, beans | | 0.94 |
| | cotton, tobacco | | 0.96 |
| | cactus | | 0.98 |
| | sugar cane | | 0.99 |
| Forests | deciduous | | 0.95 |
| | coniferous | | 0.97 |
| *Miscellaneous* | | | |
| Aluminum | foil | | 0.05 |
| Brass | polished | | 0.10 |
| Iron | polished | | 0.30 |
| Wood | oak, planed | | 0.90 |

[a]Apparent atmospheric emissivity coefficient

$\epsilon_a = 1 - 0.261 \exp \{-7.77(10^{-4})(273 - T_a)^2\}$,

Idso and Jackson (1969).

[b]If $C$ is the average fraction of cloud cover, $\epsilon'_a \simeq \epsilon_a + (1 - \epsilon_a)C$; this approximation does not account for the diversity of radiative properties among cloud types.

Combining equations 2.15 and 2.18, the net (allwave) radiation term in energy-budget equations 2.13 and 2.14 is

$$R = S + L$$
$$= (1 - r)S_t + \epsilon_s (L_i - \sigma T_s^4) \tag{2.19}$$

and, as a rule, $R < 0$ at night and $R > 0$ during the day. The components of $R$ over a forest canopy are shown diagrammatically in figure 2.3; some typical values for selected periods over vegetated land in the middle latitudes are given in table 2.7. Instruments used to measure individual incoming and outgoing fluxes of shortwave and longwave radiation, or their combined effect, net radiation, are described in section 10.2.

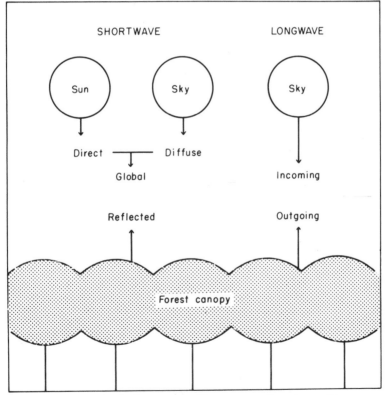

Figure 2.3. Radiant energy fluxes over a forest canopy.

**Table 2.7. Typical Values of Radiation Components over Vegetated Land in the Middle Latitudes**

| Radiation component | Clear sky, summer | | Seasonal average | | Annual total (kly/yr) |
|---|---|---|---|---|---|
| | Midday (ly/min) | Night (ly/min) | Summer (ly/day) | Winter (ly/day) | |
| *Shortwave* | | | | | |
| Direct | 1.00 | | 290 | 100 | 70 |
| Diffuse | 0.10 | | 210 | 100 | 55 |
| Reflected | -0.20 | | -100 | -60 | -30 |
| Net | 0.90 | | 400 | 140 | 95 |
| *Longwave* | | | | | |
| Atmospheric | 0.55 | 0.45 | 750 | 550 | 240 |
| Terrestrial | -0.70 | -0.55 | -850 | -600 | -265 |
| Net | -0.15 | -0.10 | -100 | -50 | -25 |
| *Allwave* | | | | | |
| Net | 0.75 | -0.10 | 300 | 90 | 70 |

Numerous theoretical and empirical methods have been used to estimate radiant energy fluxes in lieu of actual measurements (Robinson, 1966; Budyko, 1974); such methods are useful where climatological averages are sufficient and great accuracy is not required. Ordinarily the longwave fluxes and net longwave radiation can be estimated with sufficient accuracy for hydrological purposes using equations 2.16 through 2.18, tables 2.6 and A.2, and observed temperatures $T_a$ and $T_s$. Net longwave radiation increases (becomes less negative) as the fraction of cloud cover $C$ increases, so that

$$L \text{ (cloudy)} = L(1 - kC) \tag{2.20}$$

where $k = 0.5 + 0.004 \phi$ for latitude ($\phi$) in degrees.

Daily averages of global radiation at a site are highly correlated with mean cloudiness and *potential* or *extraterrestrial radiation* ($S_p$, the theoretical maximum solar radiation that could reach the site in the absence of the earth's atmosphere; see tables A.3 and A.4). A general relationship for the earth is

$$S_t = S_p (0.80 - 0.34C - 0.46C^2) \tag{2.21}$$

according to Black (1956); in a humid region of the eastern United States, at $\phi = 39°N$, Lee et al. (1979) found that throughout the year

$$S_t = S_p (0.86 - 0.65C) \qquad (2.22)$$

or in simpler form

$$S_t = 0.57S_p - 70 \qquad (2.23)$$

for monthly averages of daily totals in ly/day (correlations about 0.98, and standard errors about 2% of means). Net allwave radiation is highly correlated with the global flux:

$$R = 0.71S_t - 41 \qquad (2.24)$$

for monthly averages of 24-hour totals over grass (Lee, 1978); over a hardwood forest canopy

$$R = 0.83S_t - 0.13 \qquad (2.25)$$

with a standard error of 0.03 ly/min based on instantaneous measurements under clear skies at various times of day and year (Federer, 1968).

*Heat conduction.* Heat transfer by conduction ($B$) is important in hydrology because it represents an energy sink (−) during heating periods (daytime, summer) and an energy source (+) during cooling periods (night, winter); in this way the forest and substrata act as transient heat storage reservoirs that modify hydrologic processes (e.g., infiltration, snowmelt, and transpiration). The rate of conduction per unit cross-section of medium normal to the direction of transfer is proportional to the rate of change of temperature with distance ($z$) between the high temperature $T_s$ (source) and the low temperature $T$ (sink), or

$$B = -k \frac{dT}{dz} \qquad (2.26)$$

where $k$ is the thermal conductivity of the medium, and the negative sign indicates that heat is transferred away from the source; under steady conditions, $dT/dz$ = constant (for a homogeneous medium), and

$$B = \frac{k}{z} (T_s - T) = - h_b \Delta T_z \qquad (2.27)$$

where $\Delta T_z = T_s - T$ and $h_b = k/z$ is the *heat transfer coefficient* (i.e., the ratio of flux density to temperature difference) for conduction. The average rate of heat storage over time ($t$) for any body of volume ($V$) occupying surface area ($A$) is

$$B = - \frac{\rho c}{t} \frac{V}{A} \Delta T_t = - \frac{\rho c z}{t} \Delta T_t \qquad (2.28)$$

where $\rho c$, the product of density ($\rho$) and specific heat ($c$), is the thermal capacity; $V/A = z$ the effective thickness; and $\Delta T_t$ the change in mean temperature of the body.

Some typical thermal properties of common materials are given in table 2.8; it is significant that, despite much greater densities of some common substances, liquid water has the greatest thermal capacity. Heating a unit volume of liquid water requires about twice as much energy per degree as that for ice, rock, and soils, three times as much as that for wood, and more than 3000 times as much as that for air; this explains the fact that the thermal capacities of mineral soils and organic materials increase with moisture content. Thermal conductivity is lowest for air, dry organic soil, wood, and new snow, intermediate for liquid water, and highest for rock, wet mineral soil, and ice; organic materials and snow insulate substrata against rapid temperature fluctuations.

The thermal capacity of a forest above ground level is relatively small; the total volume of wood and organic material usually does not exceed about 5 cm³/cm² of surface, and from table 2.8 the total thermal capacity of this volume (primarily wood) would be 1.9 ly/°C. The total thermal capacity of air within the canopy volume would be 0.6 ly/°C (for a 20-meter forest height), and the total heat capacity of the forest volume (2.5 ly/°C) would be roughly equivalent to that of a 5-cm depth of soil (or snow). Clearly, therefore, the primary heat storage reservoir in the forest is soil (or snow cover).

Table 2.8. Some Typical Thermal Properties of Common Materials

| Material | Bulk density $\rho$ (g/cm$^3$) | Specific heat $c$ (cal/g · °C) | Thermal capacity $\rho c$ (cal/cm$^3$ · °C) | Thermal conductivity $k$ (cal/cm · min · °C) |
|---|---|---|---|---|
| *Miscellaneous* | | | | |
| Rock | 2.7 | 0.18 | 0.49 | 0.25 |
| Wood | 0.6 | 0.64 | 0.38 | 0.04 |
| Water (at 0°C) | 1.0 | 1.00 | 1.00 | 0.08 |
| Ice (at 0°C) | 0.9 | 0.50 | 0.45 | 0.32 |
| Snow (old) | 0.8 | 0.50 | 0.40 | 0.24 |
| Snow (new) | 0.2 | 0.50 | 0.10 | 0.02 |
| Air | 0.0012 | 0.24 | 0.0003 | 0.0036 |
| *Soils* | (% water) | | | |
| Clay | 10 / 1.7 | 0.24 | 0.40 | 0.09 |
| | 20 / 1.8 | 0.28 | 0.50 | 0.16 |
| | 30 / 1.9 | 0.32 | 0.60 | 0.19 |
| Sand | 10 / 1.7 | 0.26 | 0.44 | 0.15 |
| | 20 / 1.8 | 0.30 | 0.54 | 0.28 |
| | 30 / 1.9 | 0.34 | 0.64 | 0.31 |
| Peat | 10 / 0.4 | 0.55 | 0.22 | 0.015 |
| | 40 / 0.7 | 0.74 | 0.52 | 0.041 |
| | 70 / 1.0 | 0.82 | 0.82 | 0.062 |

*Heat convection.* Energy convection ($H$) occurs as air (or any fluid) moves across a solid surface; if the surface is warmer than the air (typical daytime condition) energy flows in the direction surface → air and convection is negative, but when the surface is cooler than the air (typical at night) the flow direction and its sign are reversed. Convection is a two-stage process of 1) heat conduction by molecular diffusion through a thin "boundary layer" of effectively still air near the surface, and 2) true convection by mass motion and turbulent diffusion of air outside the boundary layer; during steady flow the heat flux is the same for each stage, and

$$H = - \frac{k}{\delta_c} (T_s - T_a) = - \rho c K_h \frac{\Delta T}{\Delta z} \qquad (2.29)$$

where $\delta_c$ is the thickness of the boundary layer for heat transfer, $T_a$ is air temperature outside the layer, and $\Delta T / \Delta z$ is the temperature gradient in a layer of free air where the turbulent transfer coefficient is $K_h$. The boundary-layer thickness ($\delta_c$) can be determined for small geometric forms as a function of body size, shape, and wind characteristics (see, e.g., Gates, 1962; Monteith, 1973; Lee, 1978), and the turbulent transfer coefficient ($K_h$) from wind profile measurements (see, e.g., Thom, 1975).

In equation 2.29, $k/\delta_c = h_c$ is, in analogy with equation 2.27, the heat transfer coefficient for convection (here $k$ is the thermal conductivity of air); its magnitude is generally greater for greater windspeeds and smaller bodies. Under normal conditions in a forest canopy (forced convection) an approximate value of $h_c$ for single platelike bodies, e.g., hardwood leaves, is given by

$$h_c = 3.1 \, k \, (u/d)^{0.5} \qquad (2.30)$$

where $h_c$ (entire leaf, both surfaces) is in ly/min · °C for windspeed ($u$) in cm/sec and leaf width or diameter ($d$) in cm; and for clusters of pine needles

$$h_c = k(5.0 + 0.2u) \qquad (2.31)$$

as adapted from Gates, Tibbals, and Kreith (1965). Over larger areas of land, based on the data of Geiger (1965),

$$h_c = 0.27\,ku^{0.5} \qquad (2.32)$$

may serve as a rough approximation; solutions to equations 2.30 through 2.32 for the common range of values of $d$ and $u$ are listed in table 2.9.

Outside of the thin boundary layer of air near a surface wind-speed generally increases logarithmically with height, and in practice it may be convenient to use an equation of the form

$$H = -\,\rho c K_h \frac{\mathrm{d}T}{\mathrm{d}z} \qquad (2.33)$$

where $K_h$ is determined from wind profile measurements. If $\mathrm{d}T/\mathrm{d}z$ is obtained from measurements at heights $z_1$ and $z_2$ above ground level, the convection rate can be expressed in terms of temperature

**Table 2.9. Some Approximate Heat Transfer Coefficients for Convection (mly/min · °C)**

| Windspeed (cm/sec) | Pine needle cluster | Hardwood leaf | Typical land area |
|:---:|:---:|:---|:---:|
| 100 | 90 | $d =$ 1: 110 | 10 |
|  |  | 5: 50 |  |
|  |  | 10: 35 |  |
| 200 | 160 | 1: 160 | 14 |
|  |  | 5: 70 |  |
|  |  | 10: 50 |  |
| 500 | 380 | 1: 250 | 22 |
|  |  | 5: 110 |  |
|  |  | 10: 80 |  |
| 1000 | 740 | 1: 350 | 31 |
|  |  | 5: 160 |  |
|  |  | 10: 110 |  |
| 2000 | 1460 | 1: 500 | 43 |
|  |  | 5: 225 |  |
|  |  | 10: 160 |  |

and height differences as in equation 2.29. Or, in terms of wind profile parameters above a forest canopy,

$$H = - \frac{0.17\rho c \Delta T \Delta u}{\{\ln[(z_2 - x)/(z_1 - x)]\}^2} \qquad (2.34)$$

where the upward displacement $(x)$ of the wind profile is roughly two-thirds of forest height.

*Latent heat.* The common phase changes of water are accompanied by extraordinary exchanges of energy. The latent heat of fusion $(L_f)$ decreases from about 80 cal/g at 0°C to 56 cal/g at -40°C (table 2.1) and, for $T$ in °C,

$$L_f = 80 + (5/9)T \qquad (2.35)$$

is a good approximation for $T \geqslant -30$; similarly, the latent heat of vaporization $(L_v)$ is given by

$$L_v = 597 - (5/9)T \qquad (2.36)$$

over the range $0 \leqslant T \leqslant 50$ (table 2.3). Combining equations 2.35 and 2.36 yields the constant

$$L_s = L_f + L_v = 677 \qquad (2.37)$$

which, as an estimate of the latent heat of sublimation, is accurate to within 1 cal/g at temperatures down to -80°C.

Latent heat exchange associated with evaporation and transpiration is of singular importance in forest hydrology because it involves simultaneous transfers of water and energy and, in humid areas, usually accounts for a major part of the energy budget. Since the latent heat term $(L_v)$ is accurately known, any mass flux $(E)$ can be evaluated in terms of an equivalent energy flux $(L_v E)$; in the equation developed by Dalton, for example, the mass flux

$$E = C(e_s - e_a) \qquad (2.38)$$

where $e_s$ and $e_a$ are vapor pressures at the surface and in the ambient air, respectively, $C$ is a coefficient that must be determined independently in each instance, and

$$L_v E = L_v C(e_s - e_a) \qquad (2.39)$$

is the corresponding energy flux. Vaporization processes, and methods used in their quantification, are elaborated in chapter 6.

*Relative magnitudes.* Typical hourly variations of the energy-budget components over a forest during clear weather in summer are illustrated in figure 2.4; actual values vary considerably with atmospheric conditions, forest characteristics, and moisture levels. In a closed forest heat conduction or storage ($B$) is usually 10% or

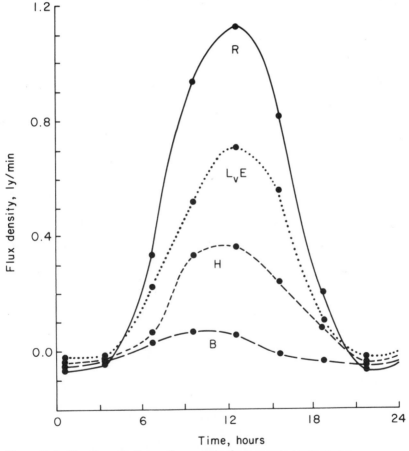

Figure 2.4. Hourly variations of energy-budget components over a forest during clear summer days (based on data from Baumgartner, 1956).

Table 2.10.  Average Energy-Budget Components over a Young Spruce Forest
During Clear Summer Days
(adapted from Baumgartner, 1956)

| Time interval (hr) | $R$ (mly/min) | $B$ (mly/min) | $H$ (mly/min) | $L_vE$ (mly/min) | $\beta$ $(H/L_vV)$ |
|---|---|---|---|---|---|
| 23-2 | -60 | 30 | 20 | 10 | 2.00 |
| 2-5 | -37 | 20 | 10 | 7 | 1.50 |
| 5-8 | 330 | -37 | -60 | -233 | 0.26 |
| 8-11 | 930 | -63 | -343 | -524 | 0.65 |
| 11-14 | 1150 | -53 | -373 | -724 | 0.52 |
| 14-17 | 813 | 3 | -250 | -566 | 0.44 |
| 17-20 | 197 | 37 | -107 | -127 | 0.84 |
| 20-23 | -60 | 40 | 13 | 7 | 2.00 |
| $R < 0$ | -52 | 30 | 14 | 8 | 1.86 |
| $R < 0$ | 684 | -22 | -227 | -435 | 0.52 |

less of net radiation $(R)$ during heating periods (daytime), and the
energy-budget equation may be written

$$R - B = H + L_vE = L_vE\,(1 + \beta) \qquad (2.40)$$

where the *Bowen ratio* $(\beta = H/L_vE)$ is of special interest. Usually
$\beta < 1$ (i.e., $H < L_vE$) under moist forest conditions with $R > 0$
(daytime), and $\beta < 0$ during the evaporation of intercepted rain
if canopy temperature drops below that of the ambient air, thereby
creating a sink for convective energy (changing the sign of $H$);
table 2.10 lists the relative magnitudes of energy-budget components over a young spruce forest as observed by Baumgartner
(1956).

## 2.3.  Hydrologic Units

In water budgeting it is useful to select natural topographic units
of land (watersheds or catchment areas) in which liquid water tends
to flow toward a common point—e.g., the mouth of a stream.
Water behavior and the magnitudes of water-budget components are
determined to a large extent by the physical properties, morphol-

ogy, and exposure of land segements; for hydrologic purposes, therefore, each watershed in unique. Forest hydrology is concerned primarily with the cover characteristics of watersheds that can be manipulated to modify the water budgets of forested areas for human purposes.

## 2.3.a. Catchment Areas

A water *catchment* or *watershed* is defined with respect to a given point, the gaging station, along a stream where surface water discharge is conveniently measured as streamflow (see section 10.7). The catchment area includes all points that lie above the elevation of the gaging station and within the *topographic divide* that separates adjacent watersheds. The topographic divide, or watershed perimeter, follows the ridge line between hydrologic units; on a topographic map it appears, as in figure 2.5, as in irregular closed traverse that is everywhere normal to the land contour.

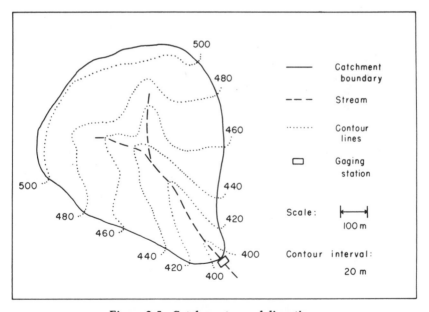

**Figure 2.5. Catchment area delineation.**

Drainage areas are frequently described as pear-shaped in plan view, as in figures 2.5 and 2.6*a*, but numerous other symmetrical and irregular forms are also encountered. In every instance, however, the watershed surface is essentially a tilted concavity or basin that determines the general direction of water flow and virtually isolates fluvial processes. The lateral section of a catchment may describe a U-shaped valley (fig. 2.6*b*), or a V-shaped one (fig. 2.6*c*), depending on the interaction of climate, rock type, and geologic structure; the transverse section (fig. 2.6*d*) reveals a characteristic increase in steepness near the upstream or headwater area.

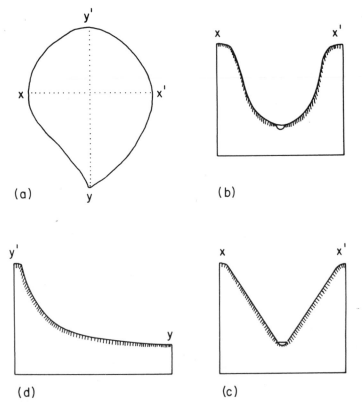

Figure 2.6. Catchment shape: *a*, plan view; *b* and *c*, lateral sections; and *d*, transverse section.

Subsurface flow ("leakage") into or out of a catchment may occur beneath the topographic divide as illustrated in figure 2.7; just as the topographic divide separates areas of surface flow, the underground or *phreatic divide* fixes the boundary for subsurface flow. In figure 2.7*a*, the dip of an impervious rock layer *toward* the stream diverts precipitation from outside the surface divide and increases basin discharge; the dip *away from* the stream diverts water to the outside and reduces streamflow. Leakage between

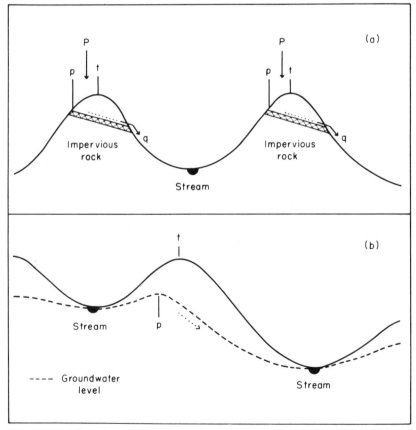

Figure 2.7. Watershed leakage caused by *a*, impervious strata and *b*, varying groundwater levels; *t*, topographic divide; *p*, phreatic divide; *P*, rainfall; *q*, discharge.

catchments may also occur when, for any reason, groundwater in adjacent basins is not at the same level; in figure 2.7b, for example, topographic and phreatic divides are not coincident, and subsurface flow increases the total inflow to the basin having the lower groundwater level.

The characteristics of catchment areas vary considerably with the composition and structure of underlying rock strata; an obvious manifestation of the lithological influence is illustrated in figure 2.8. Over relatively homogenous flat-lying rock the drainage pattern is characteristically *dendritic* (fig. 2.8a); this pattern, with local modifications, is common over much of the earth's surface. Some

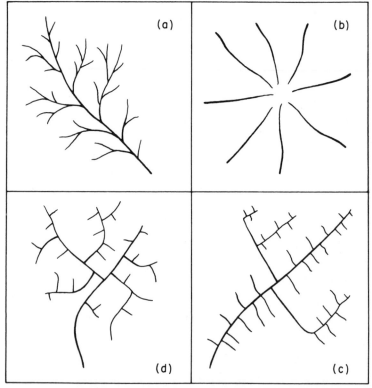

Figure 2.8. Drainage pattern types: *a*, dendritic; *b*, radial; *c*, trellised, and *d*, rectangular.

exceptions are the *radial* patterns (fig. 2.8*b*) that develop around steep domes or volcanic cones, or the *trellised* (fig. 2.8*c*) and *rectangular* patterns (fig. 2.8*d*) that form along lines of weakness on jointed or folded strata.

Catchment areas may be characterized in terms of the hierarchy of stream ordering as illustrated in figure 2.9: a *first order* stream has no tributaries, a *second order* stream has two or more tributaries of the first order, and a stream of any order has two or more tributaries of the next lower order. A catchment is described as first, second, or higher order depending on the stream order at the outlet or gaging station (i.e., the highest order stream within the watershed area). In relatively homogeneous regions basin area and other watershed parameters are highly correlated with catchment order (see section 2.3b); the forest hydrologist is usually concerned with small catchments (first to third order) that are com-

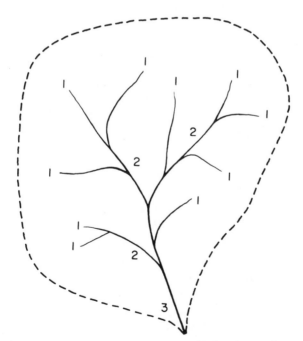

Figure 2.9. Ordering of streams in a third order catchment.

parable in size to forest management compartments (roughly 10 to 100 hectares).

Streams, or stream segments, may be classified according to temporal or spatial aspects, or in relation to groundwater levels. A *perennial* stream is one that flows continuously, an *intermittent* stream is usually dry during a part of each year, and an *ephemeral* stream flows only in direct response to precipitation or snow melt; perennial and intermittent streams can be mapped because they have well-defined channels, but ephemeral streams simply follow depressions in the natural contours of the land surface. Any larger stream segment that is perennial, intermittent, or ephemeral throughout its length is called *continuous*, but if alternating reaches are variously classified it is an *interrupted* stream; in headwater areas, first order stream segments normally change from perennial to intermittent to ephemeral as one progresses upstream.

A stream segment is said to be *effluent*, or gaining, if it is being fed by seepage from the groundwater reservoir; but if the stream is above the groundwater table and loses water to the underground reservoir, it is said to be *influent*, or losing. If the streambed is relatively impermeable so that the stream neither loses nor gains, it is an *insulated* stream; an influent or insulated stream that is separated from the groundwater reservoir by an unsaturated zone is called a *perched* stream. These static conditions are illustrated in fig. 2.10; it is important to recognize, however, that groundwater levels change continuously and that these stream classifications may be transitory (see section 5.3).

## 2.3.b. Physical Parameters

Each catchment is unique in terms of location, morphology, and other physical parameters that influence the receipt and disposition of water, the relative importance of various hydrologic phenomena, and the timing of hydrologic events. The isolated effects of individual parameters can sometimes be defined in terms of deterministic or stochastic relationships, or theoretical and empirical laws, based on many years of careful analysis and interpretation. But it is important to note that catchment uniqueness is also the result of multifarious interactions among individual

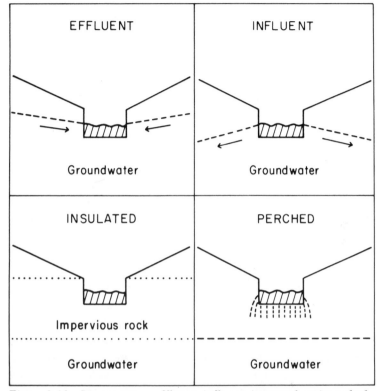

Figure 2.10. Stream types: effluent, influent, insulated, and perched.

parameters and hydrologic processes, and the combined effect is rarely the sum of isolated influences; this means that the importance of physical parameters listed in this section must depend to a large extent on the combination of factors that is specific to a particular catchment.

*Catchment location.* The geographic coordinates (latitude, longitude, and elevation) of a catchment are useful in defining regional climate—including the expected means and extremes of solar radiation, humidity, wind, temperature, precipitation, and evaporation. Of particular importance are the seasonal variations of precipitation and evaporation that determine water availability for streamflow, and temperature which is related to the fraction of annual or seasonal precipitation that occurs in solid form; the solidification of liquid water and the melting of snow; the freezing and infiltration capacity of soils; and forest phenological events. It is also important to identify the relative location of a catchment with regard to major physiographic features and large bodies of water that significantly affect climate and related hydrologic phenomena.

With respect to the small catchments that are of primary concern in forest hydrology it is usually sufficient to obtain geographic coordinates as approximate means, for example as half the sum of maximum and minimum values. In some instances, however, the elevation range is great enough to cause significant differences in climate and it may be important to determine the percentages of total catchment area that lie within discrete elevation zones. This can be accomplished by random or systematic sampling of elevations on a topographic map, or by planimetering areas between contour lines; an example of data obtained by the latter process is given in table 2.11, and the corresponding hypsometric curve (cumulative elevation frequency diagram) is shown in figure 2.11.

*Total relief.* Total catchment relief ($H$) is the difference between maximum and minimum elevations (in table 2.11 and figure 2.11, $H = 490 - 160 = 330$ m). Total relief varies widely among catchments, but average values tend to increase geometrically with catch-

Table 2.11. **Area-Elevation Data for a Small Catchment (Area = 80.8 ha)**

| Elevation range (m) | Area between contours | | Area above lower limit (% of total) |
| --- | --- | --- | --- |
| | Absolute (ha) | Relative (% of total) | |
| 160–200 | 8.1 | 10.0 | 100.0 |
| 200–250 | 16.3 | 20.2 | 90.0 |
| 250–300 | 24.0 | 29.7 | 69.8 |
| 300–350 | 17.8 | 22.0 | 40.1 |
| 350–400 | 7.9 | 9.8 | 18.1 |
| 400–450 | 4.8 | 5.9 | 8.3 |
| 450–490 | 1.9 | 2.4 | 2.4 |
| Total | 80.8 | 100.0 | — |

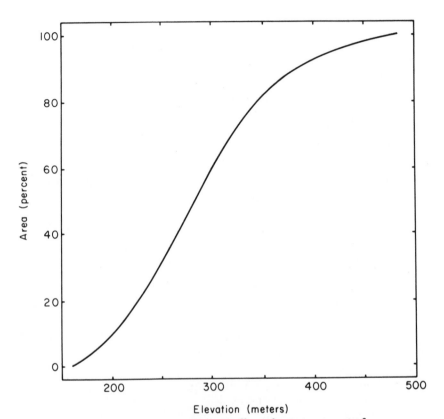

**Figure 2.11.** Hypsometric curve for a small catchment; percent of catchment area above a given elevation.

ment order; according to Morisawa (1962),

$$\overline{H}_u = \overline{H}_1 R_r^{u-1} \tag{2.41}$$

where $\overline{H}_1$ is the mean for first order catchments, $u$ is catchment order, and $R_r = \overline{H}_u/\overline{H}_{u-1}$ (i.e., $R_r$ is the ratio of mean total relief for catchments of order $u$ and the mean for the next lower order). Total relief divided by catchment length is a measure of overall basin steepness, and the latter is related to the intensity of catchment erosion processes (Schumm, 1954).

*Area relations.* Catchment area is an important parameter for the obvious reason that it is necessary in extracting volumetric data from depth measurements; it is also important in the derivation of other catchment parameters, and in various flow equations. Basin area ($A$) varies widely among catchments of the same order, but average values for progressively higher orders increase in a geometric sequence. In analogy with equation 2.41, Schumm (1956) developed a *law of stream areas* in the form

$$\overline{A}_u = \overline{A}_1 R_a{}^{u-1} \tag{2.42}$$

where $R_a$ is the ratio of mean areas for catchments of order $u$ and the next lower order.

Watershed discharge ($Q$) can be related to catchment area by an empirical equation of the form

$$Q = kA^x \tag{2.43}$$

where the magnitude of $k$ depends on precipitation and other watershed parameters, and $x$ varies with $Q$. For average discharge rates, $x \simeq 1$, and $Q/A = k$; but $x < 1$ for high discharge rates $x > 1$ for low flows. In other words the average depth of discharge is unaffected by watershed size, but in larger basins it takes longer for total flood flow to pass the gaging station (smaller peak flows) and a given flow rate is sustained longer during periods of drought (greater low flows).

*Catchment shape.* Catchment shape (plan view) is determined by geologic structure and local erosion processes; it may vary considerably from the typical pear-shaped outline shown in figure 2.5. In catchments of equal area the shape parameter can affect relative precipitation and discharge regimes; for example, a long narrow catchment is less likely to be entirely included in the area of maximum rainfall intensity of local storms, and the time required for surface flow to reach the discharge point from watershed extremities (i.e., *time of concentration*) will be greater. Theoretically, therefore, greater peak discharge rates are to be expected from catchments of more compact shape.

Numerous expressions have been used to define catchment shape in quantitative terms; some common forms are given in table 2.12 as a function of catchment "length," area, and perimeter. Length is defined variously as 1) the greatest straight-line distance between any two points on the perimeter, 2) the greatest distance

Table 2.12. Catchment Shape Expressions

| Name | Definition | Computation formula[a] | Value[b] |
|---|---|---|---|
| Form factor | $\dfrac{\text{Catchment area}}{(\text{Catchment length})^2}$ | $\dfrac{A}{L^2}$ | $<1$ |
| Shape factor | $\dfrac{(\text{Catchment length})^2}{\text{Catchment area}}$ | $\dfrac{L^2}{A}$ | $>1$ |
| Elongation ratio | $\dfrac{\text{Diameter of circle of catchment area}}{\text{Catchment length}}$ | $\dfrac{1.128\,A^{0.5}}{L}$ | $\leqslant 1$ |
| Circulatory ratio | $\dfrac{\text{Catchment area}}{\text{Area of circle of catchment perimeter}}$ | $\dfrac{12.57\,A}{P^2}$ | $\leqslant 1$ |
| Compactness coefficient | $\dfrac{\text{Catchment perimeter}}{\text{Perimeter of circle of catchment area}}$ | $\dfrac{0.2821\,P}{A^{0.5}}$ | $\geqslant 1$ |

[a] Catchment area ($A$), length ($L$), and perimeter ($P$).
[b] Based on definition of length as "greatest straight-line distance between any two points on catchment perimeter."

between the mouth and any point on the perimeter, or 3) the length of the main stream axis from its source (projected to the perimeter) to the discharge point. The *form factor* is always less than unity (using definition 1, above, for length), and its reciprocal, the *shape factor*, is always greater than unity; the *elongation ratio*, *circulatory ratio*, and *compactness coefficient* approach unity as catchment shape approaches that of a circle.

*Catchment exposure.* The exposure of catchments, and of land facets within catchment areas, includes both slope steepness and orientation; it is an especially important parameter in small catchments and in areas of greater total relief. Slope steepness affects the velocity of overland flow, catchment erosion potential, and local wind systems; it also interacts with slope orientation in determining the potential input of solar radiation. Through its influence on the receipt of radiant energy, slope orientation affects the forest microclimate and phenology, latent heat exchanges, and the timing of snowmelt; it is also important with respect to the direction of storm movements (see section 7.2) and small-scale topographic influences on the distribution of precipitation (see section 3.3.b).

Slope steepness may be expressed either as a mean value for an entire catchment, or in terms of the mean or frequency distribution of individual terrain facets within the basin. An estimate of the former may be obtained as the ratio of total relief and catchment length, or by statistically fitting a plane to the three-dimensional perimeter as described by Lee (1963); the statistical method also serves to define overall watershed orientation. The mean slope steepness ($S$) of individual terrain facets can be obtained from a topographic map by measuring the total length ($C$) of contours of interval ($I$) and computing

$$S = \frac{CI}{A} \tag{2.44}$$

where $A$ is catchment area in compatible units, and $S$ is dimensionless; if the frequency distribution of steepness categories is required, a sampling procedure analogous to that described for elevation determinations (in connection with table 2.11 and figure 2.11) may be used.

*Stream parameters.* Stream parameters are measures of drainage efficiency; these include stream numbers, lengths, and gradients, drainage density, and length of overland flow. The *law of stream numbers* (Horton, 1945) is

$$N_u = R_b{}^{s-u} \qquad (2.45)$$

where, in analogy with equations 2.41 and 2.42, $N_u$ is the number of streams of order $u$, $s$ is the catchment order (order of trunk stream), and $R_b$ is the *bifurcation ratio* (the ratio of the number of streams of order $u$ to the number of the next higher order). Since, by definition, any higher order stream has at least two tributaries of the next lower order, $R_b \geqslant 2$ must be true and, as a rule, $2 < R_b < 5$; Eagleson (1970) demonstrated a systematic increase of $R_b$ with increase in stream order.

The *law of stream lengths* (Horton, 1945) and *law of stream gradients* (Morisawa, 1962) are

$$\overline{L}_u = \overline{L}_1 R_L{}^{u-1} \qquad (2.46)$$

and

$$\overline{S}_u = \overline{S}_1 R_s^{s-u} \qquad (2.47)$$

respectively, where $\overline{L}_u$ and $\overline{S}_u$ are average lengths and gradients for streams of order $u$, $\overline{L}_1$ and $\overline{S}_1$ are the corresponding values for first order streams, $R_L = \overline{L}_u/\overline{L}_{u-1}$, $R_s = \overline{S}_u/\overline{S}_{u+1}$, and $s$ is catchment order. The ratios $R_L$ and $R_s$ define *drainage density* ($D_u$; the total length of streams per unit area in a catchment of order $u$) as

$$D_u = \frac{\overline{L}_1}{A_u} \frac{R_L^u - R_b^u}{R_L - R_b} \qquad (2.48)$$

where $A_u$ is catchment area (as adapted from Horton, 1945). It follows that the *average length of overland flow* $L_o = 1/2D$ where channel slope is small relative to ground slope in the area.

*Catchment substrata.* The composition and structure of materials underlying the surface of a catchment affect its morphology (as indicated in preceding paragraphs), infiltration and water-holding capacities, and subsurface water movements. Watershed descriptions ordinarily include at least a synopsis of the geologic history of the area, the degree of glaciation, and a summary of rock types and structural elements; where carbonate rocks predominate, subsurface discharges may preclude the application of surface water-budgeting procedures. The nature of underlying rock strata is also important because it determines, to a large extent, the properties of the catchment soil mantle.

The hydrologic properties of soils derive from their texture, organic content, and structure which determine soil porosity, infiltration and percolation capacities, capillary behavior, and the range of soil water availability to plants; the quantification of soil hydrologic properties is treated in greater detail in chapter 5. Other important parameters are soil depth, which is directly related to total water-holding capacity or catchment storage capacity, the salinity and fertility of soils, the stratification of the soil mantle, and the erodibility of surface layers. Soil scientists identify major soil groups and named types for specific purposes, but hydrologists are more concerned with classifications based on slope and infiltration capacity, or hydrologic condition based on cover characteristics and the degree of compaction and disturbance (see, e.g., Ogrosky and Mockus, 1964).

### 2.3.c. Cover Characteristics

The forest hydrologist is especially concerned with hydrologic entities that can be manipulated for human purposes. Whereas catchment physical features (sections 2.3. a and b) vary over periods of geologic time as a result of natural causes, cover characteristics are directly amenable to planned change. "Cover," in the hydrologic sense, includes all of the elements of the surface and rooting zone that are attributable to plant growth: specifically, living plants with their foliage, stems, and rooting systems, and the organic litter and humus layers that form over mineral soil as a result of plant growth.

*Forest type.* Forest type is the name given to the tree species, or group of species, that dominate a given catchment area; it is a taxonomic classification that is useful in designating some general characteristics of forest cover for hydrologic purposes. Type names suggest numerous qualitative characteristics of forest species including leaf type and arrangement, crown form and branching habit, bark characteristics, stem structure, and root form; other silvicultural parameters suggested by type names are geographic range, site preference, ecological associates, light tolerance, drought resistance, and relative growth rate and height at maturity. Of particular importance to the hydrologist are aspects of tree physiology and phenology that affect transpiration rates and the seasonal variability of water use by forest types; for example, the persistent foliage of conifers introduces a significant seasonal deviation relative to deciduous types.

*Cover density.* The density of forest cover may be expressed as a percentage of full cover, i.e., relative density as compared to a "closed" forest that provides complete cover, or completely shades the forest floor. Other measures of density are numbers of tree stems, basal area, and dry mass per unit area of surface, or the percentage of incident shortwave radiation that penetrates the cover; leaf area index, or the ratio of leaf to ground area, is an index to canopy interception for a given species, and a direct measure of transpiring surface area. Density parameters vary considerably among forest species, and with site conditions, the age and height of trees and, for deciduous types, with seasonal foliage changes.

*Energy parameters.* Forest cover, as opposed to bare soil and lower vegetation, exerts a significant effect on the energy budget, generally increasing net radiation and latent heat exchanges, insulating the soil against rapid temperature fluctuations and freezing, and delaying snowmelt. Shortwave reflectivity, or albedo, varies from about 10% for some conifers to about 20% for some hardwood types; growing-season albedoes for the ten major timber types in eastern United States, as estimated by Lee (1977), are given in table 2.13; a change of 1% is probably equivalent to a change of 1 to 2% in net radiation. Other parameters of importance in determining the net energy available for evaporation and transpiration are the aerodynamic properties (roughness) of canopies,

Table 2.13. Estimated Growing-Season
Albedoes for Major Timber
Types in Eastern United States
(Lee, 1977)

| Timber type | Albedo (%) |
|---|---|
| *Coniferous forest* | |
| White–red–jack pine | 12 |
| Spruce–fir | 10 |
| Longleaf–slash pine | 12 |
| Loblolly–shortleaf pine | 12 |
| *Deciduous forest* | |
| Oak–pine | 15 |
| Oak–hickory | 18 |
| Oak–gum–cypress | 15 |
| Elm–ash–cottonwood | 17 |
| Maple–beech–birch | 19 |
| Aspen–birch | 20 |

and the thermal properties (heat capacity and conductivity) of the forest and substrata.

*Forest floor.* The hydrologic role of forest cover is greatly augmented by the organic materials of the forest floor and rooting zone. A forest stand usually produces 1 to 10 metric tons/ha · yr of organic litter, and the net accumulation of decomposing litter under a mature stand is typically 1 to 3 g (dry matter)/cm² of surface; this material protects the soil from raindrop impact, improves its structure, inhibits freezing, greatly enhances infiltration capacity, absorbs a fraction of rainfall and melting snow, and virtually eliminates overland flow and surface erosion during all but the most intense rainfall events. Tree roots may penetrate the forest soil to a depth of 10 m or more, but most roots are found in the first meter; the depth of the primary rooting zone is an important hydrologic parameter because it limits the volume of water that is available for transpiration in a drying soil.

*Climate interactions.* The importance of any specific cover characteristic depends to a large extent on its interactions with regional or local climate; for example, forest type and tree physiology and phenology vary with a wide spectrum of climatological variables, so the hydrologic influence of a given species is not constant. Cover density is usually greater where water is plentiful relative to energy, for example in humid areas, on cooler slopes, and in coves; and cover density has a greater effect on interception loss in areas where rainfall is greater and showers more frequent. Also, forest albedoes are greater at higher latitudes for similar forest types, the insulating effects of forest cover are more significant where daily and seasonal temperature fluctuations are greater, and the importance of forest floor influences on infiltration and percolation capacities is greater in areas of greater average temperature range and precipitation intensity.

## LITERATURE CITED

Baumgartner, A. 1956. Untersuchungen uber den Warme- und Wasserhaushalt eines jungen Waldes. *Berichte des Deutschen Wetterdienstes* No. 28, Bad Kissengen, Germany.

Black, J. N. 1956. The distribution of solar radiation over the earth's surface. *Archives for Meteorology, Geophysics, and Bioclimatology* B. 7:165–89.

Budyko, M. I. 1974. *Climate and Life*. New York: Academic Press.

Eagleson, P. S. 1970. *Dynamic Hydrology*. New York: McGraw-Hill.

Federer, C. A. 1968. Spatial variation of net radiation, albedo and surface temperature of forests. *Journal of Applied Meterology* 7:789–95.

Gates, D. M. 1962. *Energy Exchange in the Biosphere*. New York: Harper & Row.

Gates, D. M., E. C. Tibbals, and F. Kreith. 1965. Radiation and convection from Ponderosa Pine. *American Journal of Botany* 52:66–71.

Geiger, R. 1965. *The Climate Near the Ground*. Cambridge: Harvard University Press.

Horton, R. E. 1945. Erosional development of streams and their drainage basins. *Geological Society of America Bulletin* 56:275–370.

Idso, S. B. and R. D. Jackson. 1969. Thermal radiation from the atmosphere. *Journal of Geophysical Research* 74:5397–403.

Lee, R. 1963. *Evaluation of Solar Beam Irradiation as a Climatic Parameter of Mountain Watersheds*. Fort Collins: Colorado State University.

Lee, R. 1977. *Opportunities for Increasing Water Supplies in the Eastern United States by Vegetation Management*. Morgantown: West Virginia University.

Lee, R. 1978. *Forest Microclimatology*. New York: Columbia University Press.

Lee, R., D. G. Boyer, V. J. Valli, and W. H. Dickerson. 1979. *Global Radiation in West Virginia*. Morgantown: West Virginia University.

Monteith, J. L. 1973. *Principles of Environmental Physics*. New York: American Elsevier.

Morisawa, M. E. 1962. Quantitative geomorphology of some watersheds in the Appalachian Plateau. *Geological Society of America Bulletin* 73:1025–46.

Ogrosky, H. O. and V. Mockus. 1964. Hydrology of agricultural lands. In V. T. Chow, ed., *Handbook of Applied Hydrology*. New York: McGraw-Hill.

Robinson, N., ed. 1966. *Solar Radiation*. London: Elsevier.

Schumm, S. A. 1954. The relation of drainage basin relief to sediment loss. *International Association of Scientific Hydrology Publication* 36:216–19.

Schumm, S. A. 1956. Evolution of drainage systems and slopes in badlands at Perth Amboy, N.Y. *Geological Society of American Bulletin* 67:597–646.

Tabata, S. 1973. A simple but accurate formula for the saturation vapor pressure over liquid water. *Journal of Applied Meteorology* 12:1410–11.

Thom, A. S. 1975. Momentum, mass and heat exchange of plant communities. In J. L. Monteith, ed., *Vegetation and the Atmosphere*, vol. 1. New York: Academic Press.

## SELECTED READINGS

Eisenberg, D. and W. Kauzmann. 1969. *The Structure and Properties of Water*. New York: Oxford University Press.

Hoover, M. D. 1962. Water action and water movement in the forest. In *Forest Influences*. Rome: Food and Agricultural Organization of the United Nations.

Jarvis, P. G., G. B. James, and J. J. Landsberg, 1976. Coniferous forest. In J. L. Monteith, ed., *Vegetation and the Atmosphere*, vol. 2. New York: Academic Press.

List, R. J. 1951. *Smithsonian Meteorological Tables*. Washington, D.C.: Smithsonian Institution.

Lull, H. W. 1964. Ecological and silvicultural aspects. In V. T. Chow, ed., *Handbook of Applied Hydrology*. New York: McGraw-Hill.

Morisawa, M. 1968. *Streams, Their Dynamics and Morphology*. New York: McGraw-Hill.

Rauner, J. L. 1976. Deciduous forest. In J. L. Monteith, ed., *Vegetation and the Atmosphere*, vol. 2. New York: Academic Press.

Reifsnyder, W. E. and H. W. Lull. 1965. *Radiant Energy in Relation to Forests*. Washington, D.C.: U.S. Forest Service.

Strahler, A. N. 1964. Quantitative geomorphology of drainage basins and channel networks. In V. T. Chow, ed., *Handbook of Applied Hydrology*. New York: McGraw-Hill.

# 3 ATMOSPHERIC WATER

## 3.1. Atmospheric Humidity

Atmospheric humidity may be expressed in absolute or relative quantities for particular purposes, or in terms of associated
atmospheric properties that are influenced by forest cover. The
humidity budget of the atmosphere is an integral part of any
large-scale comprehensive budgeting procedure; it emphasizes the
importance of advection in determining the regional availability of
moisture for precipitation and streamflow. Vapor condensation to
liquid and solid forms is a physical phenomenon that occurs in the
biosphere, but occurs to a much greater extent in upper atmospheric
air masses where most precipitation processes are initiated.

### 3.1.a. Humidity Terms

*Precipitable water* (depth) is the total mass of water vapor in
the atmosphere, expressed in equivalent liquid volume over a unit
area of surface; its depth varies from about 5 cm over tropical
oceans to 0.5 cm or less at the poles (mean value for the earth,
2.55 cm, from section 1.1.a). Mean precipitable water is generally
correlated with temperature latitudinally, and seasonally at any
particular station, especially in the middle latitudes where summer
maxima may be several times greater than winter minima. Since
atmospheric water is replenished by evaporation from the surface,
precipitable water is highly correlated with regional evaporation,
and is greater over large water bodies and in coastal areas; on the
vertical scale, water vapor concentration generally decreases directly
with distance from the surface.

Water vapor concentration is its bulk density ($\rho_v$) or *absolute humidity* (mass/volume) usually expressed in g/m$^3$; it is related to the partial pressure of water vapor, or *vapor pressure* ($e$, mb), by

$$\rho_v = \frac{217e}{T} \tag{3.1}$$

where $T$ is in °K. The mass of water vapor per unit mass of *moist* air is the *specific humidity* ($q$) given by

$$q = \frac{\rho_v}{\rho_{ma}} = \frac{0.62e}{p - 0.38e} \tag{3.2}$$

where $\rho_{ma}$ is the density of moist air and $p$ is barometric pressure. Similarly, the mass of water vapor per unit mass of *dry* air is the *mixing ratio* ($w$), where

$$w = \frac{\rho_v}{\rho_{da}} = \frac{0.62e}{p - e} \tag{3.3}$$

and $\rho_{da}$ is the density of dry air. Ordinarily $p$ is two orders of magnitude greater than $e$, and $q \simeq w$; but since $\rho_{da} < \rho_{ma}$ (for a given air mass volume), $w > q$.

In a saturated atmosphere, $e = e_s$, where $e_s$ is the *saturation vapor pressure* (equation 2.1, table 2.4); $e_s$ is strictly a function of temperature as illustrated in figure 3.1. Also in terms of $e$ and $e_s$, the *relative humidity ratio* $h = e/e_s$, relative humidity $rh = 100\,h$, and the *saturation deficit* for a space is $e_s - e$, or $e_s(1 - h)$. Since $e_s$ is a function of temperature, relative humidity depends on temperature as well as on the actual amount of water vapor that is present, and in a given air mass it is inversely proportional to temperature; figure 3.2 shows that, with constant absolute humidity, the forest is relatively more humid than an adjacent field during the day because air temperature is lower.

An example of the relationships among water vapor terms is given in table 3.1. From examination of figure 3.1 it is apparent that, for any combination of vapor pressure ($e$) and temperature ($T$) such that $e < e_s$ (or $h < 1$), there is a lower temperature $T_d$ (*dew-point temperature*) corresponding to $h = 1$; in other words,

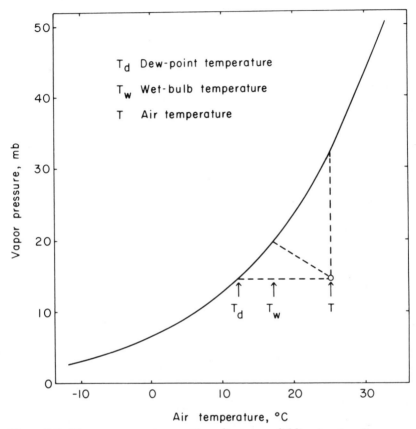

**Figure 3.1.** Vapor pressure-temperature diagram; solid line is saturation vapor pressure ($rh < 100\%$ below solid line).

at $T_d$, $e = e_s$. Atmospheric humidity can also be expressed in terms of the *wet-bulb temperature* ($T_w$) which is a measure of the maximum cooling effect of evaporation (see section 10.1); if $e = e_s$, then $T = T_w = T_d$; otherwise $T > T_w > T_d$.

Atmospheric water vapor moves in response to differences in vapor pressure between any two levels $z_1$ and $z_2$, and the rate of movement is proportional to the *vapor pressure difference* ($e_1 - e_2$, as in equations 2.38 and 2.39), or the *vapor pressure gradient* ($de/dz$). It is important to observe the distinction between "vapor

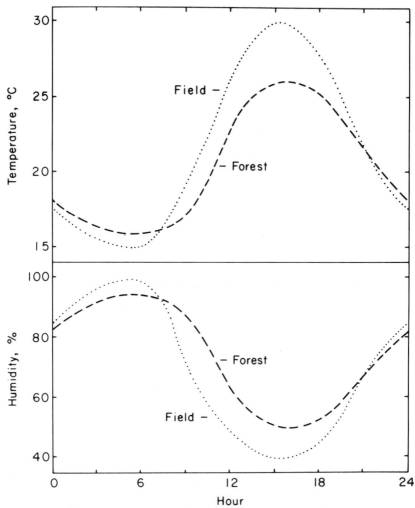

Figure 3.2. Hourly variations of air temperature and relative humidity near the ground with constant absolute humidity.

pressure difference" and "humidity deficit" because the same symbol, $e_s - e$, is frequently used for both. Vapor pressure generally decreases with height over a forest canopy during periods of positive net radiation (daytime), and vapor flow is upward (transpiration occurring); but with nocturnal cooling, or over relatively cold

**Table 3.1. Relationships Among Water-Vapor Terms at Constant Temperature (20°C) and Barometric Pressure (1000 mb)**

| Term | Units | Relative humidity (%) | | | | |
|---|---|---|---|---|---|---|
| | | 20 | 40 | 60 | 80 | 100 |
| Saturation vapor pressure | (mb) | 23.37 | 23.37 | 23.37 | 23.37 | 23.37 |
| Actual vapor pressure | (mb) | 4.67 | 9.35 | 14.02 | 18.70 | 23.37 |
| Absolute humidity | (g/m$^3$) | 3.46 | 6.92 | 10.38 | 13.84 | 17.30 |
| Specific humidity | (g/kg) | 2.91 | 5.84 | 8.77 | 11.71 | 14.67 |
| Mixing ratio | (g/kg) | 2.92 | 5.87 | 8.85 | 11.85 | 14.89 |
| Saturation deficit | (mb) | 18.70 | 14.02 | 9.35 | 4.67 | 0.00 |
| Dew-point temperature | (°C) | −3.6 | 6.0 | 12.0 | 16.4 | 20.0 |
| Wet-bulb temperature | (°C) | 9.5 | 12.6 | 15.3 | 17.7 | 20.0 |

water, snow, or ice, an inversion of the humidity profile is typical, vapor movement is downward, and dewfall may occur.

### 3.1.b. Humidity Budget

Atmospheric moisture is ultimately replenished by evaporation from the surface but, since the atmosphere is always in motion, its humidity budget over any particular area is affected by the horizontal inflow (advection) of water vapor. Symbolically, with inflows to the left of the equality sign,

$$E + A_i = P + A_o + S_{ea} \qquad (3.4)$$

where $A_i$ and $A_o$ are the inflow and outflow of advected vapor, respectively, and $S_{ea}$ is the increase in storage (precipitable water) derived from evaporated and advected moisture. As an annual average $S_{ea} = 0$, and by rearrangement and comparison with equation 2.8,

$$A_i - A_o = P - E = Q \qquad (3.5)$$

shows that liquid water discharge from the area must be equal to the net influx of advected vapor.

Water vapor that is advected from exterior regions into the atmosphere over a given locality may increase atmospheric storage, contribute to local precipitation, or be advected to leeward regions. In equation form,

$$A_i = P_a + S_a + (A_i - P_a - S_a) \qquad (3.6)$$

where $P_a$ and $S_a$ are the parts of local precipitation and atmospheric storage supplied by the advective stream, and $A_i - P_a - S_a$ is the leeward advection of moisture derived from exterior regions. It follows that

$$\frac{A_i + (A_i - P_a - S_a)}{2} = A_i - \tfrac{1}{2}(P_a + S_a) \qquad (3.7)$$

is the average flow of *externally derived moisture* in the local atmosphere.

Similarly the *total* leeward flux of water vapor is, from equation 3.4,

$$A_o = A_i + E - P - S_{ea} \qquad (3.8)$$

and

$$\frac{A_i + (A_i + E - P - S_{ea})}{2} = A_i - \tfrac{1}{2}(P + S_{ea} - E) \qquad (3.9)$$

is the average total flux (independent of source). From equations 3.7 and 3.9,

$$\frac{S_a}{S_{ae}} = \frac{A_i - \tfrac{1}{2}(P_a + S_a)}{A_i - \tfrac{1}{2}(P + S_{ea} - E)} \qquad (3.10)$$

since the average flow rates are measures of the relative amounts of water vapor stored transiently in the local atmosphere. Also,

$$\frac{P_a}{P} = \frac{A_i - \tfrac{1}{2}(P_a + S_a)}{A_i - \tfrac{1}{2}(P + S_{ea} - E)} \qquad (3.11)$$

assuming that water molecules of local and external origin are completely mixed and have equal probabilities of being precipitated. Equation 3.11 reduces to

$$\frac{P_a}{P} = \frac{2A_i}{2A_i + E} = \frac{2M}{2M + 1} \qquad (3.12)$$

where $M = A_i/E$ is the ratio of moisture inflows to the local atmosphere. Ordinarily $A_i > E$, and $(P_a/P) > 2/3$, even for entire continents. Some empirical estimates of atmospheric water-budget components for three large regions are given in table 3.2 (adapted from Sellers, 1965).

From table 3.2 it is apparent that, in the middle latitudes at least, advected moisture is by far the most important source of local precipitation, and that even the enormous quantities of water vapor diffused by forests have relatively little effect on the atmospheric water budget. Note that the ratio $P_a/P$ increases as the area of the region decreases. This suggests that in smaller drainage basins $P_a/P$ will approach unity, and that in the small catchment areas that are of primary concern in forest hydrology, the effects of forest cover on local precipitation must be virtually zero.

### 3.1.c. Vapor Condensation

Water enters the earth's atmosphere as the result of phase changes, solid → vapor (sublimation) and liquid → vapor (evapora-

Table 3.2. Atmospheric Water-Budget Components (adapted from Sellers, 1965)

| Region | Area ($10^6$ km$^2$) | $P$ (mm/yr) | $E$ (mm/yr) | $A_i$ (mm/yr) | $A_o$ (mm/yr) | $M$ ($A_i/E$) | $P_a/P$ (%) |
|---|---|---|---|---|---|---|---|
| Arizona | 0.1 | 314 | 313 | 2452 | 2451 | 7.83 | 94 |
| European Russia | 4.9 | 487 | 294 | 1189 | 996 | 4.04 | 89 |
| United States and Canada | 17.8 | 675 | 561 | 758 | 644 | 1.35 | 73 |

tion), at the surface; it returns to the surface primarily as a result of vapor → solid and vapor → liquid transformations (condensation) in upper atmospheric air masses and, to a lesser extent, as dewfall and frost in the biosphere. The prerequisite for condensation is that atmospheric vapor pressure be equal to saturation vapor pressure or $e = e_s$, *at a surface*. Condensation occurs on soil and plant surfaces in the biosphere, and in the upper atmosphere on *condensation nuclei*—tiny particles of sea salt or other hygroscopic aerosols that vary in diameter from about 0.1 to 1.0 μm.

If a plant or soil surface is cooled to the dew-point temperature ($T_d$) by the negative radiation balance at night, condensation will occur in the form of dew (if $T_d > 0°C$) or frost (if $T_d < 0°C$). The rate of condensation is strictly limited by the longwave radiation balance (equation 2.18) because release of the latent heat of condensation tends to warm the surface; typically, on clear nights, the longwave balance $L \simeq -0.1$ ly/min, which is equivalent to the energy released at a dewfall rate of about 0.1 mm/hr. Condensation rates that compensate entirely for radiational cooling are probably never achieved on plant and soil surfaces, however, because under these conditions conduction or convection will also contribute energy to the surface.

Dewfall is usually a negligible term in the water budget of a forest, especially in humid regions; when it occurs, it rarely exceeds a few tenths of a millimeter per night. Condensation of another sort (distillation) occurs when water evaporated from a moist soil diffuses upward to a cooled canopy; distillation is simply a redistribution of water within the forest ecosystem. Both dewfall and distillation deposit water on exposed surfaces from which it is freely evaporated under conditions of positive net radiation.

Water bodies, including forest streams, deep lakes, and snowpacks, frequently exhibit surface temperatures below the ambient dew-point, and consequently become condensation surfaces. In these situations the rate of condensation is not limited by the radiation deficit (with the exception of a nonmelting snowpack), and may occur continuously at much higher rates than dewfall. Condensation rates at liquid water surfaces (including melting snow) are limited only by the efficiency of turbulent transport (wind) in bringing moisture to the surface; rates exceeding 1 mm/day have been reported (Phillips, 1972; Miller, 1977).

An example of the relative frequency of condensation to a small forest stream under a closed canopy can be deduced from figure 3.3. Mean daily ambient humidity and stream temperature were observed during July days, 1973–1974, in the mountains of West Virginia; the plotted points are cumulative frequencies of the estimated differences in vapor pressure, $e_s - e$ (stream minus ambient). Condensation must have occurred when $(e_s - e) < 0$, or about 50% of the time; otherwise, with $e_s > e$, the stream was losing water through evaporation.

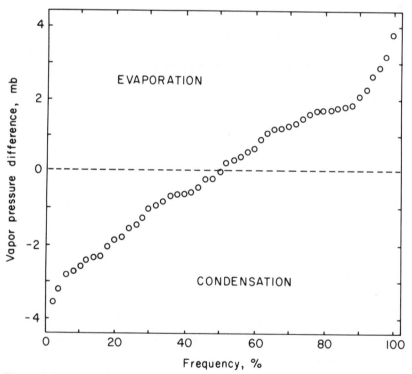

Figure 3.3. Cumulative frequency of vapor pressure differences (stream minus ambient).

Condensation of greatest hydrologic significance occurs at higher levels in the atmosphere as a precursor of precipitation; in this instance, however, the necessary condition that $e_s = e$ *at a surface* has additional meaning. At the surface of an incipient cloud droplet, vapor pressure is a function not only of temperature but also of *solute* and *curvature effects*; the solute effect arises because hygroscopic nuclei add impurities to the droplets that tend to decrease $e_s$, whereas the curvature effect increases $e_s$ as a result of greater surface tension. Condensation is more rapid on larger nuclei because the solute effect is greater and the curvature effect is smaller; both effects become negligible as cloud droplet size increases to about 2 to 3 $\mu$m.

As air moves upward in the atmosphere and is cooled by expansion (see section 3.2.a), the entrained water vapor begins to condense on hygroscopic nuclei at temperatures slightly below the dew point. With additional upward movement, expansion, and cooling of the air mass, incipient cloud droplets act as condensation nuclei and continue to grow; in the initial stages water migrates from smaller droplets (with higher $e_s$) to larger droplets (with lower $e_s$) because of the curvature effect, but this process is short-lived. With continued cooling some cloud droplets freeze (though not uniformly at 0°C because of their relative purity), and in a mixture of droplets and ice crystals the latter grow at the expense of the former because $e_s$ is greater over liquid water (see table 2.4).

Condensation theory is sufficient to explain the growth of cloud droplets to raindrop size only when condensation nuclei are exceptionally large (of the order of 5 $\mu$m), or when cloud temperatures are below the freezing point; otherwise, by condensation alone, it takes about 3 hours to form a small (1 mm diameter) raindrop. As it happens, as cloud droplets of the order of 0.1 mm diameter begin to fall, they collide with smaller drops that fall more slowly, and grow by accretion or "capture" of the smaller drops. Rain that falls from clouds at temperatures above the freezing point (typical in the tropics) is called "warm" rain, and that from clouds containing ice crystals is called "cold" rain regardless of its temperature as it arrives at the surface.

## 3.2. Precipitation Analysis

Condensation at higher levels in the atmosphere, and the growth of water droplets or ice crystals to precipitable size, are the prerequisites for precipitation; these processes occur primarily when moist air masses are forced upward. The temporal and spatial variations of precipitation are basic hydrologic parameters that can be described for general purposes in terms of climatological means, extremes, and frequency distributions that vary with location, topography, and related air mass properties. Local precipitation data must be interpreted with reference to their inherent limitations, and in terms of their consistency relative to data from surrounding areas.

### 3.2.a. Causal Factors

Atmospheric moisture in sufficient quantities, cooling to the dew-point temperature, the presence of condensation nuclei, cloud formation, and droplet or ice crystal growth to precipitable size are the necessary conditions for precipitation (occult precipitation, section 2.2.a, is a minor exception). These conditions are not always sufficient, however, as clouds may dissipate as a result of warming, or raindrops (virga) may evaporate while falling. Meteorological textbooks should be consulted for more thorough elaboration of storm causes; here it will suffice to review the lifting mechanisms that are largely responsible for air-mass cooling and precipitation.

In an area of low barometric pressure at the surface there is necessarily an inflow (convergence) of external air and subsequent lifting of the local air mass; the air expands as it rises and the work of expansion absorbs energy and cools the mass. The large-scale circulation of air around this "low" (counterclockwise as viewed from over the North Pole) is called a cyclone. Cyclonic cooling may extend over millions of square kilometers in the middle latitudes, and produce moderate precipitation intensities for a period of several days; hurricanes (originating over tropical waters) and tornadoes (much smaller vortices over land) are also cyclones.

Lifting and cooling may also occur as air masses of different densities collide. At the leading edge (front) of a moving cold air mass (fig. 3.4a), more dense (cold) air forms a wedge under the less dense (warm) air, and the discontinuity surface is relatively steep (1–4%); short-duration storms of high intensity may result if the warm air is sufficiently moist. At the leading edge of a moving warm air mass (fig. 3.4b) the front is less steep (<1%), and more gradual lifting tends to produce less intense storms of greater duration.

Air that is forced to converge upward on the windward side of a mountain range will expand and cool as it rises to a lower pres-

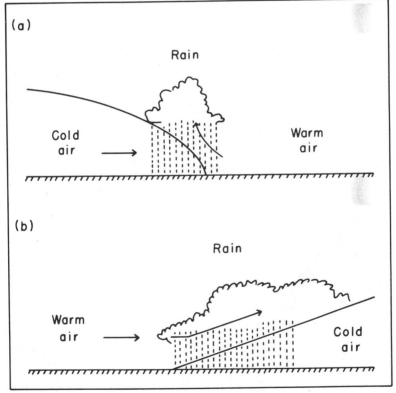

Figure 3.4. Frontal storms: a, cold front; b, warm front.

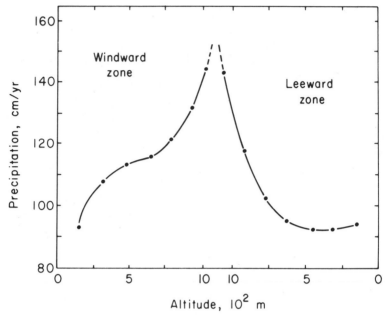

Figure 3.5. Mean orographic effect on windward and leeward slopes of the Appalachian Mountains in West Virginia.

sure level; condensation and precipitation will generally occur beginning at the level where the dew-point temperature is attained. Increases in precipitation with elevation on windward slopes vary considerably among regions, and among elevation zones in a given region; at intermediate elevations in eastern United States the increase ranges from about 4 to 8 cm/yr · 100m. On leeward slopes descending air contracts and warms producing the typical "rain shadow" effect; the leeward gradient is usually steeper than the windward (fig. 3.5).

Intense uneven heating at the surface may produce a localized low pressure area and rapid upward movement of the heated (less dense) air; as the rising air reaches its dew-point temperature, heat released in the condensation process tends to maintain instability and continued upward movement. Isolated convective (thunderstorm) activity of this sort usually persists for only 1 to 2 hrs, but associated cloud formations may extend to heights of

10 to 15 km and produce intense rainfall over areas of 10 to 50 km². These small-scale convective disturbances frequently occur in conjunction with more extensive orographic and frontal storms, and intensify their precipitation-producing processes.

### 3.2.b. Precipitation Variability

The temporal and spatial variability of precipitation can be described in general terms for most land areas of the earth based on measurements at numerous stations. It is important to recognize that individual station measurements are simply *point samples* that suffer from inherent inaccuracies (see section 10.1.a) and lack of areal representativeness. Nevertheless, the available data are extremely useful as indices of precipitation variability in time and space.

*Annual totals.* It is common knowledge that precipitation varies considerably from year to year at particular stations, or as an average for individual regions; the annual variation over a 50-year period (1927–1976) for 35 stations in West Virginia is shown in figure 3.6 (Lee et al., 1977). In this example the 50-year mean is 1110 mm, and about two-thirds of the annual values are within the range from 970 to 1260 mm (coefficient of variation 13.0%); during the wettest year (1972) the 35-station mean was 1370 mm, or more than twice as great as that for the driest year (1930) with 670 mm. Attempts to describe annual variations of this sort in terms of climatological "cycles," or as a correlation with other periodicities (e.g., sunspot cycles) have failed, evidently either because precipitation is acyclic or its annual variability is too great to permit definitive interpretations based on available data.

Annual (or monthly) precipitation, averaged over many years, is called *normal precipitation*; *current normals* in the United States are based on the 30-year period, 1931–1970 (Environmental Data Service, 1973). An example of the errors involved in attempting to estimate long-term average precipitation on the basis of shorter records is given in table 3.3; relative errors are generally greater in areas of lower precipitation, and smaller in areas of higher precipitation. In the example, if a period of record of from 5 to 10 years is chosen to estimate the 50-year mean, most of the errors will

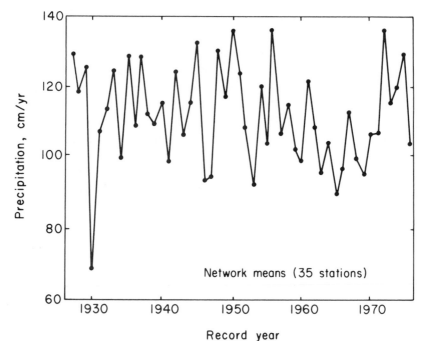

Figure 3.6. Annual variation of mean precipitation for 35 stations in West Virginia (1927–1976).

Table 3.3. Relative Error Involved in Estimating 50-Year Mean Precipitation from Shorter Records in a Humid Region (West Virginia)

| Interval (years) | Mean error (%) | Error range (95% confidence) |
|---|---|---|
| 5 | 17.6 | 14.1–21.1 |
| 10 | 11.3 | 9.6–12.9 |
| 15 | 8.1 | 7.0–9.2 |
| 20 | 6.3 | 5.5–7.1 |
| 25 | 4.5 | 3.8–5.2 |
| 30 | 3.7 | 3.2–4.3 |
| 40 | 2.4 | 2.0–2.8 |

fall within the range from about 10 to 20%; if the period of record is 30 years the expected error is reduced to 3 to 4%.

Normal precipitation depth varies over the earth's land surfaces from less than 50 mm/yr to more than 5000 mm/yr; in general the values decrease from the equator toward the poles, but there are secondary maxima at 50° to 60° N and S (latitudes of predominantly rising air), and secondary minima at 20° to 30° N and S (latitudes of descending air). Within any particular latitudinal zone precipitation varies with altitude (as a result of the orographic effect), with proximity to windward moisture sources (primarily warm ocean currents), with position relative to mountain ranges, and with the relative temperatures of land and bordering oceans. Within more restricted climatological zones much of the variability of normal annual precipitation among stations can usually be explained on the basis of altitudinal differences alone; the relationship illustrated in figure 3.5 accounted for 60% of the variation among stations in West Virginia (Chang and Lee, 1975).

Normal precipitation depth for the conterminous United States is 760 mm/yr, but it varies among regions from less than 100 mm/yr in southwestern desert areas to more than 3000 mm/yr in the coastal mountain ranges of the Northwest. Along the east coast there is a general increase from *north* to *south* (from about 1000 to 1500 mm/yr), but along the west coast the increase is from *south to north* (from about 500 to 2500 mm/yr). Internally there is a general decrease from east to west; typical values for selected regions (in mm/yr) are: Appalachian Mountains (higher elevations), 1500 to 2000; Gulf Coast, 1000 to 1500; Lake States, 700 to 800; Central Plains (north), 400 to 800; Great Plains (south), 500 to 1000; Rocky Mountains, 400 to 600; and Great Basin and southwestern deserts, 100 to 400.

*Seasonal totals.* The significance of annual precipitation in forestry and hydrology depends to a large extent on its seasonal variation; some typical seasonal patterns in the United States are illustrated in figure 3.7. Along the west coast (San Francisco) most rainfall occurs in winter under the influence of Pacific cyclones that bring moist air over the cooler land mass; contrastingly, the Great Plains (Omaha) are too far inland to be affected by the mari-

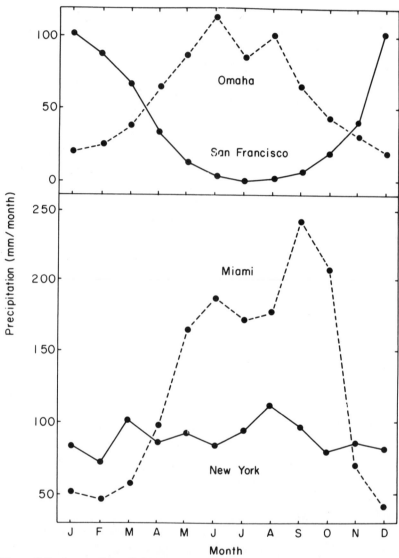

Figure 3.7. Seasonal precipitation patterns at stations in different climatological regions of the United States.

time influence, and here most precipitation occurs during warmer
months as convective showers and thunderstorms. Along the east
coast (New York), under the influence of Atlantic cyclones, precipitation is relatively evenly distributed throughout the year; to the
south (Miami) the influence of tropical hurricanes is evident in the
late summer rainfall maximum.

A method of analyzing mean seasonal variations in precipitation
is illustrated in figure 3.8 (based on monthly normals in West
Virginia); the percentage deviations of monthly totals from the
annual total (each expressed as daily averages) are plotted by
months. The figure shows that the normals are higher than average
from March through August when evapotranspiration losses are

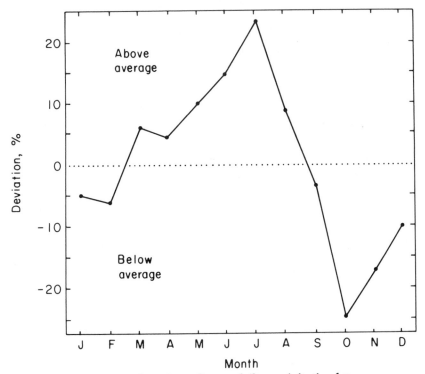

Figure 3.8. Percentage deviations of mean daily precipitation by
months from the annual mean in West Virginia.

greater, and lower than average from September through February. Precipitation is about 25% greater than average during July, and 25% below average during October.

Seasonal variations, as well as the annual totals of precipitation, are frequently influenced by altitude. Figure 3.9 is a plot of the ratios of mean monthly precipitation totals at two stations in northern West Virginia; the forest station at Coopers Rock (C), 13 km east of Morgantown Airport (M), is on a ridge about 300 m above the airport. Annual precipitation at the airport station is only 77% of that at the forest, yet the ratios (M/C) vary from less than 0.7 in winter to more than 1.0 in summer; greater annual precipitation measured at the forest station is largely the result of a winter excess that occurs in the form of snow.

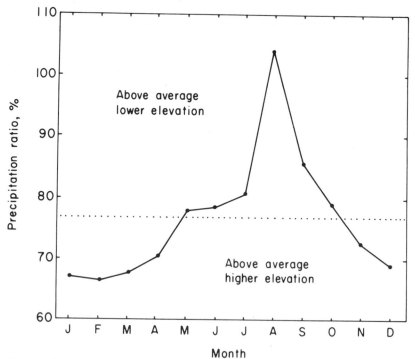

Figure 3.9. Ratios (100 M/C, see text) of mean monthly precipitation totals for neighboring stations at different elevations.

*Daily totals.* Precipitation is commonly measured in nonrecording gages (see section 10.1.a) as daily totals. The characteristics of daily precipitation at a station can be expressed in terms of the frequency of occurrence of measurable amounts, the frequency of various levels of daily totals, the mean level, or the maximum recorded total per day—all of which may show distinct seasonal variations; table 3.4 is an example of this analysis at one station. At this station (Charleston, W.Va.) precipitation occurs most frequently during winter months, but mean and maximum precipitation per day are much greater during summer; also, there are more days with light precipitation ($P \leqslant 5$ mm/day) in winter, but heavy precipitation ($P \geqslant 25$ mm/day) is more frequent during the summer months.

*Rainfall extremes.* Maximum recorded point rainfall depths (the highest values ever recorded) generally follow the relationship

$$P = 389t^{0.486} \tag{3.13}$$

adapted from Jennings (1950), where $P$ (in mm) is roughly proportional to the square root of storm duration ($t$, in hrs). In simpler form

$$P \simeq 50t^{0.5} \tag{3.14}$$

for $t$ in minutes; also, as a corollary, maximum observed rainfall intensity is

$$i \simeq 50t^{-0.5} \tag{3.15}$$

Table 3.4. **Characteristics of Daily Precipitation at Charleston, W. Va. (1948–1972)**

| Period | Mean number of days with $P$ (mm): $P \leqslant 5$ | $5 < P < 25$ | $P \geqslant 25$ | $P > 0$ | One-day totals Mean | Maximum |
|---|---|---|---|---|---|---|
| Spring | 24.5 | 15.7 | 1.7 | 41.9 | 6.7 | 70 |
| Summer | 17.5 | 13.8 | 2.9 | 34.2 | 9.2 | 142 |
| Autumn | 17.5 | 10.6 | 1.5 | 29.6 | 7.3 | 61 |
| Winter | 26.8 | 14.4 | 1.2 | 42.4 | 6.1 | 49 |
| Annual | 86.3 | 54.5 | 7.3 | 148.1 | 7.2 | 142 |

94 / ATMOSPHERIC WATER

where $i = P/t$. Equations 3.13 and 3.14 show that point precipitation may exceed the depth of precipitable water during the first minute, and that the limiting value of $P$ is largely determined by the amount of advected moisture (see section 3.1.b); from equation 3.15, maximum rainfall intensity must decrease with storm duration, and $i$ is limited by the inflow rate of advected moisture.

The maximum recorded point rainfall depths and intensities defined by equations 3.13 through 3.15 are exceptional events (world records); hydrologists are more directly concerned with the probability of occurrence of extreme rainfall events in given localities. Ordinarily the probability ($p$) is given with reference to a single year (e.g., $p = 0.10$ means that there is a 10% chance of occurrence in any given year), or in terms of its reciprocal

$$t_r = \frac{1}{p} \tag{3.16}$$

where $t_r$ is the *return period* or *recurrence interval*; $t_r$ is the average number of years between rainfall events (of given duration) that equal or exceed a given depth. If, for example, a rainfall depth of 100 mm in 6 hrs is equaled or exceeded once in 50 years, on the average, then $t_r = 50$, $p = 0.02$ and, in hydrological jargon, 100 mm is the "50-year 6-hour storm"; rainfall depths for various return periods and storm durations in the United States are available in atlas form (Hershfield, 1961; Miller, 1964).

The probabilistic nature of the recurrence interval concept means that it is capable of deductive development for broader applicability in hydrologic planning. A specified return period for a given rainfall event does not mean that the event will occur at regular intervals; in fact, the probability ($p_n$) that an event will occur at least once in a given interval of $n$ years is

$$p_n = 1 - q^n \tag{3.17}$$

where $q$ is the probability of nonoccurrence, or $q = 1 - p$. For example, letting $t_r = 50$, $p = 0.02$, and $q = 0.98$,

$$p_n = 1 - (0.98)^n \tag{3.18}$$

and there is a 50% chance that the 50-year storm will recur within 34 years, and there is only an 87% chance that it will recur within 100 years.

The return period idea based on annual occurrences can be extremely misleading in that it ignores seasonal variations. Extreme rainfall events are frequently restricted to a particular season, as shown in table 3.4 for example, where maximum 1-day precipitation is almost three times as great in summer as in winter. This means that a storm having a relatively high probability of occurrence (short annual recurrence interval) as a result of high intensity summer storms may be a rare event in winter; estimated seasonal rainfall probabilities for various subregions in the eastern United States were given in graphical form by Hershfield (1961).

Hydrologists are also concerned with the combinations of rainfall depths and durations as related to the dimensions of the areas that are directly influenced by rainfall events. Table 3.5 lists maximum recorded depth-area-duration data for the United States

Table 3.5. Maximum Recorded
Depth-Area-Duration and
Intensity-Area-Duration Data for the
United States (adapted from Shands and
Ammerman, 1947)

| Area | Storm duration (hrs) | | | |
|---|---|---|---|---|
| $(km^2)$ | 6 | 12 | 24 | 48 |
| *Depth (mm)* | | | | |
| $10^2$ | 572 | 721 | 881 | 914 |
| $10^3$ | 411 | 561 | 696 | 780 |
| $10^4$ | 226 | 320 | 424 | 572 |
| $10^5$ | 74 | 119 | 180 | 259 |
| *Intensity (mm/hr)* | | | | |
| $10^2$ | 95 | 60 | 37 | 19 |
| $10^3$ | 69 | 47 | 29 | 16 |
| $10^4$ | 38 | 27 | 18 | 12 |
| $10^5$ | 12 | 10 | 8 | 5 |

Table 3.6. Mean Storm-Wind Data, Morgantown, W. Va. (1966–1970)

| Wind direction | Number of storms | | Windspeed (cm/sec) | | Precipitation percentage | |
|---|---|---|---|---|---|---|
| | Summer | Winter | Summer | Winter | Summer | Winter |
| N | 8 | 15 | 340 | 349 | 3.5 | 8.6 |
| NE | 5 | 9 | 291 | 308 | 2.0 | 5.5 |
| E | 5 | 10 | 308 | 362 | 4.8 | 7.2 |
| SE | 14 | 16 | 304 | 371 | 12.3 | 12.2 |
| S | 27 | 28 | 349 | 384 | 25.6 | 19.4 |
| SW | 44 | 59 | 371 | 474 | 34.8 | 25.2 |
| W | 9 | 28 | 375 | 469 | 9.6 | 12.1 |
| NW | 7 | 17 | 380 | 411 | 5.6 | 9.0 |
| Calm | 4 | 2 | <100 | <100 | 1.8 | 0.8 |
| All | 123 | 184 | 340 | 416 | 100.0 | 100.0 |

NOTE: A storm period is defined here as any period during which measurable precipitation occurred each successive hour.

(adapted from Shands and Ammerman, 1947). For any given storm duration, rainfall depth decreases as the area covered by the storm increases; rainfall intensities are greater for smaller areas and shorter time periods.

*Wind relations.* Windspeed and direction during periods of precipitation affect the accuracy of point precipitation measurements (section 10.1.a), the small-scale distribution of precipitation at ground level (section 3.3.b), the amount of canopy interception (section 4.1.a), and the timing of streamflow (section 7.2.a and b). An example of storm wind analysis is given in table 3.6. At this station the prevailing wind direction is from the southwest as indicated by both the numbers of storms and the percentages of precipitation that arrive with southwest winds; windspeeds are generally greater during the winter half-year and with westerly flow.

### 3.2.c. Data Interpretation

Raw precipitation data from standard climatological networks must be interpreted realistically as indices rather than true quantitative measures of water input. Such data are usually expressed in increments of from 0.1 to 0.5 mm depth (0.25 mm is common in the United States), but the suggested precision is far greater than the accuracy of point measurements can support (see section 10.1.a); in addition, the extreme local and microscale variability of precipitation at ground level (see section 3.3.b) introduces a profound degree of uncertainty with regard to the interpretation of point-sample data. Moreover, even in an intensive network of precipitation gages, the area sampled usually exceeds the total collecting areas of the gages by a factor of from $10^6$ to $10^9$; this means that the representativeness of sample data is a critical consideration in area averaging to obtain mean values for catchment areas (see section 3.3.c).

Despite inaccuracies and lack of representativeness, there is generally a significant positive correlation of monthly and annual precipitation totals among stations in close proximity. The data show that the degree of correlation decreases with both horizontal and vertical distance between stations. Lee et al. (1977) found that, in a mountainous precipitation network (West Virginia) covering $6(10^4)$ km$^2$ with total relief greater than 1 km, the correlation coefficient ($r$) among monthly totals was

$$r = 0.829 - 0.109X - 0.069Z \qquad (3.19)$$

where $X$ (in $10^2$ km) is horizontal distance, and $Z$ (in km) is elevation difference (standard error = 0.042); also

$$r = 0.803 - 0.049X - 0.180Z \qquad (3.20)$$

for annual totals (standard error = 0.081).

Given the degree of correlation among stations, it is feasible to extend a short-term record at a given station by comparing it with the data from surrounding stations in an established network. It may be desired, for example, to estimate the 30-year average, or normal precipitation ($P_n$), for a new station that has only 5 years of record; if $\bar{P}_n$ is the mean normal precipitation for a group of surrounding stations, and $\bar{P}_s$ is their 5-year mean during the new station record period, then

$$P_n = (\overline{P}_n / \overline{P}_5) P_5 \qquad (3.21)$$

where $P_5$ is the 5-year mean at the new station. The relative accuracy of the estimated value will be greater when the network stations are closer to the new station with respect to both horizontal distance and elevation; its absolute accuracy cannot, of course, be expected to exceed the accuracy of the measured values.

A similar procedure can be used to estimate data that are missing from the record of a station that has been in existence for a longer period. It is important to recognize, however, that the correlation of precipitation among stations, as in equations 3.19 and 3.20, is much weaker for shorter time periods. If data from a single day or storm event are missing, it is necessary to study the areal pattern of precipitation, and to interpolate between surrounding stations rather than rely on average relationships.

Observed precipitation at a site is affected by wind, and therefore by the degree of protection from wind afforded by surrounding obstructions; if the surroundings are changed over time, for example by the growth or removal of trees in the immediate vicinity, the precipitation record may be internally inconsistent. The long-term record at a station is said to be consistent if annual precipitation totals at the station $(P_s)$ retain a relatively constant proportionality with the mean values $(\overline{P}_g)$ for a group of neighboring stations in the network (i.e., if $P_s / \overline{P}_g \simeq$ constant). If the record is consistent, accumulated totals of $P_s$ versus $\overline{P}_g$ will plot as a straight line; if there is a significant deviation from linearity the station record can be adjusted for consistency based on the change in slope of the *double-mass plot*.

The procedure of *double-mass analysis* is illustrated in figure 3.10, and the pertinent data are listed in table 3.7; the neighboring control stations were located in forest openings, and the forest station was located in a forest opening until 1961 when the adjacent forest was cut. The slope of the double-mass plot, or $P_s / \overline{P}_g$, was 1.02 before cutting (1950–1961) and 0.86 after cutting (1962–1970), so the forest station data for 1962–1970 were adjusted ac-

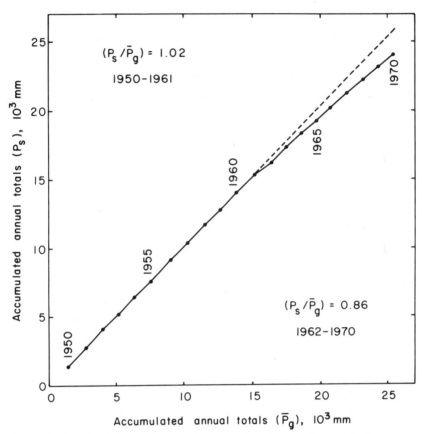

**Figure 3.10.** Slope change in a double-mass plot of annual precipitation following forest cutting.

cording to the rule

$$P_s \text{ (adjusted)} = (1.02/0.86) P_s \text{ (observed)} \qquad (3.22)$$

to maintain the consistency of the record. Chang and Lee (1974) developed an objective computerized method of double-mass analysis in which plotting is unnecessary and adjustments are made automatically for persistent deviations from proportionality, either single or multiple, in a long-term record.

Table 3.7. Data for Double-Mass Analysis of Annual Precipitation
Totals ($P$ in mm)

| Year | Group mean ($\overline{P}_g$) | | Forest station ($P_s$) | | |
|---|---|---|---|---|---|
|  | Annual | Accumulated | Annual | Accumulated | Adjusted |
| 1950 | 1402 | 1402 | 1430 | 1430 | − |
| 1 | 1360 | 2762 | 1384 | 2814 | − |
| 2 | 1212 | 3974 | 1237 | 4051 | − |
| 3 | 1087 | 5061 | 1106 | 5157 | − |
| 4 | 1266 | 6327 | 1281 | 6438 | − |
| 5 | 1195 | 7522 | 1215 | 7653 | − |
| 6 | 1393 | 8915 | 1422 | 9075 | − |
| 7 | 1201 | 10116 | 1223 | 10298 | − |
| 8 | 1248 | 11364 | 1279 | 11577 | − |
| 9 | 1179 | 12543 | 1200 | 12777 | − |
| 1960 | 1174 | 13717 | 1188 | 13965 | − |
| 1 | 1270 | 14987 | 1322 | 15287 | − |
| 2 | 1208 | 16195 | 1035 | 16322 | 1228 |
| 3 | 1143 | 17338 | 981 | 17303 | 1164 |
| 4 | 1186 | 18524 | 1014 | 18317 | 1203 |
| 5 | 1037 | 19561 | 897 | 19214 | 1064 |
| 6 | 1099 | 20660 | 943 | 20157 | 1118 |
| 7 | 1235 | 21895 | 1062 | 21219 | 1260 |
| 8 | 1142 | 23037 | 989 | 22208 | 1173 |
| 9 | 1126 | 24163 | 976 | 23184 | 1158 |
| 1970 | 1196 | 25359 | 1027 | 24211 | 1218 |
| *Means:* | | | | | |
| 1950–61 | 1249 | − | 1274 | − | − |
| 1962–70 | 1152 | − | 992 | − | 1176 |
| 1950–70 | 1208 | − | 1153 | − | − |

## 3.3. Catchment Precipitation

Precipitation in forested areas is caused almost exclusively by physical factors that are unrelated to the existence of forest cover, but the forest influences the measurement process and the distribution of rain and snow in openings and along edges. Small-scale topographic elements interact with windspeed and direction to produce distinctive patterns of precipitation at ground level, and to influence the representativeness of measurement sites. The local variability of precipitation, and the associated influences of forest cover and local topography, complicate the task of obtaining useful area estimates of depth for water budgeting in small catchment areas.

### 3.3.a. Forest Influences

The forests of the earth are restricted to areas of relatively high precipitation; the causes for this are natural for the most part, but forest removal from lowlands (areas of lower relative precipitation) for agriculture and other land uses may also be a contributing factor. According to Petterssen (1969) the dividing line between geographic zones of steppe and forest climate in terms of annual precipitation is

$$P_m = 20T_a + 140 \tag{3.23}$$

where $P_m$ (in mm/yr) is the minimum requirement for tree growth (assuming that precipitation is not strongly seasonal), and $T_a$ (in °C) is the mean annual air temperature. In the conterminous United States, Anderson, Hoover, and Reinhart (1976) estimated that forested areas receive twice as much precipitation (depth) as other land (1140 versus 570 mm/yr), which is the same total volume as other land on half as much area (forests occupy one-third of the total land area); the forested land generates three-fourths of the annual streamflow volume.

The natural coincidence of forest cover and higher precipitation has undoubtedly caused, or at least reinforced, the popular notion that forests increase or "attract" rain and other precipitation forms. Acceptance of the forest as a causal factor leads naturally to the conclusion that forest cutting will reduce precipitation, or that afforestation will increase it; this conclusion played a major role in the development of forest policy in the United States and elsewhere, and is still the basis of considerable concern among environmentalists. Objectively, however, the arguments in favor of a positive forest influence are severely weakened when the alleged mechanisms for the influence are critically reviewed.

It is frequently alleged that, since forests use (evaporate and transpire) more water than other cover types, total precipitation must be greater with forest cover in order to satisfy the relation $P = E$ (equation 2.6); this argument is irrefutable, taken on the global scale, but is appears almost meaningless when the relative magnitude of the effect is seen. A proper perspective can be achieved by noting that, from table 1.3, evaporation from *all* of the land area of the earth amounts to only 14.3% (71/496) of the total; this means that if all land evaporation were stopped, total precipitation over the earth would decrease by 14.3% (providing that ocean evaporation remained constant). But since forests occupy only one-fourth of the earth's land area, and forest removal does not stop evaporation but only reduces it (by one-third or less, on the average), the global effect of complete forest removal probably would not exceed 1 to 2% of precipitation.

The global argument for an equality of precipitation and evaporation clearly does not apply to individual land segments, except perhaps in some tropical areas where internal circulations are dominant. Water evaporated from a particular segment is mixed by atmospheric turbulence and moved downwind, usually at the rate of several hundred kilometers per day. Consequently the contribution of evaporation to precipitation in the same general area is small, ranging from 6 to 27% for the extensive land masses ($10^5 - 10^7$ km$^2$) described in table 3.2, and any increases in precipitation that are attributable to forest transpiration in areas of $10^2$ to $10^3$ km$^2$ must be immeasurably small.

Since forests tend to add to the effective elevation of upland areas, it is conceivable that total precipitation will increase with forest height as a direct result of the orographic effect. Assuming that the effect varies from 40 to 80 mm/yr · 100 m in an area where normal precipitation is 1000 mm/yr, an increase of 10 to 20 mm/yr, or 1 to 2%, might occur over a 25-m tall forest; the forest is not an impermeable barrier, so the effect may be even smaller, especially over deciduous forest types during dormant periods. It is also conceivable that the aerodynamic roughness of a forest canopy may cause additional turbulence and promote upward movement of the local air mass.

When fog moves horizontally into a forest canopy, fog droplets are deposited by contact on the foliage. In coastal fog belts or mountainous areas the total accumulation of droplets at the leading edge of a forest may add a depth of water approaching the total for other forms of precipitation. The forest influence is undeniable with regard to this "occult" precipitation, but the phenomenon is severely limited in geographic extent.

Apparently, with trivial exceptions, precipitation in forested areas is caused by physical factors that are unrelated to the existence of forest cover; contrary opinions persist, however, and it is instructive to consider the difficulties involved in obtaining a definitive answer from experimental data. Ground-level precipitation is not uniformly distributed at a site, even over a few square meters of surface area, because falling raindrops and snowflakes are scattered by turbulent air movements that arise as the result of surface roughness and physical obstructions in the windfield. Compounding the problem is the fact that standard rain gages also constitute obstructions in the windfield, causing additional variability in the quantity to be measured.

An example of the complexity of the problem can be seen in the data collected by Hursh (1948) in a study of local climate as influenced by forest cover. Hursh selected an appropriate area in the Copper Basin in eastern Tennessee where 2800 ha of forest land had been denuded by smelter fumes; between the denuded area and the surrounding forest there was a 4800-ha zone, 1 to 3 km wide, that supported grass cover. Precipitation and windspeed were measured over a 4-yr period at two stations in each zone; the annual averages given in table 3.8 show that forest precipitation

Table 3.8. Copper Basin Data (Hursh, 1948) and Adjusted Precipitation

| Zone | Mean windspeed (cm/sec) | Annual precipitation (mm) | |
|---|---|---|---|
| | | Observed | Adjusted |
| Denuded | 226 | 1277 | 1458 |
| Grass | 167 | 1339 | 1462 |
| Forest | 33 | 1459 | 1466 |

exceeded that in the denuded area by 14.3%, and in the grassed area by 9.0%.

Table 3.8 also shows that mean windspeed was inversely related to observed precipitation depth; windspeed was much smaller at the forest stations which were located in forest openings. Numerous investigations have demonstrated that wind decreases the catch of rainfall in a standard gage, and that the deficiency in catch is greater at greater windspeeds; the relationship between windspeed and catch deficiency has not been precisely defined, but theoretical considerations and experimental data have provided useful correction formulae (see section 10.1.a). The precipitation data, adjusted to eliminate the effects of wind at measurement sites in the Copper Basin (table 3.8), suggest that true precipitation depth was relatively uniform among sites and that any influence of forest cover was negligible.

Since rain gages exposed in small forest openings usually indicate a greater depth of rain than those in adjacent unsheltered areas, and since the catch in unsheltered gages is characteristically deficient, the former are usually assumed to be more accurate. But rainfall catch also varies with the relative dimensions of forest openings, and there is no universal agreement with regard to an "optimum" size; a common rule of thumb is that the radius of a circular opening (with a gage at the center) should be 1 to 2 times tree height, corresponding to a vertical angle (screening angle) from the gage to tree tops of 27 to 45°. In a study of model obstructions Repa (1977) found that, for a series of 25 summer storms with mean storm windspeeds ranging from 1.2 to 5.4 m/sec, the greatest catch occurred with screening angles between 15 and 30°; but since the aerodynamic characteristics of forest openings are poorly understood, and undoubtedly vary with the structure of the surrounding forest, it would be naive to equate maximum catch to true rainfall.

The distribution of rainfall in forest openings and along edges is determined to a large extent by air movements and the mass and aerodynamic properties of the drops. Blowing rain is carried beneath the canopy at the windward edge of a forest, adds to vertical throughfall, and creates a rain-rich zone, the width of which depends on the angle of inclination of the falling drops; just outside the forest at the leeward edge there is a deficit zone of the same width. The area of maximum rainfall is toward the leeward edge of a forest opening, and the deficit area is toward the windward; a formal analysis of raindrop trajectories is given in section 10.3.

### 3.3.b. Topographic Effects

The spatial distribution of precipitation is influenced by both large-scale and small-scale topographic features. The large-scale influence, discussed in section 3.2.a, causes an increase in precipitation on windward slopes (the orographic effect) and a decrease to the leeward (the rain shadow effect); these effects are related to the expansion and contraction of large air masses. On a much smaller scale, around hills or mountain ridges where elevation differences are too small to produce a significant orographic effect, there is a reversal of the large-scale pattern that is associated with the irregular distribution of precipitation by wind near the ground.

Precipitation falls through moving air, and any disruption of the normal windfield caused by an obstruction at the surface will affect the distribution of precipitation at ground level. On the windward side of an obstruction, whether a rain gage, tree, or small hill, air is forced to converge upward and windspeed ($u$) increases; this causes an increase in the angle of inclination ($I$) of falling raindrops, where

$$\tan I = \frac{u}{v} \tag{3.24}$$

and $v$ is the terminal (fall) velocity of the drops (see section 10.1.a). With increasing $u$ and $I$, precipitation intensity decreases in the downwind direction because raindrops are spread over a greater local area; to the leeward of the obstruction the air stream diverges and, as $u$ and $I$ are decreasing, precipitation increases.

The small-scale topographic effect on summer rainfall was observed by S. C. Hill over a 4-month period (May–September) along a cleared utility transect that traversed a small hill near Harmony

Grove, West Virginia; the transect bearing was SW → NE, following the direction of prevailing winds. Duplicate rain gages were installed at each of 20 observation sites along the cleared area, near ground level, at the approximate height of existing shrubs and herbaceous cover. The results for storms during which the mean southwesterly flow exceeded 3 m/sec are shown in figure 3.11; near the ridge the windward slope was a "blow-over" zone with a 5% deficiency in catch, and the leeward slope was a "dump" zone with a 5% excess.

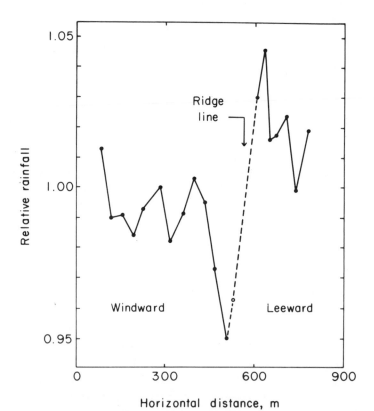

Figure 3.11. Relative rainfall (fraction of mean) at stations on windward and leeward slopes of a small hill (Harmony Grove, West Virginia).

### 3.3.c. Area Averaging

Point precipitation data are used in quantitative hydrology to estimate mean depths or volumes of precipitation input to catchment areas; the accuracy of such estimates depends on both the accuracy and representativeness of individual point samples. Point sample inaccuracy is a problem of continuing concern in forest hydrology; there is no standard method of obtaining accurate measurements at critical locations (over a forest canopy, for example), and so current network data are useful primarily as indices. A point measurement of precipitation is said to be representative for a given land segment if it is equal to the mean precipitation depth over the area; but the area mean for a land segment is an unknown quantity except as an estimate based on point samples, so the representativeness of any particular sample must either be assessed independently or by comparison with other samples—each of which suffers from inherent inaccuracy.

The uncertainty involved in area averaging of precipitation can be alleviated to a considerable extent by careful network design and independent assessment of the accuracy of point measurements (see sections 10.1.a and 10.3). Also, the problems are less acute when dealing with the precipitation totals that are needed to describe monthly, seasonal, or annual variations, or to estimate changes in the water balance of an area caused by forest management activities or cover-type changes. Assuming that individual point samples are accurate enough for the intended purpose, or that they are to be used primarily as indices, useful area averages can be obtained using the standard procedure that is most appropriate in any particular instance.

Area averages of precipitation for catchments are computed either as arithmetic means or weighted means based on the available station data and, in some cases, personal judgment. The *arithmetic mean* $(P_a)$ is simply

$$P_a = \frac{1}{n} \sum_{s=1}^{n} P_s \qquad (3.25)$$

where $P_s$ is station precipitation and $n$ is the total number of stations. This method is easiest to use and may be accurate enough if the network of gages is dense, precipitation is relatively uniform among sites, or gage sites are carefully selected for representativeness; the latter may be achieved by intense preliminary sampling to locate the most appropriate stations to be retained in a permanent network.

If network stations are relatively few in number or poorly placed, greater accuracy may be achieved by weighting each station value by the area ($A_s$) of that part of the catchment that is nearest the station. Area weighting may be accomplished in an approximate manner by direct examination of a station location map, or more accurately by constructing polygons (Thiessen polygons) around each station as in figure 3.12$a$; the sides of the polygons are perpendicular bisectors of lines between adjoining stations. The *Thiessen mean* ($P_t$) is then

$$P_t = \frac{1}{A} \sum_{s=1}^{n} P_s A_s \qquad (3.26)$$

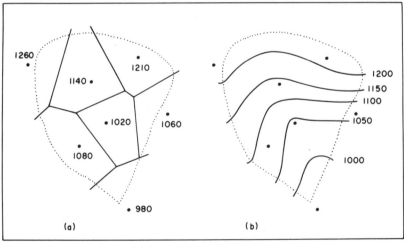

Figure 3.12. Thiessen polygons, $a$, and isohyets, $b$, used in averaging annual catchment precipitation (precipitation in mm).

where $A$ is total catchment area; the Thiessen method assumes a linear variation of precipitation among stations, making no allowance for topographic influences.

In areas of complex topography the skilled hydrologist may choose to develop an area weighting scheme based on lines of equal precipitation (isohyets) as in figure 3.12$b$; this method provides a means of considering both large-scale and small-scale topographic influences that cause nonlinear variations of precipitation between stations. If $A_c$ is the partial catchment area that lies between two isohyets, and $P_c$ is the mean precipitation in this area, then

$$P_i = \frac{1}{A} \sum_{c=1}^{n} P_c A_c \qquad (3.27)$$

where $n$ is the number of partial areas and $P_i$ is the *isohyetal mean;* ordinarily $P_c$ is taken as the arithmetic mean of bounding isohyets, but greater accuracy is attained by computing a weighted mean based on the lengths of the individual isohyets. The isohyetal method is potentially most accurate, but it is subjective, dependent upon the skill of the analyst, and not adaptable to automatic data processing.

## LITERATURE CITED

Anderson, H. W., M. D. Hoover, and K. G. Reinhart. 1976. *Forests and Water: Effects of Forest Management on Floods, Sedimentation, and Water Supply.* General Technical Report PSW-18. Berkeley, Cal.: U.S. Forest Service.

Chang, M. and R. Lee. 1974. Objective double-mass analysis. *Water Resources Research* 10:1123–26.

——— 1975. *Representativeness of Watershed Precipitation Samples.* WRI Bulletin 4, Morgantown: West Virginia University.

Environmental Data Service. 1973. *Monthly Averages of Temperature and Precipitation for State Climatic Divisions 1941-1970.* Asheville, N.C.: National Climatic Center.

Hershfield, D. M. 1961. *Rainfall Frequency Atlas of the United States.* Washington, D.C.: U.S. Department of Commerce.

Hursh, C. R. 1948. *Local Climate in the Copper Basin of Tennessee as Modified by the Removal of Vegetation.* Circular 774. Washington, D.C.: U.S. Department of Agriculture.

Jennings, A. H. 1950. World's greatest observed point rainfalls. *Monthly Weather Review* 78:4–5.

Lee, R., S. Tajchman, D. G. Boyer, and E. W. Repa. 1977. Normal precipitation in West Virginia. *West Virginia Agriculture and Forestry* 7:12–18.

Miller, D. H. 1977. *Water at the Surface of the Earth.* New York: Academic Press.

Miller, J. P. 1964. *Two to Ten-Day Precipitation for Return Periods of 2 to 100 Years in the Contiguous United States.* Technical Paper 49, Washington, D.C.: U.S. Department of Commerce.

Petterssen, S. 1969. *Introduction to Meteorology.* New York: McGraw-Hill.

Phillips, D. W. 1972. Modification of surface air over Lake Ontario in winter. *Monthly Weather Review* 100: 662–70.

Repa, E. W. 1977. "The Effect of Circular Obstructions on Rainfall Catch." Master's thesis, Morgantown: West Virginia University.

Sellers, W. D. 1965. *Physical Climatology.* Chicago: University of Chicago Press.

Shands, A. L. and D. Ammerman. 1947. *Maximum Recorded United States Point Rainfall for Five Minutes to 24 Hours at 207 First Order Stations.* Technical Paper 2. Washington, D.C.: U.S. Weather Bureau.

## SELECTED READINGS

Anthes, R. A., H. A. Panofsky, J. J. Cahir, and A. Rango. 1978. *The Atmosphere.* Columbus, Ohio: Charles E. Merrill.

Budyko, M. I. 1974. *Climate and Life.* New York: Academic Press.

Corbett, E. S. 1967. Measurement and estimation of precipitation on experimental watersheds. In W. E. Sopper and H. W. Lull, eds., *International Symposium on Forest Hydrology.* New York: Pergamon Press.

Johnson, J. C. 1960. *Physical Meterology.* New York: Wiley.

Lee, R. 1978. *Forest Microclimatology.* New York: Columbia University Press.

Penman, H. L. 1958. *Humidity.* New York: Reinhold Publishing Corporation.

Penman, H. L. 1963. *Vegetation and Hydrology.* Technical Communication 53. Farnham Royal, England: Commonwealth Agricultural Bureaux.

Stanhill, G. 1970. The water flux in temperate forests: precipitation and evapotranspiration. In D. E. Reichle, ed., *Analysis of Temperate Forest Ecosystems.* New York: Springer.

# 4 PRECIPITATION DISPOSAL

## 4.1. Canopy Interception

Precipitation that falls on a forest canopy is redistributed and reduced in quantity as it moves toward the forest floor. The amount of reduction (canopy interception) is determined by the amount and frequency of precipitation, and by canopy storage capacity and drying rate; empirical studies have shown that it varies widely, not only among climatological regions and forest types, and with stand density and age, but also with position relative to tree stems in any particular stand. Water that is intercepted by tree crowns is also important hydrologically because it causes nonuniform wetting of the forest soil, inhibits transpiration and reduces the draft on soil moisture, evaporates more rapidly than transpiration can occur in the same microclimate, and adds significantly to total vaporization loss.

### 4.1.a. Storage Capacity

Canopy storage capacity is the quantity of water that can be held on the aerial portions of a forest stand; it is expressed, in the same units as precipitation, as an average depth for the stand in terms of liquid water equivalent. The magnitude of canopy storage capacity depends on the surface area of leaves and bark, their roughness, orientation, arrangement, and wettability, and on the forces of wind and gravity that tend to dislodge precipitation particles. The problem seems hopelessly complicated from the physical standpoint and, as a practical expedient, the overall effect is usually inferred from measurements of precipitation ($P$), throughfall ($T$), and stemflow ($S$); symbolically,

$$C = (1 - \alpha) P - T - S \qquad (4.1)$$

where $C$ is storage capacity (assuming $P > C$), and $\alpha$ is the fraction of precipitation that evaporates during the storm.

Equation 4.1 may be reduced to the form

$$C = I_c - \alpha P \qquad (4.2)$$

where $I_c$ is canopy interception (see equation 4.3), but both equations 4.1. and 4.2 pose additional problems. First, $\alpha \simeq 0$ during periods of uninterrupted rainfall, but otherwise it is not a constant ($\alpha$ is generally smaller for more intense storms) and must be evaluated independently; and second, $C$, as a residual, is burdened with all of the errors associated with measurements of $P$, $T$, and $S$. It is not surprising, therefore, that published estimates of $C$ show considerable variation for similar forest stands.

If it is assumed that $P$ and $I_c$ are linearly related, and if both variables are measured over a wide range of $P$, $C$ and $\alpha$ in equation 4.2 can be taken as the intercept and slope, respectively, from an estimated regression; in fact, the true relationship is curvilinear, but the scatter of plotted points is so great, and measurement accuracy so poorly defined, that the assumption of linearity is useful as a means of obtaining a first approximation. Table 4.1.

Table 4.1. **Mean Values and Ranges of Canopy Storage Capacity ($C$) and the Evaporation Component ($\alpha$) of Canopy Interception for Major Forest Types Based on Summaries by Helvey and Patric (1965) and Zinke (1967)**

| Type | $C$ (mm) | | $\alpha$ (dimensionless) | |
|---|---|---|---|---|
| | Mean | Range | Mean | Range |
| *Deciduous* (Rainfall) | | | | |
| Dormant season | 0.5 | 0.1–1.0 | 0.07 | 0.02–0.16 |
| Growing season | 1.0 | 0.1–2.0 | 0.09 | 0.04–0.22 |
| *Coniferous* | | | | |
| Rainfall | 2.0 | 0.5–9.0 | 0.13 | 0.06–0.20 |
| Snowfall | 3.0 | 0.3–8.0 | 0.13 | 0.05–0.28 |

lists mean values and ranges of $C$ and $\alpha$ for major forest types based on summaries of numerous studies by Helvey and Patric (1965) and Zinke (1967). The data show that canopy storage capacity is generally greater for deciduous species in leaf, greater for conifers than for hardwoods, and greater for snow than for rain; nevertheless the ranges of values are so great that the averages may have little meaning as applied to any particular stand.

### 4.1.b. Empirical Equations

Canopy interception is the part of precipitation that does not reach the forest floor; quantitatively it is the difference between precipitation and the sum of throughfall and stemflow, i.e.,

$$I_c = P - T - S \tag{4.3}$$

and

$$I_c = C + \alpha P \tag{4.4}$$

by rearrangement of equation 4.2. Since $I_c$ cannot be measured directly in the field, it is inferred from measurements of $P$, $T$, and $S$; data from many regions and forest types show that seasonal or annual averages of $I_c$ are much smaller than either $P$ or $T$ (generally $0.1 < I_c/P < 0.4$, and $0.1 < I_c/T < 0.7$). This means that a small measurement error in either precipitation or throughfall will introduce a much larger relative error in the estimate of canopy interception; for example, if it is assumed, optimistically, that the error in $P$ is 5%, then the error in $I_c$ will range from about 10 to 50% (an error of 5% in *both* $P$ and $T$ can produce an error of almost 100% in the estimate of $I_c$).

Equation 4.4 is the common form used to express canopy interception as a linear function of precipitation; in this case the coefficients $C$ and $\alpha$ are assumed to be constant for a season or year, and their physical meanings are obscure. Taking $\hat{C}$ as the statistical counterpart of $C$, and $\hat{\alpha}$ as that of $\alpha$, total canopy interception for a longer period is estimated as

$$I_c = \hat{C}N + \hat{\alpha}P \tag{4.5}$$

when $N$ is the total number of "storms," or wetting cycles (wetting and complete drying of the canopy), and $P$ is total precipitation for the period. The definition of "storm" is arbitrary, and is usually based on tradition or the researcher's judgment concerning the time interval between storms that would be required for complete canopy drying; usually a drying interval of from 6 to 24 hrs is adopted to separate discrete storm periods, but sometimes $N$ is taken simply as the total number of days with measurable precipitation.

The amount and frequency of precipitation, expressed by $P$ and $N$ in equation 4.5, are strictly climatological variables, but the coefficients $\hat{C}$ and $\hat{\alpha}$ depend more on forest characteristics. Niederhof and Wilm (1943) demonstrated the effect of forest structure by measuring canopy rainfall interception in thinned stands of lodgepole pine; the results, given in table 4.2, show that the coefficients tend to vary systematically with stand density parameters. Similar effects for undisturbed forests are evident in the data

Table 4.2. Regression Equations for Canopy Rainfall Interception as Related to Stand Characteristics in Lodgepole Pine (Niederhof and Wilm, 1943) and Mixed Hardwoods and White Pine (Helvey, 1967)

| Forest type | Description | | Regression equation[a]<br>$I_c = \hat{C}N + \hat{\alpha}P$ |
|---|---|---|---|
| *Lodgepole pine* | Basal area<br>(m²/ha) | No. trees<br>(1/ha) | |
| | 9.2 | 360 | $I_c = 0.38N + 0.01P$ |
| | 14.9 | 450 | $= 0.33N + 0.09P$ |
| | 15.2 | 510 | $= 0.18N + 0.11P$ |
| | 22.0 | 550 | $= 0.38N + 0.13P$ |
| | 36.5 | 940 | $= 0.74N + 0.20P$ |
| *Mixed hardwoods* | Age | Season | |
| | Mature | Winter | $I_c = 0.51N + 0.06P$ |
| | Mature | Summer | $= 1.02N + 0.08P$ |
| *White pine* | 10 yrs | Annual | $I_c = 1.27N + 0.08P$ |
| | 35 yrs | Annual | $= 1.27N + 0.12P$ |
| | 60 yrs | Annual | $= 1.52N + 0.18P$ |

[a] $I_c$ and $P$ are in mm; $N$ is the number of storms.

of Helvey (1967): $\hat{C}$ and $\hat{\alpha}$ are greater in mixed hardwoods during the growing season with greater canopy density, and tend to increase systematically with age (10–60 yrs) in white pine stands.

### 4.1.c. Related Processes

In addition to reducing average precipitation depth at the forest floor, tree canopies diversify the areal pattern by channeling flows (throughfall and stemflow) in a discriminatory manner. Interception is greatest near tree stems where the total surface area of foliage and branches is greatest, and is least near crown edges; consequently throughfall is greatest near crown edges, or in small canopy openings, and least near tree stems. An additional discontinuity is introduced by the influx of water to the forest floor in the form of stemflow (section 4.3), especially during larger storms, with smooth-barked trees, and in deciduous forests during the dormant season.

Canopy interception is, by definition, the fraction of precipitation that is evaporated from external plant surfaces; during the evaporation process, canopy air is humidified, and the energy consumed is not available for transpiration. Consequently, during these periods, there is a reduced draft on soil moisture (reduced transpiration), but the reduction is not equivalent to the rate of evaporation because intercepted water is exposed directly to the air, and it evaporates more rapidly than transpiration can occur under the same atmospheric conditions (see section 6.2.c). Canopy interception is important hydrologically, therefore, because it modifies the water balance, increasing total vaporization loss and reducing streamflow.

## 4.2. Canopy Throughfall

Throughfall is the part of precipitation that reaches the forest floor directly or by dripping from leaves, twigs, and branches; quantitatively it is the difference between precipitation and the sum of canopy interception and stemflow. Throughfall depth varies inversely with the density of forest stands, and generally increases with distance from tree stems, mirroring the density effect on canopy interception; in dense forest stands throughfall patterns may be associated with patterns of soil moisture content. The average intensity of throughfall is smaller than that of rainfall, but its drop sizes are larger, and its total potential impact as an erosive force is greater.

### 4.2.a. Total Throughfall

Throughfall must be measured (actually sampled) because it cannot be expressed entirely in terms of other measured values; symbolically

$$T = (1 - \alpha) P - C - S \qquad (4.6)$$

by rearrangement of equation 4.1, and

$$T = P - I_c - S \qquad (4.7)$$

from equation 4.3, where the only measured quantities on the right of the equality signs are $P$ and $S$. From equation 4.7, throughfall as a percentage of precipitation is

$$T(\%) = 100 - I_c(\%) - S(\%) \qquad (4.8)$$

or

$$T(\%) \simeq 100 - I_c(\%) \qquad (4.9)$$

because $S$ is small (usually 1 to 5%; see section 4.3). Since seasonal or annual averages of canopy interception vary between 10 and 40% (section 4.1.b), throughfall averages for a wide variety of forest types must be restricted to the range from 60 to 90%.

Since total throughfall decreases as canopy interception increases, it must be inversely related to canopy density; it is generally greater in more open forest types, in stands of intolerant, pioneer, and subclimax species, and in hardwood (versus coniferous) stands—especially during the dormant season. In any particular stand the relationship between rainfall and throughfall may be difficult to define because of measurement problems (see sections 10.1.a and 10.4), or because of variations in canopy drying and rewetting during storm periods; usually the relationship is assumed

Table 4.3. Regression Equations for Throughfall as Related to Rainfall in Mixed Hardwoods (Helvey and Patric, 1965), White Pine (Helvey, 1967), and Loblolly Pine (Rogerson, 1967)

| Forest type | Description | Regression equation $T = aP - bN^a$ |
|---|---|---|
| *Mixed hardwoods* | Mature stands: winter | $T = 0.91P - 0.38N$ |
| | summer | $= 0.90P - 0.79N$ |
| *White pine* | Annual; age: 10 yrs | $T = 0.85P - 1.27N$ |
| | 60 yrs | $= 0.83P - 1.27N$ |
| *Loblolly pine* | Annual; basal area: 9.2 m²/ha | $T = 0.94P - 0.46N$ |
| | 43.6 m²/ha | $= 0.80P - 0.46N$ |

[a] $T$ and $P$ are in mm; $N$ is the number of storms.

to be linear for all except very small storms, and regression analysis is used to determine the *mean* quantitative relationship. Regression equations applicable to selected forest types and conditions in the eastern United States are given in table 4.3; the application of such formulas to any particular forest stand or rainfall event would obviously be precarious.

In throughfall regression equations of the form

$$T = aP - bN \qquad (4.10)$$

from table 4.3, the fraction of precipitation that appears as throughfall is

$$T(\%) = 100a - \frac{100b}{P} \qquad (4.11)$$

for any particular storm ($N = 1$). It follows that throughfall percentage must approach zero for very small storms, and increase with increasing storm size; theoretically $T(\%) \rightarrow 100$ for very large storms, but the limiting value based on regression (average conditions) is $100a$ where $a < 1$. Throughfall percentages for the forest types listed in table 4.3 are given in table 4.4 for selected storms sizes in the range $P \geqslant 5$ mm.

Table 4.4.  Throughfall as a Percentage of Precipitation for Various Storm Sizes Based on the Regression Equations of Table 4.3

| Forest type | Description | Storm size (mm) | | | | | |
|---|---|---|---|---|---|---|---|
| | | 5 | 10 | 15 | 20 | 25 | ∞ |
| *Mixed hardwoods* | Mature stands: winter | 83 | 87 | 88 | 89 | 89 | 91 |
| | summer | 74 | 82 | 85 | 86 | 87 | 90 |
| *White pine* | Annual; age: 10 yrs | 60 | 72 | 77 | 79 | 80 | 85 |
| | 60 yrs | 58 | 70 | 75 | 77 | 78 | 83 |
| *Loblolly pine* | Annual; basal area: 9.2 m$^2$/ha | 85 | 89 | 91 | 92 | 92 | 94 |
| | 43.6 m$^2$/ha | 70 | 75 | 76 | 77 | 78 | 80 |

Table 4.5.  Throughfall Depth as Related to Residual Stand Characteristics in Lodgepole Pine (Wilm and Dunford, 1948) and Black Spruce (Weitzman and Bay, 1959)

| Forest type | Description | Throughfall[a] | | Relative throughfall[a] | |
|---|---|---|---|---|---|
| | | Rain | Snow | Rain | Snow |
| *Lodgepole pine* | Relative density | | | | |
| | 6 | 233 | 193 | 75 | 79 |
| | 3 | 270 | 214 | 87 | 88 |
| | 2 | 287 | 219 | 93 | 90 |
| | 1 | 285 | 231 | 92 | 95 |
| | 0 | 310 | 244 | 100 | 100 |
| *Black spruce* | Cutting method | | | | |
| | Uncut | | 64 | | 56 |
| | Selection | | 66 | | 58 |
| | Shelterwood | | 81 | | 71 |
| | Clearcut strip | | 102 | | 89 |
| | Clearcut patch | | 114 | | 100 |

[a]Absolute depth in mm liquid water equivalent (snow depth is seasonal accumulation); relative depth in percent of maximum.

Average throughfall depth is affected by silvicultural operations that modify stand density—either uniformly by thinning, or otherwise as prescribed by an adopted cutting method; some examples of the effects are given in table 4.5. The data of Wilm and Dunford (1948) show that, in thinned stands of lodgepole pine, throughfall percentage increases almost linearly with decreases in relative density: $T(\%) \simeq 100 - 4$ (density); the effect is virtually the same for rain and snow. Weitzman and Bay (1959) found that maximum snowfall accumulations in an uncut stand of black spruce, and in a stand where the single tree selection method was used, were less than 60% of that in a clearcut area; intermediate accumulations occurred in stands where shelterwood and strip cutting methods were applied.

## 4.2.b. Throughfall Variability

The uneven distribution of throughfall at the forest floor is caused by the small-scale variability of precipitation above the canopy, and by mechanical effects of foliage and branches in redistributing raindrops and snowflakes. The "topography" of a canopy surface undoubtedly creates microscale "blowover" and "dump" zones, analogous to those that occur over local terrain (see section 3.3.b), but this aspect of the problem has received little attention. Most studies have been directed toward an understanding of the overall effect as it appears from through-fall samples collected at the surface.

Throughfall tends to be less variable in stands of lower average density; in hardwood stands, for example, the standard deviation of measured values may be 10 to 20% of the mean during the leafless period, but 20 to 30% or more during the growing season. At the other extreme, in stands of very high average density, it is not uncommon to find maximum values that are 2 to 3 times as great as the minima during any particular storm; throughfall maxima frequently exceed above-canopy precipitation by 50% or more. Throughfall depth tends to be less variable during storms of greater average depth and intensity.

One measure of throughfall variability is the number ($N$) of gages or sampling points that are needed to estimate a mean value with a given level of statistical reliability; ordinarily an error of 5% is assumed to be acceptable, and

$$N = \frac{s^2}{(0.05 \, \overline{T})^2} \tag{4.12}$$

can be used to determine $N$ as a function of the sample standard deviation ($s$) and mean throughfall ($\overline{T}$). Reynolds and Leyton (1963) found that even with 20 stationary gages in a 0.2-ha plot (1 gage per 100 m$^2$) of Norway spruce, the error term was 11% for a 4-month series, and 9 to 14% for shorter periods; the statistical error for the same number of trough gages was relatively constant at about 6%. Rogerson (1967) used a more dense network (3 gages per 100 m$^2$) to reduce the error to less than 5% in a loblolly pine stand; Helvey and Patric (1965) proposed that 6 standard gages in winter and 15 in summer would provide an adequate sample in mixed hardwood stands if the gages were moved periodically to randomly selected locations.

Storm throughfall depth at any particular site in a stand is largely unpredictable, but distinct patterns can be observed in the mean values. The fraction of precipitation that appears as throughfall generally increases with increasing distance from tree stems, and is greatest near crown edges where there is a concentration of dripping; the effects are more pronounced under denser forest canopies (for example, snow accumulation is relatively uniform under leafless deciduous trees). Wind may affect the throughfall pattern, especially of snow, and greater accumulations sometimes occur leeward of boles.

A plot of average throughfall catch ($T$) as a function of distance ($D$) from tree stems in a dense forest stand usually shows a wide scatter of points that can be reduced to a straight line represented by the regression equation

$$T = a + bD \qquad (4.13)$$

where the coefficients ($a$ and $b$) are almost always positive; the assumption of linearity is questionable, but the scatter of points is characteristically so great that no other general form can improve the statistical fit. Assuming that the axis of the tree is at the center of a circular plot in which $X$ is the distance from plot center,

$$T = a + b(X - r) \qquad (4.14)$$

where $r$ is stem radius, and the volume of throughfall ($T\,dA$) in any narrow concentric ring around the tree is

$$T\,dA = T\,2\pi X\,dX \qquad (4.15)$$

where $dX$ is ring width; also,

$$\int_r^x T\,2\pi X\,dX = \left[ \pi X^2 \left( a + \frac{2bX}{3} - br \right) \right]_r^x \qquad (4.16)$$

which can be evaluated for $X$ equal to half the average distance between trees (or $X = X_p$) to determine the total volume of throughfall for the plot. It follows that mean throughfall depth ($\overline{T}$) for the stand is given by

$$\overline{T} = \frac{1}{A} \int_r^{x_p} T\, 2\pi X\, dX = \frac{1}{\pi(X_p^2 - r^2)} \int_r^{x_p} T\, 2\pi X\, dX \quad (4.17)$$

where $A$ is throughfall area per tree; ordinarily $0.03X_p < r < 0.1X_p$ (corresponding to basal areas of from 0.1 to 1.0% of stand area); and evaluation of equation 4.17 shows that

$$\overline{T} \simeq a + bX_p \left( \frac{2}{3} - \frac{r}{X_p} \right) \quad\quad\quad (4.18)$$

or in general that average throughfall depth occurs at $X \simeq 0.6X_p$.

### 4.2.c. Related Phenomena

Throughfall, with the exception of a minor contribution from stemflow, represents all of the water that is available to the forest soil, and the fact that there are systematic patterns of throughfall suggests the possibility of similar patterns in the distribution of soil moisture. Any coincidence of the two patterns should be most evident immediately following rain or snowmelt, because areas of greater throughfall tend to coincide with those of greater penetration of radiation and wind, and would therefore be subjected to more rapid drying. The relationship between throughfall and soil moisture was reviewed by Eschner (1967), but in general the subject has received very little attention among hydrologists and foresters; some important quantitative implications are discussed in section 5.2.c, and the relationships to soil water quality and internal nutrient cycling are treated in section 8.3.c.

Direct throughfall begins with the onset of precipitation, but dripping is delayed while canopy storage capacity is being filled; likewise, after the storm has passed, throughfall continues as wind and gravity dislodge excess storage, or as snow held in the canopy begins to melt. Consequently the duration of throughfall is greater than that of rain or snowfall, and its average intensity must be smaller. The forest canopy also moderates ground-level precipitation throughout the storm period, causing a more uniform intensity by reducing the peaks and providing additional increments during lulls.

It has been convincingly demonstrated that raindrop impact is the major force in initiating erosion from bare soils (see, e.g., Young and Wiersma, 1973) and, prior to the work of Chapman (1948), it was generally assumed that a forest canopy protects the soil by reducing the impact. Chapman compared the size distribution of raindrops under a red pine canopy with that in an adjacent open area; in the open the ranges of drop diameters, and median sizes for rainfall intensities between 2 and 35 mm/hr, were much smaller than those under the forest canopy (range: open 0–4 mm, forest 0–7 mm; median: open 0.7–2.1 mm, forest 2.8–3.6 mm). Large drops have much greater impact, or kinetic energy ($KE$),

$$KE = \frac{mv^2}{2} \qquad (4.19)$$

since drop mass ($m$) increases with the cube of diameter, and the terminal velocity ($v$) increases with mass (see table 10.2).

The kinetic energies of individual raindrops can be computed from equation 4.19, but rain normally consists of an assemblage of various drop sizes, the distribution of which depends on rainfall intensity (see table 10.1); Wischmeier and Smith (1958) found that total kinetic energy for the assemblage could be given as

$$KE = 11.9 + 3.79 \ln i \qquad (4.20)$$

where $KE$ is in Joules/m² · mm of rainfall depth when the intensity ($i$) is in mm/hr (equation 4.20 is a modification of the original). The size distribution of throughfall drops is apparently independent of storm intensity and, provided that the live canopy is 8 m or more above the surface, drops attain 95% of terminal velocity before striking the ground. Solutions to equation 4.20 are plotted in figure 4.1. along with Chapman's (1948) data which show that $KE$ in the red pine stand was virtually constant at 26.8 J/m² · mm of rainfall; this means that raindrop impact would be greater under

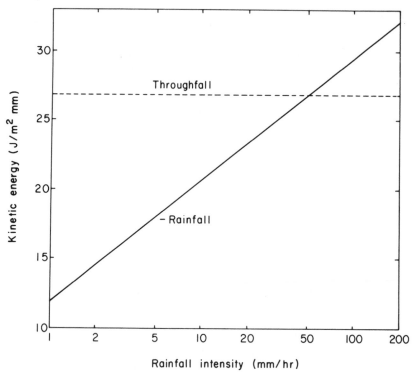

**Figure 4.1. The kinetic energy of rainfall and throughfall as a function of intensity.**

the canopy than in the open for all storms of intensity less than about 50 mm/hr.

## 4.3. Stemflow Characteristics

Stemflow is a minor element in the water budget of a forest; it is the residual

$$S = P - I_c - T \qquad (4.21)$$

which is usually an order of magnitude smaller than throughfall. Stemflow may be important ecologically because it is absorbed by

**Table 4.6.** Approximate Average Values of Stemflow as a Percentage of
Precipitation for Selected Hardwood and Coniferous Stands

| Hardwoods | $S$ (%) | Conifers | $S$ (%) |
|---|---|---|---|
| Understory | 12 | Cedar | 6 |
| Beech | 11 | White pine | 5 |
| Beech–birch–maple | 6 | Southern pine | 4 |
| Birch | 5 | Hemlock | 3 |
| Maple | 5 | Spruce–fir | 3 |
| Mixed species | 4 | Cypress | 3 |
| Ash | 4 | Norway spruce | 3 |
| Elm | 3 | Ponderosa pine | 2 |
| Oaks | 2 | Red pine | 2 |
| Oak–maple | 2 | Canary Island pine | 2 |
| Basswood | 2 | Juniper | 1 |
| Aspen | 1 | Douglas fir | <1 |
| Hickory | <1 | Lodgepole pine | <1 |

the soil of the primary rooting zone at the base of the tree, but the usefulness of stemflow data in quantitative hydrology is questionable because the magnitudes are of the same order as the errors in other measurements. Stemflow volume, expressed as a percentage of seasonal or annual percipitation for comparisons of forests growing in different climates, varies considerably among forest types and species, and even among individuals of the same species; as a result it is difficult to obtain accurate estimates of mean values, and the existing data must be viewed as first approximations.

Table 4.6 lists approximate average values of stemflow percentages for selected mature hardwood and coniferous stands; values reported by individual authors may vary by several percentage points from those listed. Stemflow is consistently greater for beech and young (understory) trees which have smoother bark; rough-barked hickory is almost always at the bottom of any ranked list, and values for most other species range between 1 and 5%. Tree form, attitude, and relative height with respect to surrounding trees have been suggested as additional influencing factors, and stemflow is usually greater during the dormant season in hardwood stands.

## 4.4. Litter Interception

Net precipitation $(P_n)$ is the sum of throughfall and stemflow, and effective precipitation $(P_e)$ is that which reaches the mineral soil; the difference (litter interception, $I_f$)

$$I_f = P_n - P_e \qquad (4.22)$$

is intercepted and subsequently evaporated from the forest floor. It follows that, since

$$P_n = P - I_c \qquad (4.23)$$

the difference between above-canopy precipitation $(P)$ and effective precipitation is

$$P - P_e = I_c + I_f \qquad (4.24)$$

where the sum of canopy interception $(I_c)$ and $I_f$ is the total initial depletion caused by the existence of forest cover. Ordinarily $I_f$ is an order of magnitude smaller than $I_c$, and its quantitative role in the forest water budget is small.

The magnitude of litter interception depends on litter storage capacity (its depth and water holding characteristics), and on the frequency of wetting and rate of drying. The storage capacity of litter has been studied infrequently, but the available data suggest that it is comparable to canopy storage capacity; wetting frequency and drying rate are a function of local climate. Litter interception losses usually do not exceed 50 mm/yr, and generally vary between 1 and 5% of annual precipitation; in the eastern United States losses from hardwood stands are 2.5% of precipitation in summer and 3.5% in winter (Helvey and Patric, 1965), and for white pine the losses increase from 2 to 4% as stands increase in age from 10 to 60 years (Helvey, 1967).

## 4.5. Infiltration Potential

Infiltration $(F)$ is the portion of precipitation that is finally absorbed by the mineral soil; its maximum or potential value is effective precipitation ($P_e$), and in an undisturbed forest it is almost always true that $F = P_e$ (since overland flow is negligible). The relationship of $F$ to other precipitation disposal processes can be derived in terms of

$$P = T + S + I_c \qquad (4.25)$$

which is a rearrangement of equations 4.3, 4.7, and 4.21, and

$$I_f = P - P_e - I_c \qquad (4.26)$$

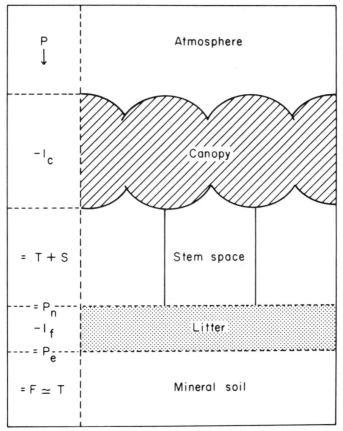

Figure 4.2. Precipitation disposal processes.

from equation 4.22; combining these two forms yields

$$P_e = T + (S - I_f) \qquad (4.27)$$

or

$$F = T + (S - I_f) \qquad (4.28)$$

for $P_e = F$. But since, from sections 4.3 and 4.4, both $S$ and $I_f$ are small (1 to 5% of $P$), the quantity $S - I_f$ will usually be negligible, and

$$F = T \qquad (4.29)$$

can be assumed for all practical purposes; figure 4.2 is a diagrammatic representation of precipitation disposal processes.

## LITERATURE CITED

Chapman, G. 1948. Size of raindrops and their striking force at the soil surface in a red pine plantation. *Transactions American Geophysical Union* 29:664–70.

Eschner, A. R. 1967. Interception and soil moisture distribution. In W. E. Sopper and H. W. Lull, eds., *International Symposium on Forest Hydrology*. New York: Pergamon Press.

Helvey, J. D. 1967. Interception by eastern white pine. *Water Resources Research* 3:723–29.

Helvey, J. D. and J. H. Patric. 1965. Canopy and litter interception of rainfall by hardwoods of eastern United States. *Water Resources Research* 1:193–206.

Niederhof, C. H. and H. G. Wilm. 1943. Effect of cutting mature lodgepolepine stands on rainfall interception. *Journal of Forestry* 41:57–61.

Reynolds, E. R. C., and L. Leyton. 1963. Measurement and significance of throughfall in forest stands. A. J. Rutter and F. W. Whitehead, eds., *The Water Relations of Plants*. New York: Wiley.

Rogerson, T. L. 1967. Throughfall in pole-sized loblolly pine as affected by stand density. In W. E. Sopper and H. W. Lull, eds., *International Symposium on Forest Hydrology*. New York: Pergamon Press.

Weitzman, S. and R. R. Bay. 1959. *Snow Behavior in Forests*. Forest Service Station Paper 69. St. Paul, Minn.: U.S. Department of Agriculture.

Wilm, H. G. and E. G. Dunford, 1948. *Effect of Timber Cutting on Water Available for Stream Flow from a Lodgepole Pine Forest*. Technical Bulletin 968. Washington, D.C.: U.S. Department of Agriculture.

Wischmeier, W. H. and D. D. Smith. 1958. Rainfall energy and its relationship to soil loss. *Transactions American Geophysical Union* 39:285–91.
Young, R. A. and J. L. Wiersma. 1973. The role of rainfall impact in soil detachment and transport. *Water Resources Research* 9:1629–36.
Zinke, P. J. 1967. Forest interception studies in the United States. In W. E. Sopper and H. W. Lull, eds., *International Symposium on Forest Hydrology*. New York: Pergamon Press.

## SELECTED READINGS

Anderson, H. W., M. D. Hoover, and K. G. Reinhart. 1976. *Forests and Water: Effects of Forest Management on Floods, Sedimentation, and Water Supply*. Forest Service Technical Report PSW-18. Berkeley, Calif.: U.S. Department of Agriculture.
Geiger, R. 1965. *The Climate Near the Ground*. Cambridge, Mass.: Harvard University Press.
Helvey, J. D. 1971. A summary of rainfall interception by certain conifers of North America. In E. J. Monke, ed., *Biological Effects in the Hydrological Cycle*. West Lafayette, Ind.: Purdue University.
Kittredge, J. 1948. *Forest Influences*, ch. 11. New York: McGraw-Hill.
Lull, H. W. 1964. Ecological and silvicultural aspects. In V. T. Chow, ed., *Handbook of Applied Hydrology*. New York: McGraw-Hill.
Miller, D. H. 1977. *Water at the Surface of the Earth*. New York: Academic Press.

# 5 SUBSURFACE WATER

## 5.1. Infiltration Process

Infiltration is important hydrologically because it marks the transition from fast-moving surface water to slow-moving soil and groundwater. The infiltration capacity of a soil is affected by its physical properties and degree of compaction, the moisture content and permeability of subsurface layers, the relative purity of infiltrating water, and soil microclimate; optimum conditions usually prevail in undisturbed woodlands. Infiltration capacity is a dynamic property that may change markedly during any particular storm event, in response to seasonal changes in soil moisture, temperature, and vegetative cover, or as a result of forest management activities.

### 5.1.a. Infiltration Concept

Infiltration is the downward movement of water through the surface of mineral soil; its rate is usually expressed in the same units as precipitation intensity (e.g., in mm/hr). The *infiltration rate* obviously cannot exceed the intensity of precipitation over a bare soil, and in the forest it cannot exceed the intensity of effective precipitation as defined by equations 4.24 and 4.27. *Infiltration capacity*, on the other hand, is the highest rate at which water can be absorbed by a given soil, and in an undisturbed forest it may exceed even the greatest rainfall intensities.

Water infiltrates a forest soil under the influences of gravity and capillary attraction, or in some instances as the result of pressure created by ponding of water at the surface. Ordinarily the soil surface layer is most permeable and, once it is saturated, the infiltration rate is limited by the rate of subsurface flow, or percolation, through less permeable underlying strata. On level land, once the entire soil profile is saturated, the infiltration rate is reduced to a rate determined by the permeability of underlying rock; but on sloping land, as the percolating water encounters greater resistance to flow in the vertical direction, it is diverted laterally within more permeable soil layers (see section 5.3.a).

The velocity of water movement is much reduced as it makes the transition from surface to subsurface flow; consequently, infiltration is much less likely to contribute to the direct runoff (quickflow) that results from specific rainfall events. If it is assumed that infiltration does not contribute at all, then the total volume of quickflow ($Q_d$) is

$$Q_d = P - (I_c + I_f + F) \qquad (5.1)$$

or

$$Q_d = P_e - F \qquad (5.2)$$

since effective precipitation $P_e = P - I_c - I_f$ (from equation 4.24); that the assumption is generally invalid is evident from the fact that quickflow occurs in undisturbed forested catchments where all of effective precipitation infiltrates the soil (i.e., $P_e = F$, but $Q_d \neq 0$). The very high infiltration capacities that characterize forested land do account for the facts that quickflow is a smaller percentage of total discharge in these areas, and that peak discharge rates are reduced by the presence of forest cover (see section 7.3.c).

## 5.1.b. Infiltration Determinants

The infiltration capacity of soil depends on the combined effects of many factors; it is highly variable among sites, and exhibits seasonal and aperiodic fluctuations at any given site. For these reasons, and because of measurement difficulties (see section 10.5), it is impossible to characterize infiltration capacities or rates in a precise manner; descriptive terms and a range of values, as given by Kohnke (1968), are listed in table 5.1. It is important to recognize

Table 5.1. Classification of Soil Infiltration and Percolation Rates (Kohnke, 1968)

| Description | Infiltration (mm/hr) | Percolation (mm/hr) |
|---|---|---|
| Very slow | $<1$ | $<1$ |
| Slow | 1-5 | 1-5 |
| Moderately slow | 5-20 | 5-16 |
| Moderate | 20-65 | 16-50 |
| Moderately rapid | 65-125 | 50-160 |
| Rapid | 125-250 | $>160$ |
| Very rapid | $>250$ | |

that surface infiltration capacities, per se, may be much greater than percolation capacities for the entire soil profile, and that the latter must limit the former except during the initial stages of rainfall.

Average infiltration capacities are correlated with the physical properties of soils; the correlation is positive with respect to soil porosity and organic matter content, and negative with clay content and soil bulk density. Some typical infiltration capacities for various soil textures are given in table 5.2; values for vegetated soils are characteristically higher, depending on vegetation type and other factors. Compaction by rain, animals, or heavy equipment can drastically reduce the water-absorbing capability of soils by eliminating noncapillary pore space.

Rainfall and soil moisture content affect infiltration capacity in

Table 5.2. Typical Values of Infiltration Capacity as Related to Soil Texture and Cover

| Texture | Infiltration capacity (mm/hr) | |
|---|---|---|
| | Bare soil | Vegetated |
| Clay | 0-5 | 5-10 |
| Clay loam | 5-10 | 10-20 |
| Loam | 10-15 | 20-30 |
| Sandy loam | 15-20 | 30-40 |
| Sand | 20-25 | 40-50 |

a variety of ways. Raindrop impact tends to destroy soil surface structure, and fine materials from the surface may be washed into soil voids, plugging the pores; also, during periods of high rainfall (or low evaporation and transpiration) soil moisture levels are higher, soil pore space is water-filled, and infiltration cannot exceed the rate of subsurface flow (percolation) in the least permeable stratum. At very high soil moisture levels infiltration may also be retarded because it is difficult for soil air to escape to make room for additional water; when soils are exceptionally dry they may be hydrophobic (water-repellent), which reduces infiltration capacity.

Vegetated land is generally more absorbent because surface litter reduces raindrop impact effects, and organic material, microorganisms, and plant roots tend to increase soil porosity and stabilize soil structure. Vegetation also depletes soil moisture to greater depths, increasing the water storage opportunity and favoring higher infiltration rates; these effects are more pronounced under forest cover where roots penetrate deeper and evapotranspiration rates are greater. Forest cover, litter, and lower vegetation also moderate soil microclimate, in particular the depth and frequency of soil frost; infiltration can occur in frozen soil if the large pores are not filled with ice, but when saturated soils freeze they become impermeable.

The uncertainty involved in estimating infiltration capacities for land areas has led to the adoption of various ranking procedures; for example, Ogrosky and Mockus (1964) classified more than 3000 soils according to "hydrologic soil groups" based on relative infiltration capacities when throughly wetted (group A, high; B, moderate; C, slow; and D, very slow). In practice such rankings may be used to develop numerous subcategories, or "soil-cover complexes," based on the ranking of other parameters; for example, infiltration capacity generally increases with the cover-type sequence from bare soil → row crops → grain → pasture → meadow → forest, with hydrologic condition from poor (<50% plant cover) → fair (50–75%) → good (>75%), and with categories of increasing litter depth. Infiltration capacity is inversely related to soil moisture content, and the latter is usually indexed (by seasons) according to various levels of antecedent rainfall; soil-cover complex and other rankings have been widely used by the U.S. Soil Conservation Service to estimate direct runoff from catchments based on the infiltration approach suggested in connection with equations 5.1 and 5.2.

### 5.1.c. Dynamic Aspects

The infiltration capacity of a catchment area cannot be understood simply in terms of the physical determinants discussed in the previous section; not only are there great variations among sites, but lateral water movements ensure that site phenomena will be interdependent. As a result, and because the overall land response is usually of primary concern, catchment infiltration is commonly inferred from measurements of precipitation and storm discharge. The average infiltration rate $(\bar{f})$ for a given storm or storm segment may be evaluated in terms of the $\phi$-index as

$$\bar{f} \simeq \phi = i_v \qquad (5.3)$$

where $i_v$ is the rainfall intensity above which rainfall volume is equal to storm discharge volume, as illustrated in figure 5.1; more precisely, in terms of equation 5.2, the $W$-index is

$$\bar{f} \simeq W = \frac{P_e - Q_d}{t_f} \qquad (5.4)$$

where $t_f$ is the interval of time during which rainfall intensity is greater than the average infiltration rate.

The $\phi$- and $W$-indexes are applicable only to situations in which storm discharge is derived entirely from overland flow, so that

$$F = P_e - Q_d = S \qquad (5.5)$$

where $S$ is the increase in soil and groundwater storage. But in catchments where subsurface flow contributes to storm discharge, $F \neq S$, rather

$$F = S + Q_i \qquad (5.6)$$

where $Q_i$ is interflow; in undisturbed forested catchments, $Q_i \simeq Q_d$ because overland flow is negligible. Nevertheless a small fraction of

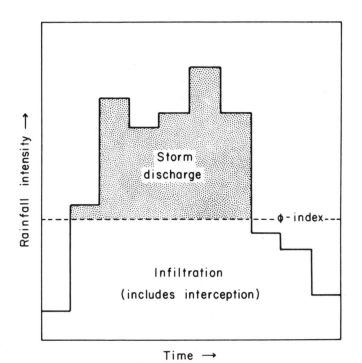

Figure 5.1. Derivation of the infiltration index ($\phi$-index) from rainfall and storm discharge records.

total precipitation (channel precipitation) falls directly into stream channels, and

$$F = P_e + (Q_i - Q_d) \qquad (5.7)$$

is applicable in any case; it follows that the average infiltration rate with interflow considered ($\bar{f}_i$) is

$$\bar{f}_i = \frac{P_e - Q_d + Q_i}{t_p} \qquad (5.8)$$

and usually $\bar{f}_i$ for the period of actual rainfall ($t_p$) will be much greater than $\phi$ or $W$.

Infiltration capacity is a dynamic property; it is greatest as rainfall begins, and decreases progressively as soil colloids swell and reduce pore sizes, fine materials from the surface wash into pores and restrict water movement, the soil approaches saturation, and the hydraulic gradient is reduced. This trend is frequently described as an exhaustion process (after Horton, 1940) in which the initial infiltration rate ($f_o$) approaches a lower limit ($f_c$) as a function of time ($t$), i.e.,

$$f = f_c + (f_o - f_c)e^{-kt} \tag{5.9}$$

where $k$ is a constant for a particular soil; a sample solution is shown in figure 5.2$a$. In logarithmic form

$$\ln(f - f_c) = \ln(f_o - f_c) - kt \tag{5.10}$$

and a plot of $\ln(f - f_c)$ as a function of $t$ will be a straight line with slope $k$ and intercept $\ln(f_o - f_c)$ as shown in figure 5.2$b$.

Seasonal variations in the infiltration capacity of a catchment are related to changes in physical determinants and generally follow the regimen of soil moisture; where precipitation is not strongly seasonal, maximum infiltration rates occur toward the end of the growing season. Temperature affects the viscosity of water (viscosity doubles as temperature decreases from 25 to 0°C; see table 2.3), but the seasonal influence is usually confounded by changes in other factors; at very low temperatures soil freezing may drastically reduce the infiltration capacity, especially at high soil moisture levels. Seasonal changes are generally smaller for coarser-textured soils, and under forest cover (especially conifers), where infiltration capacities are higher throughout the year.

The infiltration capacity of forest land may decrease abruptly as the result of forest fire that destroys the organic layer (litter and humus) at the forest floor, following careless cutting and harvesting operations that compact the soil, or when significant areas of mineral soil are exposed by poorly designed roadbuilding and surface mining activities. More gradual decreases have been observed following light fires, intensified grazing, and limited or carefully controlled cutting. Gradual increases in infiltration capacity have been demonstrated following conservation measures, natural successional changes in vegetation types, and with increases in the age, density, depth of litter, and organic matter content of forest soils.

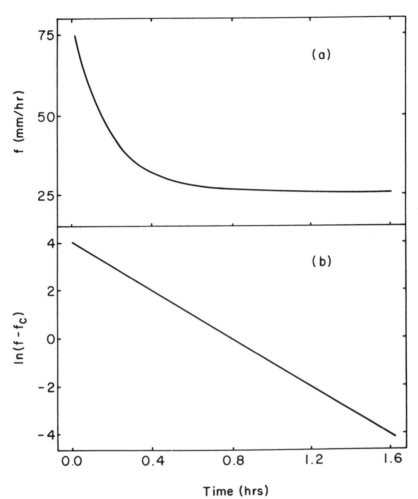

Figure 5.2. Infiltration capacity as a function of time following the
onset of rainfall: *a*, linear coordinates; *b*, semilogarithmic
coordinates.

## 5.2. Subsurface Storage

Water that infiltrates the soil surface may be discharged quickly
as interflow, percolate to underlying rock strata and the groundwater reservoir, or be transiently stored as soil moisture; soil mois-

ture performs vital functions in dissolving nutrients and supporting plant life, but hydrologically it represents a rapidly fluctuating storage reservoir from which water is extracted by plant roots for transpiration, and by direct evaporation from the surface. The volume of groundwater storage, which is roughly 10, 100, and 1000 times greater than that of lakes, soils, and streams, respectively (see table 1.2), fluctuates less rapidly but maintains streamflow during periods of deficient precipitation. Forest cover generally reduces the levels of soil moisture and groundwater—compared with corresponding levels under other vegetation types—especially during periods of negative water balance (i.e., when evapotranspiration exceeds precipitation).

### 5.2.a. Soil Moisture

Soil is that part of the earth's crust from which water can be returned to the surface through plant roots or by capillary movement; its depth may be 10 m or more in some instances, but most upward movement (exfiltration) usually occurs from within 1 to 2 m of the surface. The volume of water held by a soil ($V_w$) may be expressed as a fraction of total soil volume ($V$), or its mass ($M_w$) as a fraction of dry soil mass ($M$), and the equality of ratios is

$$\frac{V_w}{V} = \frac{\rho_s}{\rho_w} \frac{M_w}{M} = \rho_s \frac{M_w}{M} \tag{5.11}$$

where $\rho_s$ is the bulk density of the soil ($\rho_w = 1$ in cgs units). In hydrology it is most convenient to express soil moisture in units of equivalent water depth, or storage ($S$), analogous to precipitation depth; in terms of soil depth ($d$),

$$S = \frac{V_w}{V} d = \rho_s \frac{M_w}{M} d \tag{5.12}$$

where $d$ and $S$ are in the same units.

The volume of water held in a saturated soil, expressed as a fraction of total soil volume, is equal to *soil porosity* ($\epsilon_s$), or

$$\epsilon_s = \frac{V - V_s}{V} \tag{5.13}$$

where $V_s$ is the total volume of solids; soil porosity generally varies between 0.3 and 0.6. If a saturated soil is permitted to drain freely for a few days under the force of gravity it will attain a relatively stable moisture condition called *field capacity;* field capacity is not a rigorous constant for a given soil, but the term has been widely used to describe moisture conditions on well-drained sites at 1 to 3 days following heavy rain. Another nonrigorous term, *permanent wilting point,* is used with reference to moisture conditions after soil has dried to a point where plant roots cannot extract sufficient moisture to maintain leaf turgidity, and *available soil moisture* (for plant growth) is taken as the difference between field capacity and permanent wilting point.

The status of soil moisture can be more rigorously defined in terms of its free energy as compared with a plain surface of pure water; water held by soil is said to have negative free energy, or to be under negative pressure, tension, or suction, and *soil moisture potential* ($\psi_s$, mb) is a measure of work required per unit mass to bring it to the condition of pure free water. Soil moisture status may also be expressed in terms of $pF$ ($pF \simeq \log |\psi_s|$), and in these terms the upper and lower limits of water availability to plants are frequently taken as $\psi_s = -0.3$ bar, $pF = 2.5$, and $\psi_s = -15$ bar, $pF = 4.2$, respectively. The amount of water held by soil at these limits depends to a large extent on soil texture; some typical values for a range of textural classes are listed in table 5.3.

Table 5.3. Soil Moisture in Millimeters per Meter of Soil Depth

| Textural class | Field capacity | Wilting point | Available moisture |
|---|---|---|---|
| Sand | 100 | 25 | 75 |
| Fine sand | 116 | 33 | 83 |
| Sandy loam | 158 | 50 | 108 |
| Fine sandy loam | 217 | 67 | 150 |
| Loam | 267 | 100 | 167 |
| Silty loam | 283 | 116 | 167 |
| Light clay loam | 300 | 133 | 167 |
| Clay loam | 317 | 150 | 167 |
| Heavy clay loam | 325 | 175 | 150 |
| Clay | 325 | 208 | 117 |

Soil water may be classified according to specific forces that affect the status of individual components: *gravitational water* moves from noncapillary soil spaces as gravity flow in a free drainage field, *capillary water* is held by the cohesive forces among water molecules that create surface tension at air-water interfaces in the capillaries, and *hygroscopic water* is held at very high tension by molecular forces and is largely unavailable to plants. Soil water may also be unavailable to plants if it contains dissolved salt; in saline soils the water potential ($\psi_s$) may be much greater (negatively) than normal, and the range of available moisture much reduced. A minor component of soil moisture, water vapor, occurs in the air spaces of nonsaturated soils where the relative humidity ($rh_s$) is

$$rh_s = 100 + 7(10^{-5}) \, \psi_s \tag{5.14}$$

over the normal range of $\psi_s$ (expressed in mb); even at $\psi_s = -50$ bars, $rh_s > 96\%$, which means that the concentration of water vapor in soil must be approximately equal to that at saturation, and therefore largely determined by soil temperature.

### 5.2.b. Groundwater Storage

Subsurface water occurs primarily in the interstices of the earth's crust, or in the *zone of rock fracture* (see figure 5.3). Air and water occur together in the voids of the upper segment, the *zone of aeration*, which includes soil and underlying rock strata containing suspended (vadose) water. Groundwater occurs in the *zone of saturation*, the upper level of which is called the *water table.*

Virtually all groundwater is precipitation that has infiltrated the soil and percolated through the zone of aeration; it may be stored either in intergranular spaces in solid rock, in larger spaces among unconsolidated sand and gravels, or in the massive spaces of rock fractures and solution channels. Any geologic formation that is capable of storing and transmitting significant quantities of water is called an *aquifer;* otherwise it is an *aquiclude.* Groundwater is said to be *free* if its upper boundary is a water table supporting a *capillary fringe* (pore water at atmospheric pressure), *confined* or *artesian* if overlain by an aquiclude, and *perched* if underlain by an aquiclude that is not continuous over a very large area but lies above the main groundwater body.

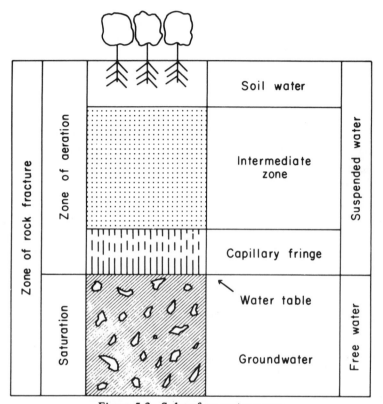

Figure 5.3. Subsurface water zones.

The *porosity* of an aquifer ($\epsilon_a$), in analogy with equation 5.13 for soil porosity, is defined as

$$\epsilon_a = \frac{V - V_a}{V} = S_r + S_y \tag{5.15}$$

where $V_a$ is the aggregate volume of solids. *Specific retention* ($S_r$), analogous to the field capacity of soil, is the fractional volume of water held against the force of gravity, or

$$S_r = \frac{V_r}{V} = \frac{V - V_a - V_y}{V} \tag{5.16}$$

where $V_r$ is the absolute volume retained; also, the *specific yield* $(S_y)$ or "effective" porosity is

$$S_y = \frac{V_y}{V} = \frac{V - V_a - V_r}{V} \tag{5.17}$$

where $V_y$ is the volume of water drained by gravity flow. The typical values of $\epsilon_a$, $S_r$, and $S_y$ listed in table 5.4 show that whereas fine-grained clay has the highest porosity, sand and gravel aquifers are most productive in terms of water yield.

Groundwater is by far the largest component of catchment storage, as indicated by the data of table 1.2, but hydrologically its absolute magnitude is less important than its relative immobility. Groundwater storage fluctuates slowly in response to precipitation and percolation inflow, and to the seepage outflow that is responsible for the existence of springs and base flow in streams; as a result the groundwater reservoir moderates effects of precipitation extremes, storing periodic excesses which are released gradually during periods of drought. Average seasonal variations in groundwater storage are highly correlated with the climatic balance between precipitation and evaporation; short-term fluctuations (discussed in section 5.3.b) are most apparent in valley bottoms or along streambanks, especially where trees or other plants (phreatophytes) draw water directly from the saturated zone or its capillary fringe.

Table 5.4. Typical Values of Porosity, Specific Retention, and Specific Yield for Various Aquifers (in %)

| Aquifer type | Porosity | Specific retention | Specific yield |
|---|---|---|---|
| Clay | 50 | 45 | 5 |
| Sand | 35 | 10 | 25 |
| Gravel | 30 | 5 | 25 |
| Gravel and sand | 25 | 5 | 20 |
| Sandstone | 15 | 7 | 8 |
| Solid limestone | 5 | 3 | 2 |
| Granite | 1 | <1 | <1 |

## 5.2.c. Forest Influences

Forest influences on subsurface storage can be inferred from evapotranspiration and discharge relationships (chapters 6 and 7); in summary, it is generally true that forests use (evaporate and transpire) more water, and yield less to streamflow, than other cover types in the same regional climate. When water use exceeds precipitation, soil moisture storage becomes a negative term in the water balance equation (equations 2.9–2.12), and greater soil drying (reduced storage) is associated with greater water use. Also, during rainless periods (periods of base flow or groundwater discharge), streamflow is directly related to the ground water level, and the lower flow in forest streams must be associated with reduced groundwater storage.

The role of subsurface storage in seasonal water budgeting is suggested by the highly idealized climatographs shown in figure 5.4; with an even distribution of precipitation throughout the year, and a bell-shaped curve of evapotranspiration that exceeds precipitation during some of the warmer months, there will be typical periods of soil moisture depletion and recharge, and (in a humid climate) a period of water excess. Greater total depletion of soil moisture (greater storage decrease) occurs under forest cover, and the period of recharge is correspondingly greater; groundwater depletion and recharge (not shown) lag behind the surface phenomena. Minimum streamflow rates usually occur following soil moisture depletion periods, and the maxima toward the end of periods of water excess.

Plant cover reduces direct evaporation by insulating the soil against radiant heating and wind, but overcompensates for this effect by drawing moisture from deeper levels; consequently, whereas surface layers may be more moist under forest cover during a period of drying, the deeper layers will be drier. The forest influence depends partly on the depth and proliferation of the rooting system, but also on growing season length; coniferous trees extract soil moisture after deciduous types have become dormant. Numerous studies have shown that in areas where the groundwater table is near the surface, forest cutting will cause it to rise; conversely, reforestation can eliminate semiswamp conditions.

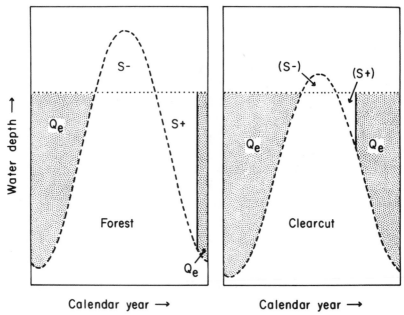

Figure 5.4. Climatographs for forest and clearcut areas: $S-$, soil moisture depletion; $S+$, soil moisture recharge; $Q_e$, water excess; dotted line, precipitation; dashed line, evapotranspiration.

Forest interception (canopy and litter interception) reduces the total amount of precipitation that can infiltrate the soil, but throughfall causes systematic variations within the stand, and stemflow delivers water to the central rooting area where the greatest storage opportunity ordinarily exists. The infiltration capacity of forest floor is generally greater than that in outlying areas, so a greater proportion of effective precipitation actually enters the mineral soil; but this circumstance occurs in part because of greater antecedent drying. Also, the greater permeability of the rooting zone facilitates percolation only to a certain depth where, especially in steep terrain, lateral flow (interflow) diverts much of the excess water toward steam channels before it can move vertically toward the groundwater reservoir.

## 5.3. Subsurface Flow

Water movements in porous media (soils and aquifers) are formally described in terms of the general mass-flow equation

Flow rate = (Conductivity) (Driving force)       (5.18)

which is analogous to the energy-flow equations of section 2.2.c; it is equally applicable under conditions of saturated and unsaturated liquid flow, or to the movement of water vapor. The conductivity term is an empirical coefficient used to characterize the intrinsic permeability of the medium and the properties (density and viscosity) of water; the driving force is a potential gradient (hydraulic energy gradient) that depends primarily on the forces of suction (negative pressure) and gravity. Subsurface flows are three-dimensional, and are strongly influenced by active plant processes and the configuration of local terrain.

### 5.3.a. Soil Water

Soil water potential ($\psi_s$) was defined in section 5.2.a as the negative pressure (tension) with which moisture is held at any point in the soil; in nonsaline soils $\psi_s$ is referred to as the *matric* or *capillary potential*. Within the capillary fringe above a pool of free water, water is held by surface tension in capillaries and in thin films adhering to soil particles; *at equilibrium* $\psi_s$ is opposed by the *gravity potential* ($\psi_g$, mb) which is equal and opposite in sign:

$$\psi_s = -\psi_g = -\rho_w gz(10^{-3})\qquad(5.19)$$

where $\rho_w$ (g/cm$^3$) is the density of water, $g$ is the accleration of gravity (981 cm/sec$^2$), and $z$(cm) is distance above the free water surface. If water is extracted from the soil by plant roots or evaporation, $\psi_s$ increases (negatively) creating an unbalanced force and causing upward movement from the pool of free water; conversely, if water is added by infiltration and percolation from above, flow within the capillary fringe will be downward.

The thickness ($z$) of a capillary fringe at equilibrium is inversely proportional to the "effective diameter" ($d$) of soil capillaries:

$$z = \frac{4s}{\rho_w\, gd} \qquad (5.20)$$

where $s$ is surface tension; both $s$ and water density ($\rho_w$) vary slightly with temperature (see table 2.3), but at 15°C

$$zd = 0.30 \qquad (5.21)$$

($z$ and $d$ in cm) and the change with temperature is only about $-0.2\%/°C$. Capillary rise extends to greater heights above the water table in fine-textured soils, and the moisture content at any given height is also greater (see fig. 5.5). During nonequilibrium condi-

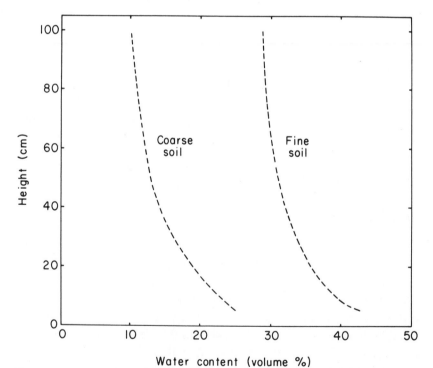

Figure 5.5. Typical profiles of moisture content as a function of height above the water table.

tions (the usual circumstance, with either additions or extractions of moisture occurring from above), the rate of water movement ($q$) at any level is

$$q = -k_u \frac{d\psi_u}{dz} \qquad (5.22)$$

where $\psi_u = \psi_s + \psi_g$, and $k_u$ is the *hydraulic conductivity for unsaturated flow;* $q$ is the volume of flow per unit time and cross-sectional area normal to the direction of flow (volume/time · area, or depth/time, e.g., mm/hr), and $k_u$ is in the same units when $\psi_u$ is expressed in terms of equivalent water depth (1 mb = 1.02 cm $H_2O$).

In equation 5.22 the negative sign means that flow is upward ($q$ positive) when the potential gradient is negative; in reduced form

$$q = -k_u \left[ \frac{d\psi_s}{dz} + 1 \right] \qquad (5.23)$$

since the rate of change of the gravity potential with height is unity. The hydraulic conductivity ($k_u$) must be determined empirically; it increases markedly with soil water content and potential, and also varies with soil type (texture and structure), and with water temperature because of its effect on viscosity. Ordinarily the upward flow of water is insufficient to support vegetation if the rooting zone is more than 1 m above the water table; some maximum flow rates at various heights (taken from graphs reproduced by Ward, 1967) are given in table 5.5.

Table 5.5. **Maximum Capillary Movement Related to Approximate Height Above the Water Table and Soil Texture**

| Flow rate (mm/day) | Height above water table (cm) | |
|---|---|---|
| | Coarse texture | Fine texture |
| 1 | 90 | 90 |
| 2 | 75 | 60 |
| 3 | 65 | 45 |
| 4 | 60 | 40 |
| 5 | 55 | — |

When rainfall infiltrates a relatively dry soil, both capillary (suction) and gravity potential gradients cause downward movement of water, and ponding (surface detention) may create an additional pressure potential at the surface and increase the driving force. The problem of devising an exact formal solution in this case is further complicated by the layered structure of natural soil, by the variability of soil properties with time during infiltration, and by the inconstancy of rainfall intensity during storm periods; as a result, hydrologists ordinarily use infiltration indexes (equations 5.3 and 5.4) or formulations similar to the Horton equation (equation 5.9). In the limiting case, after long-continued rainfall and saturation of the soil profile, the infiltration rate ($f_c$ from equation 5.9) is constant, and the vertical gravity-flow equation is simply

$$q = f_c = k_s \tag{5.24}$$

where $k_s$ is the *hydraulic conductivity for saturated flow.*

Subsurface water moves from higher to lower water potentials, but by no means exclusively in the vertical direction: soil moisture extraction by plant roots may cause a capillary potential gradient in any direction, and in hilly terrain percolating water is diverted along a plane parallel to the topographic slope by the reduced permeability of lower soil horizons. Unsaturated horizontal flow is proportional to the matric or capillary potential gradient, but under saturated conditions, $\psi_s = 0$, and strictly horizontal flow can occur only in response to a difference in *pressure potential* ($\psi_p$)— based on gas pressure or the weight of impounded water. Along sloping surfaces there are both horizontal and vertical components of flow, and for unsaturated conditions

$$q = -k_u \left[ \frac{d\psi_s}{dx} + \frac{d\psi_u}{dz} \right] \tag{5.25}$$

or

$$q = -k_s \left[ \frac{d\psi_p}{dx} + \frac{d\psi_h}{dz} \right] \tag{5.26}$$

for saturated flow, where $\psi_h = \psi_p + \psi_g$ is called the *hydraulic potential;* for formal analysis of omnidirectional flow parameters, and applications of theory to flow problems, see Baver, Gardner, and Gardner (1972).

Unsaturated flow may also be defined in terms of a *water content gradient*, $dS/dx$, the driving force, and diffusivity ($D_m$):

$$D_m = k_u \frac{d\psi_s}{dS} \tag{5.27}$$

so that

$$q = -D_m \frac{dS}{dx} \tag{5.28}$$

and the gradient of soil moisture content is more easily measured; equations of this form are particularly appropriate in describing the flow of water vapor. Vapor flow is complicated because it depends on gradients of both moisture and temperature, and the existing theory is less satisfactory (liquid and vapor flow may occur simultaneously in opposite directions); in general the flow is from high to low *water vapor potential* ($\psi_V$ in mb):

$$\psi_v = 4615 T \ln h \tag{5.29}$$

where $T$ is absolute temperature and $h$ is relative humidity expressed as a decimal. In general there is a movement of water vapor from warm to cold soil, upward through the soil surface at night and in winter, and downward during summer days except near the surface when evaporation is occurring; upward flow can add significantly to soil moisture in the surface layer when it is frozen, or to the moisture content of an overlying snow cover.

Water movement to plant roots is proportional to the potential difference ($\Delta\psi_s$) between the soil and the root-soil boundary; as adapted from an expression by Baver, Gardner, and Gardner (1972),

$$q = k_u \Delta\psi_s \, 4\pi \ln(r^2/x^2) \tag{5.30}$$

where $q$ is the volume rate of flow per unit root length, $r$ is root radius, and $x$ is the distance over which $\Delta\psi_s$ obtains (i.e., half the distance between adjacent roots). Equation (5.30) is an approximation for conditions under which a steady flow rate can be assumed, and the value of the relationship is more theoretical than practical. When the distance between rootlets is small the potential gradient is very small except in dry soil; in fact, in estimating water transport rates through the plant itself, $\Delta\psi_s = 0$ is usually assumed.

### 5.3.b. Groundwater Movement

Water movement in the zone of saturation occurs in response to a difference in hydraulic potential ($\psi_h$) or *head* ($h$). In a sloping aquifer the change in $h$ with distance ($x$) is called the *hydraulic gradient* ($s = h/x$), and the groundwater flow rate (volume/time · area, in units of velocity) is usually described as

$$q = k_s s = k_s' \frac{\rho_w}{u} s \qquad (5.31)$$

in terms of *Darcy's law*. The hydraulic conductivity for saturated flow ($k_s$) depends on the properties of the medium (aquifer) and the density ($\rho_w$) and viscosity ($\mu$) of water, but $k_s'$ is the *intrinsic permeability* of the medium.

The intrinsic permeability of an aquifer depends on the effective porosity of rock and unconsolidated material, and the free space created by fracturing and solution. Effective porosity is determined by grain size distribution, the shape and roughness of individual particles, and packing arrangement; but since these properties are rarely uniform, the hydraulic conductivity of an extended aquifer is limited by permeability of individual layers or zones, and may vary considerably depending on the direction of water movement (e.g., in a layered medium hydraulic conductivity may be much greater along horizontal, versus vertical, planes). Some approximate average conductivities (from Linsley, Kohler, and Paulhus, 1975) and estimated discharge rates of various materials are given in table 5.6; the effective velocity of groundwater movement varies over a wide range, from on the order of $10^{-6}$ to $10^3$ m/day.

Water is discharged from the groundwater reservoir by drainage into effluent streams and rivers, or at other points (springs) where the surface intersects the groundwater table; springs are common at the outflow points of perched water tables in upland areas. Wa-

Table 5.6. Typical Hydraulic Conductivities and Discharge Rates of Various Materials (after Linsley, Kohler, and Paulhus, 1975)

| Material | Conductivity $(m^3/day \cdot m^2)$ | Discharge velocity |
|---|---|---|
| Granite | $4(10^{-4})$ | 4 μm/day |
| Clay | $4(10^{-4})$ | 4 μm/day |
| Dense limestone | $4(10^{-2})$ | 400 μm/day |
| Sandstone | $4(10^{0})$ | 4 cm/day |
| Sand | $4(10^{1})$ | 40 cm/day |
| Gravel and sand | $4(10^{2})$ | 4 m/day |
| Gravel | $4(10^{3})$ | 40 m/day |

ter sometimes rises above the level of a confined aquifer to create a flowing artesian spring, and pumping for human purposes has become a major factor in reducing groundwater levels in areas where municipal and agricultural demands exceed the surface water supply. Shallow groundwater is discharged rapidly when streambank storage drains following periods of high flows or flooding, and more slowly as it moves upward in the capillary fringe to support surface evaporation, or to be absorbed by the roots of phreatophytic plants; the latter is responsible for a minor daily cycle in groundwater discharge to streams (see section 6.3.a).

### 5.3.c. Topographic Influences

The gravity potential of water in a catchment is strictly a function of elevation above the discharge point, and

$$\frac{d\psi_g}{dz} \simeq 1 \qquad [\rho_w g = \text{constant}] \qquad (5.32)$$

by differentiation of equation 5.19; this means that the hydraulic gradient, and the driving force for unsaturated flow, will be greater in areas of greater relative relief, and that soils and subsurface strata will drain more rapidly. Subsurface flow components as influenced by land form are illustrated in figure 5.6. Soil water drainage is characteristically more rapid, not only because soil hydraulic conductivities are greater, but also because the water moves along

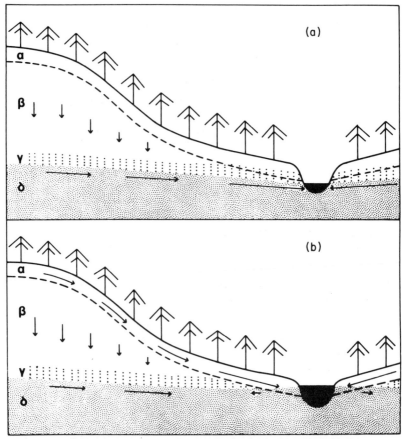

Figure 5.6. Subsurface flow in hilly terrain during *a*, rainless periods; and *b*, with rapid infiltration; *α*, soil; *β*, intermediate zone; *γ*, capillary fringe; *δ*, groundwater.

a steeper gradient parallel to the surface slope; configuration of the groundwater table tends to follow surface contours, but in much subdued form.

During rainless periods with zero surface infiltration (fig. 5.6*a*), subsurface water moves slowly through the intermediate zone, feeding the groundwater reservoir which supports base flow in streams; the capillary fringe may extend into the plant rooting zone. During periods of rainfall or snow melting (fig. 5.6*b*), water moves rapidly into the undisturbed forest soil; once the upper horizons are saturated and the wetting front extends to less permeable layers, flow is diverted along paths of least resistance (formally paths where the product $k_s s$ is greatest), and interflow produces a sharp rise in the streamflow hydrograph. Vertical flow through the intermediate zone is still very slow and the groundwater table, except where it is near the surface, may not respond for days or even months following initial infiltration; near streams the water table may extend into the rooting zone or, occasionally (during flooding), above the surface itself.

## LITERATURE CITED
Baver, L. D., V. H. Gardner, and W. R. Gardner. 1972. *Soil Physics*. New York: Wiley.

Horton, R. E. 1940. An approach toward a physical interpretation of infiltration capacity. *Soil Science Society of America Proceedings* 5:399–417.

Kohnke, H. 1968. *Soil Physics*. New York: McGraw-Hill.

Linsley, R. K., M. A. Kohler, and J. L. H. Paulhus. 1975. *Hydrology for Engineers*. New York: McGraw-Hill.

Ogrosky, H. O. and V. Mockus. 1964. Hydrology of agricultural lands. In V. T. Chow, ed., *Handbook of Applied Hydrology*. New York: McGraw-Hill.

Ward, R. C. 1967. *Principles of Hydrology*. New York: McGraw-Hill.


## SELECTED READINGS
Davis, S. N. and R. J. M. DeWiest. 1966. *Hydrogeology*. New York: Wiley.

Musgrave, G. W. and H. N. Holtan. 1964. Infiltration. In V. T. Chow, ed., *Handbook of Applied Hydrology*. New York: McGraw-Hill.

Slatyer, R. O. 1967. *Plant-Water Relationships*. New York: Academic Press.

Walton, W. C. 1970. *Groundwater Resource Evaluation*. New York: McGraw-Hill.

# 6 VAPORIZATION PROCESSES

## 6.1. Evaporation Principles

Evaporation is the physical process of liquid → vapor conversion; it occurs whenever liquid water is in contact with an unsaturated atmosphere, whether internally in plant leaves (transpiration) or externally on wet surfaces. Evaporation involves the transfer of both energy and mass, so any mass flux (mass/time) can be evaluated in terms of an equivalent energy flux (energy/time); also, since for water $1 \text{ g} \simeq 1 \text{ cm}^3$, the mass flux per unit area ($E$, volume/area · time, depth/time) is in units of velocity and

$$L_v E \text{ (ly/min)} \simeq E \text{ (mm/hr)} \qquad (6.1)$$

where $L_v E$ is the flux density, or energy flux per unit area. Regardless of the units employed, evaporation can be viewed as a process of either 1) energy exchange at the evaporation surface, 2) molecular diffusion across a thin boundary layer of air near the surface, or 3) turbulent diffusion in the free air; in some instances the formal relationships involve a combination of mass and energy transfer approaches.

### 6.1.a. Boundary Layer

Molecular diffusion of water vapor in still air is analogous to heat conduction; the flux per unit area ($E$, $\text{g/cm}^2$ · sec) is related to a vapor density ($\rho_v$) gradient:

$$E = - D \frac{d\rho_v}{dz} \qquad (6.2)$$

where $D$ (cm$^2$/sec) is the diffusion coefficient for water vapor in air (see equation 2.2 and table 2.4), and the negative sign indicates that vapor flow is in the direction of lower density. The steady-state form of equation 6.2 may be written in terms of a vapor density difference (as in the first part of equation 2.29 for boundary layer convection):

$$E = - \frac{D}{\delta_v} (\rho_s - \rho_a) = - \frac{\rho_s - \rho_a}{r_a} \qquad (6.3)$$

where $\rho_s$ (g/cm$^3$) is vapor density at the evaporation surface, $\rho_a$ the density at distance $\delta_v$ above the surface, and $r_a = \delta_v/D$ (in sec/cm) is the resistance of air to water vapor diffusion; here $\delta_v$ (cm) is the thickness of the boundary layer for water vapor diffusion, analogous to $\delta_c$ for convection (section 2.2.c), and $\delta_v \simeq 1.04 \, \delta_c$ is known from theoretical considerations. Air resistance ($r_a$) can be evaluated in terms of the heat transfer coefficient for convection ($h_c$) as used in equations 2.30 and 2.31; at common growing season temperatures in the middle latitudes, $0.23 < D < 0.27$ cm$^2$/sec, and since $h_c = k/\delta_c$, and $k = 0.0036$ cal/cm $\cdot$ min $\cdot$ °C (from table 2.8),

$$h_c r_a = \frac{\delta_v}{\delta_c} \frac{k}{D} \simeq 15 \qquad (6.4)$$

for $h_c$ in mly/min $\cdot$ °C as in table 2.9.

In terms of equivalent energy exchange, equation 6.3 is written

$$L_v E = - 60 \, L_v \frac{\Delta\rho_v}{r_a} \qquad (6.5)$$

where the flux density ($L_v E$) is in ly/min, $L_v$ in cal/g (from equation 2.36 or table 2.3), $r_a$ in sec/cm, and $\Delta\rho_v = \rho_s - \rho_a$ is the vapor density difference. The latter is frequently evaluated in terms of an equivalent vapor pressure difference ($\Delta e = e_s - e_a$); utilizing the pressure-density relationship

$$\rho_v = 2.17(10^{-4}) \frac{e}{T} \qquad (6.6)$$

for $e$ in mb, $T$ (temperature) in °K, and $\rho_v$ in g/cm$^3$,

$$L_v E = -0.013 \frac{L_v}{T} \frac{\Delta e}{r_a} \qquad (6.7)$$

in the units of equation 6.5. At 20°C ($T = 293°$K), $L_v/T = 2.00$, and the variation with temperature is less than 0.5%/°C, so

$$L_v E = -0.026 \frac{\Delta e}{r_a} \qquad (6.8)$$

is accurate to within 5% at temperatures between 10 and 30°C.

Ordinarily vapor density and pressure at the surface cannot be measured directly, but must be inferred from other data. Over a plane surface of pure water, $\rho_s$ and $e_s$ are the saturation density and pressure, respectively, both of which are known functions of surface temperature and can be obtained from tables (e.g., table 2.4) or by computation (equations 2.1 and 6.6); saturation levels are reduced slightly by the curvature of water surfaces in fine capillaries, and as a function of the concentration of solutes in soil water and plant sap. In leaves, dead organic material, or soil, where water surfaces are not freely exposed to the open air, $r_a$ may be a small part of total resistance in the diffusion pathway, and equation 6.7 must take the form

$$L_v E = -0.013 \frac{L_v}{T} \frac{\Delta e}{r_a + r_s} \qquad (6.9)$$

where $r_s$ is the additional surface (pore or stomatal) resistance.

### 6.1.b. External Layer

Outside the boundary layer vapor transport occurs as turbulent exchange, and numerous techniques have been devised for estimating the flux. Following equation 2.39,

$$L_v E = -L_v C (e_s - e_a) = -L_v C \Delta e \qquad (6.10)$$

where the coefficient ($C = E/\Delta e$) may be derived empirically and expressed as a function of windspeed; ordinarily $e_a$ and windspeed are measured at about 2 m above a wet surface, and $e_s$ is taken as saturation vapor pressure at surface temperature. This "mass transport" method is used primarily over ponds and reservoirs to obtain daily and monthly estimates, and the coefficient ($C$) is applicable only to a particular site and season.

More basic evaporation formulas are based on aerodynamic methods, analogous to those used for convective exchange (section 2.2.c). In the form of equations 2.29 and 2.33,

$$L_v E = - \rho L_v K_v \frac{\Delta q}{\Delta z} \qquad (6.11)$$

where $\rho$ is air density and $K_v$ is the turbulent transfer coefficient for water vapor ($K_v \simeq K_h$); $\Delta q$ is the difference in specific humidity for a height difference ($\Delta z$) in the free air. Alternatively, in the form of equation 2.34,

$$L_v E = - \frac{0.17\rho L_v \, \Delta q \, \Delta u}{\{\ln [(z_2 - x)/(z_1 - x)]\}^2} \qquad (6.12)$$

in terms of wind profile parameters, where $\Delta u$ is the windspeed difference between heights $z_2$ and $z_1$.

A simpler method that avoids the necessity of measuring surface temperature (equation 6.10) and windspeed (equation 6.12), or estimating $K_v$ (equation 6.11), is based on the Bowen ratio ($\beta = H/L_v E$); if $K_v = K_h$, dividing equation 2.29 by equation 6.11 yields

$$\beta = \frac{H}{L_v E} = \frac{c}{L_v} \frac{\Delta T}{\Delta q} = \gamma \frac{\Delta T}{\Delta e} \qquad (6.13)$$

where $c$ is the specific heat of air and $\gamma$ (mb/°C) is the psychrometer constant (equation 10.11). Since it can usually be assumed that net radiation ($R$) is totally expended in conductive ($B$), convective ($H$), and latent heat exchanges,

$$R - B = H + L_v E \qquad (6.14)$$

from equation 2.14. But since, from equation 6.13, $H = \beta L_v E$,

$$L_v E = - \frac{R - B}{1 + \beta} \qquad (6.15)$$

by combination with equation 6.14; this method also provides an alternative means of estimating the convective exchange ($H$).

Combining the equations (6.10, 6.13, and 6.14) for energy and mass transfer yields

$$L_v E = -\frac{f(T)(R - B) + L_v C(e_{sz} - e_z)}{f(T) + 1} \qquad (6.16)$$

where $f(T)$ is strictly a function of temperature, and $e_{sz} - e_z$ is the *humidity deficit* at height $z$. Equation 6.16, a form of Penman's (1948) "combination equation," eliminates the need for surface temperature measurement. The temperature function is

$$f(T) = \frac{1}{\gamma} \frac{de_s}{dT} \qquad (6.17)$$

where $de_s/dT$ is the slope of the saturation vapor pressure-temperature relationship illustrated in figure 3.1; numerical solutions for standard barometric pressure (1000 mb) were given by Van Bavel (1966), but

$$f(T) = \frac{e_s}{T^2} (12280 - 15T) \qquad (6.18)$$

with $e_s$ in mb and $T$ in °K gives the same answers over the temperature range from 0 to 60°C.

### 6.1.c. Evaporation Determinants

As suggested by the formal relationships of sections 6.1.a and 6.1.b, evaporation rates depend on a variety of atmospheric and surface determinants. When viewed as a mass transfer process, $E$ depends on 1) the relative "availability" of water, 2) the magnitude of the vapor pressure or density difference between the evaporation surface and the ambient atmosphere, and 3) the efficiency of the transport mechanism; alternatively, when viewed as energy exchange, $L_v E$ depends on the magnitudes and signs of other energy transfers. But evaporation determinants are also interdependent, and act in concert, so that whereas it may be true, for example, that doubling the vapor pressure difference or net radiation *can* (holding all else constant) double the evaporation rate, concomitant changes in other factors are virtually assured, and the relative change in $E$ or $L_v E$ will ordinarily be much smaller than might be assumed from simple examination of the formulas.

With the exception of perennial water bodies, the availability of water for evaporation depends to a large extent on the amount and frequency of precipitation, and on the drying rate; since evaporation is essentially a drying process, it tends to be self-limiting, reducing the availability of water at the surface. In catchments, gravity-induced movements of water maximize its presence in valleys and other local depressions, and prolong periods of moisture excess. The effective availability of water also depends on 1) its proximity to the surface where energy is more abundant and transport processes are more efficient, 2) its temporal correlation with available energy, and 3) the surface resistance to water vapor movement; consequently evaporation rates tend to be greater when the zone of saturation is nearer the surface, when the rainy season corresponds with the warmer growing period, and when plant canopies are wet with intercepted water or stomatal resistances are smaller.

The vapor pressure difference ($\Delta e = e_s - e_a$) between an evaporation surface and the ambient atmosphere is a basic determinant of the evaporation rate; the ambient vapor pressure ($e_a$) is relatively constant for a given air mass and may be considered as strictly an atmospheric determinant (in fact $e_a$ usually increases somewhat during the day as evaporation adds moisture to the local atmosphere). Surface vapor pressure ($e_s$), or saturation vapor pressure at a wet surface, however, is a function of surface temperature (see figure 3.1), and any property or circumstance that tends to increase the radiant energy load or temperature at the surface will also increase $e_s$ and the vapor pressure difference ($e_s - e_a$), since $e_a$ is relatively unaffected. As a rule, therefore, lower surface albedo, more direct exposure to solar radiation, and lower thermal conductivity and heat capacity of the surface will tend to produce higher surface temperatures, vapor pressure differences, and evaporation rates.

The efficiency of transport mechanisms for water vapor exchange depends on the speed and turbulence of air movement, and on the aerodynamic characteristics of the evaporating surface. The thickness of the boundary layer for molecular diffusion ($\delta_v$), a measure of air resistance ($r_a$), increases directly with surface size and inversely with windspeed, so that in general the evaporation rate must be greater from smaller surfaces and with greater windspeeds; surface drying of soils and dead organic materials lengthens the diffusion pathway and increases the resistance to vapor flow (plant canopy and stomatal resistances are treated in greater detail in section 6.2). Windspeed varies considerably among exposures in complex topography, and the interactions among local winds, small-scale topographic features, and forest cover produce a complicated array of windy and sheltered sites; the turbulent transfer coefficient for water vapor ($K_v$) increases with both windspeed and the aerodynamic roughness of the surface.

A selected list of evaporation determinants is given in table 6.1; "positive factors" are those for which an increase in the factor is generally associated with a higher evaporation rate, but any in-

Table 6.1. Evaporation Determinants

| Positive factor | Negative factor |
| --- | --- |
| Surface vapor pressure, $e_s$ | Ambient vapor pressure, $e_a$ |
| Surface vapor density, $\rho_s$ | Ambient vapor density, $\rho_a$ |
| Diffusivity coefficient, $D$ | Relative humidity, $rh$ |
| Turbulent transfer coefficient, $K_v$ | Relative humidity ratio, $h$ |
| Mass transport coefficient, $C$ | Dew-point temperature, $T_d$ |
| Heat transfer coefficient, $h_c$ | Air resistance, $r_a$ |
| Solar radiation, $S$ | Surface resistance, $r_s$ |
| Net radiation, $R$ | Boundary layer thickness, $\delta_v$ |
| Surface temperature, $T_s$ | Surface dimension, $d$ |
| Air temperature, $T_a$ | Convective exchange, $H$ |
| Temperature function, $f(T)$ | Bowen ratio, $\beta$ |
| Windspeed, $u$ | Conductive exchange, $B$ |
| Latent heat of vaporization, $L_v$ | Surface albedo, $r$ |
| Soil moisture content, $V_w$ | Depth to water table, $z$ |
| Vegetated land | Barren land |

crease in a "negative factor" is generally associated with a reduction in evaporation. It is important to recognize that, as indicated earlier, any single-factor analysis will almost always be an exaggeration, and in some instances may be misleading even with regard to the positive-negative relationship, or the direction of an assumed change. Greater windspeed or solar radiation, or lower ambient humidity, cannot increase the evaporation rate from a surface to which the water supply is limited by capillary movement in the soil; moreover, excessive atmospheric stress frequently causes physiological reactions (e.g., stomatal closure) that reduce the rate of water movement through forest trees.

## 6.2. Forest Transpiration

A dense forest canopy shields the underlying surface from the effects of solar radiation and wind, raises the level of the active surface for energy exchange above the level of water concentration in the soil, and drastically reduces evaporation at the lower level. Consequently water for evaporation must be conducted from soil to roots to stems to leaves through living plants where it is subject to biological control mechanisms. Transpiration is essentially an evaporation process, and is controlled by the same factors, but in this case the effective area for evaporation is much greater and surface resistance plays a much larger role.

### 6.2.a. Plant Mechanisms

Transpiration is a soil-drying process, but plant mechanisms impose conditions that alter the regimen and total volume of water loss; typical drying curves for bare soil and forest land are illustrated in figure 6.1. Evaporation from bare soil is initially rapid, but surface drying lengthens the diffusion pathway and increases the total resistance to vapor flow; in fine-grained materials water may move toward the surface by capillarity, but eventually the liquid water surface recedes. Also, under typical daytime conditions, the vapor pressure difference ($e_s - e_a$) is reduced because soil tempera-

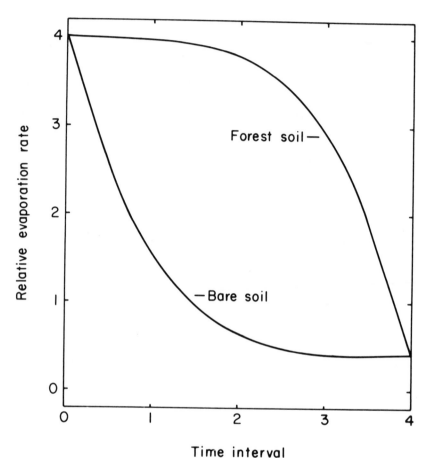

Figure 6.1. Typical drying curves for bare soil and forest land under relatively constant atmospheric conditions.

ture, and consequently saturation vapor pressure ($e_s$), decrease with depth; this, and increasing resistance, cause the evaporation rate to decrease, rather abruptly at first, then more slowly as the diffusion pathway lengthens.

Under forest cover some direct evaporation occurs, but the surface dries much more slowly because it is shaded; in this case, however, the drying process is not so severely restricted to upper horizons because tree roots occupy a considerable depth of soil.

Forest soil drying continues at a high rate until transpiration is restricted by plant mechanisms in response to reduced water potential in the rooting zone; as a result, the total volume of water removed from the forest soil is much greater (see fig. 6.2). Following a period of drying, soil moisture levels are generally much lower in the forest than in adjacent clearcut areas or forest openings; the typical situation is illustrated in figure 6.3.

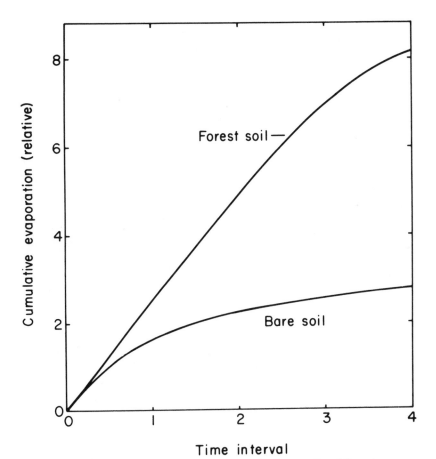

Figure 6.2. Accumulated soil moisture losses for bare soil and forest land during a period of drying (idealized for constant atmospheric conditions).

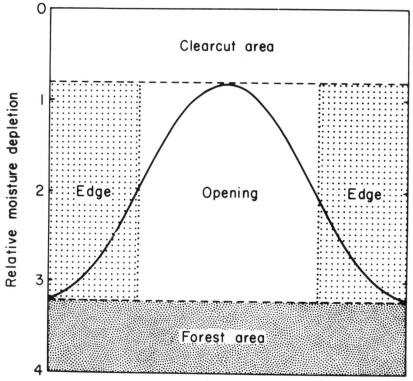

Figure 6.3. Soil moisture depletion following an extended drying period.

The effect of soil moisture content, or soil water potential ($\psi_s$), on the transpiration rate has been (and apparently still is) a matter of controversy; the controversy can be resolved by evaluating both direct and indirect effects. The direct effect of $\psi_s$ on the transpiration rate is limited to its effect on leaf water potential ($\psi_l$). Liquid water moves from soil to leaves in response to the potential difference, $\psi_s - \psi_l$, but since this difference cannot exceed the absolute value of $\psi_l$ (assuming $\psi_s = 0$), the maximum direct effect can be evaluated in terms of $\psi_l$.

Vapor pressure within a leaf is usually assumed to be equal to saturation vapor pressure ($e_s$) at leaf temperature; actually, since $\psi_l$ is usually less than zero, vapor pressure at the evaporation surface within the leaf is $h(e_s)$ where

$$\ln h = 2.17(10^{-4}) \frac{\psi_l}{T} \qquad (6.19)$$

for $\psi_l$ in mb and $T$ in °K. This means that the vapor pressure difference between the leaf and the ambient atmosphere is somewhat less than would otherwise be assumed, but for all practical purposes the reduction is negligible. The relative transpiration rate is $(he_s - e_a)/(e_s - e_a)$ for constant $e_a$ and leaves at air temperature; relative transpiration rates for $T = 20°C$ are given in table 6.2 for a range of ambient humidities and leaf water potentials.

Since leaf water potential is relatively unimportant in determining the vapor pressure difference, leaf cells might easily be dehydrated were it not for the role of leaf stomata; stomatal closure increases the resistance to vapor flow, and is the only *directly* effective physiological control of transpiration. But the absolute necessity for stomatal control must not be interpreted to exclude the *indirect* effects of soil water potential or plant resistance to liquid water movement; in fact, stomatal movements are usually initiated at relatively high leaf or soil water potentials and, when atmospheric stresses are great, rapid transpiration may reduce $\psi_l$ to a point where stomata begin to close even when liquid water is

Table 6.2. Relative Transpiration Rates as
a Function of Ambient
Humidity and Leaf Water
Potential (Leaves and
Air at 20°C)

| $\psi_l$ (bars) | $h$ | Relative humidity (%) | | |
|---|---|---|---|---|
| | | 25 | 50 | 75 |
| 0 | 1.000 | 100 | 67 | 33 |
| -10 | 0.992 | 99 | 66 | 32 |
| -20 | 0.985 | 98 | 65 | 31 |
| -30 | 0.978 | 97 | 64 | 31 |
| -40 | 0.971 | 96 | 63 | 30 |
| -50 | 0.964 | 95 | 62 | 29 |

readily available at root-soil interfaces. Light and carbon dioxide are also effective stomatal regulators that act indirectly, in concert with soil moisture potential and other environmental factors, to control transpiration rates.

### 6.2.b. Stomatal Control

Maintenance of normal cell turgidity in growing leaves requires the control of water loss (transpiration) in the vapor phase. The biological mechanism for such control is the system of leaf stomata. Diffusion of water vapor through tree leaf stomata under a given vapor pressure difference is controlled primarily by the size, configuration, and number of these pores, and to a lesser extent by the boundary layer or air resistance ($r_a$).

In terms of equation 6.9, the transpiration rate ($E_t$) in energy units (ly/min) is

$$L_v E_t = -0.013 \frac{L_v}{T} \frac{e_s - e_a}{r_s + r_a} \qquad (6.20)$$

where $e_s$ is saturation vapor pressure at leaf temperature, and $r_s$ is the leaf or stomatal resistance. Stomatal resistance is of primary importance because, in woody vegetation, it is usually an order of magnitude greater than boundary-layer resistance ($r_a$) over a leaf; in general, $0.1 < r_a < 1.0$ sec/cm, and $1 < r_s < 10$ sec/cm for unstressed tree leaves (open stomata). Also, leaf resistance represents a biological control that varies with tree species as a function of leaf anatomy, age, and phenology, and with stomatal reactions to environmental conditions.

Air resistance can be estimated using equation 6.4 and the data of table 2.8; for single leaves it increases with leaf size and decreases with windspeed. For a flat deciduous leaf,

$$r_a = 2.7 \frac{d^{0.5}}{u^{0.5}} \qquad (6.21)$$

gives the right order of magnitude, where $d$ (cm) is called the leaf characteristic dimension (width or diameter), and $u$ (cm/sec) is windspeed. Solutions to equation 6.21 for a range of common

Table 6.3. Boundary-Layer Resistance (sec/cm)
over a Flat Deciduous Leaf

| Windspeed (m/sec) | Leaf width (cm) | | | |
|---|---|---|---|---|
| | 1 | 2 | 5 | 10 |
| 1 | 0.27 | 0.38 | 0.60 | 0.85 |
| 2 | 0.19 | 0.27 | 0.43 | 0.60 |
| 5 | 0.12 | 0.17 | 0.27 | 0.38 |
| 10 | 0.09 | 0.12 | 0.19 | 0.27 |

values are given in table 6.3; as $d/u$ varies between 0.1 and 0.001 sec, $r_a$ varies between 0.085 and 0.85 sec/cm.

Assuming that stomata are straight circular pores of length $l$ and radius $s$ the resistance per unit area of leaf surface is

$$r_s = \frac{4l + \pi s}{4\pi n D s^2} \tag{6.22}$$

where $D \simeq 0.25$ cm²/sec is the diffusion coefficient, and $n$ is stomatal density (number/area); ordinarily $l$ (the thickness of leaf epidermis) is of the order of $10^{-3}$ cm, and equation 6.22 might be reduced to

$$r_s = \frac{12.7 + s}{n(10^{-4})s^2} \tag{6.23}$$

for $s$ in $\mu$m (microns). Choosing realistic values for tree leaves (i.e., $n = 10^4$/cm² and $s$-maximum = $l/3$), the data of table 6.4 illustrate the effect of stomatal movements on the transpiration rate; of course, to the extent that leaf temperature and $e_s$ increase as transpiration decreases, table 6.4 exaggerates the stomatal effect. Also, since stomata are not straight circular pores (more commonly they are elliptical in plan view and hyperbolic in section), and are frequently filled with a porous waxy material that modifies their diffusive capacity, stomate modeling is at best a crude attempt to characterize the effects of stomatal movements or resistance differences among leaf types.

Direct observation of leaf resistance has become possible with

Table 6.4. Estimated Transpiration Rate as a Function of Stomatal Opening

| s (%) | $s^2$ (%) | $r_s$ (sec/cm) | $r_a$ (sec/cm) | $L_v E_t$ (mly/min · mb) | $L_v E_t$ (%) |
|---|---|---|---|---|---|
| 20 | 4 | 30.1 | 0.5 | 0.8 | 6 |
| 40 | 16 | 7.9 | 0.5 | 3.1 | 23 |
| 60 | 36 | 3.7 | 0.5 | 6.2 | 47 |
| 80 | 64 | 2.2 | 0.5 | 9.8 | 73 |
| 100 | 100 | 1.4 | 0.5 | 13.4 | 100 |

NOTE: Rate computed from equation 6.20 with $L_v/T = 2.00$ (at 20°C), $r_a$ = 0.5 sec/cm (constant), and s-maximum = $l/3$ = (10/3) μm; since s is small relative to $l$, $L_v E_t$ is more nearly proportional to $s^2$, or the area of stomatal opening.

the recent development of sophisticated measurement techniques. The data of table 6.5 were all obtained using the diffusion porometer method (Kanemasu, Thurtell, and Tanner, 1969); the data for hardwood species were reported by Federer (1977); and Jarvis, James, and Landsberg (1976) summarized the observations of various investigators for conifers. Leaf resistances for conifers

Table 6.5. Minimum Resistances of Forest Tree Leaves

| Hardwoods (Federer, 1977) | | Conifers (Jarvis et al., 1976) | |
|---|---|---|---|
| Species | $r_s$ (sec/cm) | Species[a] | $r_s$ (sec/cm) |
| Gray birch | 2.7 | Douglas fir (c) | 1.2 |
| Big-tooth aspen | 3.0 | Sitka spruce (c) | 1.4 |
| White oak | 3.0 | Sitka spruce (1) | 2.2 |
| Yellow birch | 3.2 | Sitka spruce (2) | 3.3 |
| Black oak | 3.3 | Grand fir (c) | 2.4 |
| American elm | 3.4 | Red pine (c) | 3.1 |
| Quaking aspen | 3.5 | Red pine (1) | 4.3 |
| Black cherry | 3.5 | Red pine (2) | 8.6 |
| Red maple | 3.5 | Red pine (3) | 8.9 |
| American beech | 4.0 | Red pine (4) | 11.0 |
| White ash | 4.1 | Western hemlock (c) | 4.5 |
| Sugar maple | 4.5 | Ponderosa pine (c) | 9.5 |

[a]Symbols refer to leaf age: c, current year; and 1–4, previous years.

show a wider range of values and are usually characterized as being somewhat greater than those for deciduous species.

### 6.2.c. Canopy Models

Transpiration from a forest canopy covering horizontal area $(A_h)$ is the sum of individual vapor fluxes from a greater total area of leaf surface $(A_s)$; the ratio $A_s/A_h$ is called the *leaf area index*. If the mean transpiration rate for individual leaves is $\overline{E}_t$ then

$$E_t = \overline{E}_t \, \frac{A_s}{A_h} \qquad (6.24)$$

is the combined rate for the canopy. Also, if $\overline{r}_s$ is the mean leaf resistance,

$$r_c = \overline{r}_s \, \frac{A_h}{A_s} \qquad (6.25)$$

must be the total canopy resistance to water vapor diffusion; in this sense the canopy resistance $(r_c)$ represents the overall physiological control of transpiration.

The formal relations of section 6.1.b can be written in terms of resistances to identify the physiological role of forest cover; $L_v E_t$ (in ly/min) is given by

$$L_v E_t = -60 \, \frac{\rho c}{\gamma} \, \frac{e_s - e_a}{r_c + r_a} \qquad (6.26)$$

where $\rho c$ (in cal/cm$^3 \cdot {}^\circ$C) is the thermal capacity of air (table 2.8), and $e_s$ is saturation vapor pressure corresponding to canopy temperature at the level where the above-canopy windspeed profile extrapolates to zero. Alternatively, using the combination formula (equation 6.16),

$$L_v E_t = -\frac{r_a (de_s/dT)(R - B) + \rho c (e_{sz} - e_z)}{r_a (de_s/dT) + \gamma (r_a + r_c)} \qquad (6.27)$$

by substitution of equations 6.17 and 6.26. All such physically based models are difficult and expensive to apply to forest canopies, especially in areas of complex terrain where parameters vary considerably with site, season, and time of day; more practical methods are elaborated in section 6.3.

Precipitation that is intercepted by a forest canopy constitutes a source of water for evaporation that is basically unlike any other source; it is not only directly exposed to the atmosphere but also spread over a much larger area than, for example, a pool of free water at the surface. The rate of evaporation of intercepted water ($E_i$) compared to the transpiration rate under the same atmospheric conditions is given by the ratio

$$\frac{E_i}{E_t} = \frac{r_c + r_a}{r_a} \tag{6.28}$$

because $E_i$ occurs from *exterior* surfaces where direct physiological control is absent. Since as a rule, $r_c > r_a$, it can usually be assumed that $E_i > 2E_t$; in fact various studies have shown that $E_i/E_t$ varies between about 3 and 5 when both are measured under similar atmospheric conditions (see, e.g., Rutter, 1967).

## 6.3. Total Vaporization

The physical principles, formal relationships, and boundary conditions elaborated in sections 6.1 and 6.2 are basic to deductive development and continuing progress in scientific evaporation hydrology, but immediate needs of the practicing hydrologist usually call for more rudimentary, or currently feasible, approaches to specific problems. Water-budgeting methods as applied to catchments and smaller plots have provided the most accurate information with regard to total evaporation from forest land and the influences of forest management practices on latent heat exchange. Empirical formulations based on the correlation of evapotranspiration to "weather" are useful as indices of seasonal and annual variations in specific situations, but extrapolations are extremely unreliable and frequently misleading.

### 6.3.a. Water Balance

Water volumes and movements are inherently easier to measure and evaluate when dealing with the liquid phase; this fact has encouraged, or in some instances dictated, the use of water-budgeting methods in forest evapotranspiration studies. In terms of equation 2.9, total evaporation from a catchment area (including $E_t$ and $E_i$) is

$$E = P - Q - S \qquad (6.29)$$

assuming that precipitation ($P$) is the only input and that stream discharge ($Q$) is an adequate measure of outflow; over a period of a year or more,

$$E = P - Q \qquad (6.30)$$

assuming that the change in storage ($S$) is zero. The accuracy of these equations depends, of course, on the accuracy of catchment precipitation estimates and streamflow measurements as well as the validity of the assumptions; when subsurface flow ($L$) is significant, the associated error in $E$ is $L_o - L_i$ (subsurface inflow, $L_i$ and outflow, $L_o$, as defined by equation 2.11).

Long-term averages of $E = P - Q$ are weakly correlated with mean precipitation, air temperature, and other climatological and catchment parameters; in any particular catchment, annual evaporation is relatively conservative but tends to follow variations in total precipitation. Table 6.6 lists annual totals of $P$, $Q$, and $E = P - Q$ for a small (40 ha) undisturbed forest catchment during a 15-year period (1955–1969) of decreasing precipitation. The trends (fig. 6.4) show that $P$ decreased at an average rate of 27 mm/yr, but $E$ at only 12 mm/yr, so that $E/P$ gradually increased from 56 to 61%.

Despite its obvious deficiencies, the quantity $P - Q$ is useful as a first approximation of total annual evaporation in carefully selected catchments; it also serves as a basis for estimating changes in $E$ that occur as the result of forest cutting or cover-type conversion. Ordinarily stream discharge is more sensitive (than $E$) to variations in annual precipitation; for example, from linear regression of the data of table 6.6,

$$Q = 0.833P - 602 \qquad (6.31)$$

with a positive correlation of 0.987. Consequently the effects of forest management practices are usually evaluated in terms of

Table 6.6. Annual Water-Budget Components for a Small Catchment During a Period of Decreasing Precipitation

| Year | P (mm) | Q (mm) | E = P - Q (mm) |
|------|--------|--------|----------------|
| 1955 | 1664 | 729 | 935 |
| 6 | 1478 | 584 | 894 |
| 7 | 1725 | 851 | 874 |
| 8 | 1384 | 521 | 863 |
| 9 | 1572 | 716 | 856 |
| 1960 | 1466 | 587 | 879 |
| 1 | 1539 | 655 | 884 |
| 2 | 1458 | 625 | 833 |
| 3 | 1524 | 691 | 833 |
| 4 | 1476 | 648 | 828 |
| 1965 | 1394 | 579 | 815 |
| 6 | 1097 | 307 | 790 |
| 7 | 1273 | 544 | 729 |
| 8 | 1288 | 538 | 750 |
| 9 | 1298 | 521 | 777 |
| Mean | 1442 | 606 | 836 |

changes in $Q$ (this topic is treated in greater detail in sections 7.2.c and 7.3).

In controlled experiments on small plots, short-term evapotranspiration loss can be estimated from the generalized water budget (equation 2.11); or, during a drying period with negligible precipitation,

$$E = \Delta Q + \Delta L + S \qquad (6.32)$$

from equation 2.12 where $\Delta Q$ and $\Delta L$ are net inflows to the plot. It is important to note that $S$ takes a negative sign when storage increases (see section 2.2.b). During an extended drying period, if both surface and subsurface flows are restricted (i.e., are not factors in the plot water budget), total evaporation is equal to the storage decrease, and

$$E = S \qquad (6.33)$$

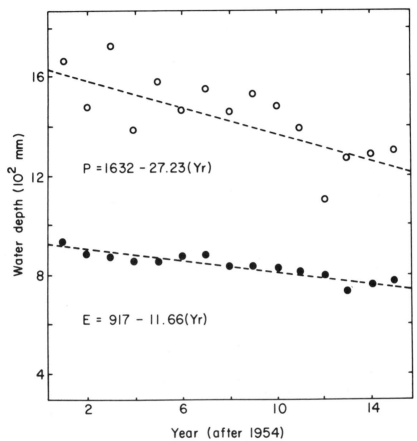

Figure 6.4. Trends in annual water-budget components during a period of decreasing precipitation.

may be taken as the change in soil moisture within the rooting zone of an isolated plot.

In areas where groundwater is near the surface, trees draw water from the capillary fringe causing fluctuations in the level of the groundwater table; near small headwater streams, diurnal cycles of water level and stream discharge are distinct. The pattern of fluctuation (fig. 6.5) can be used to estimate the total "pumping" effect (water use) of the forest. Assuming that evapotranspiration is

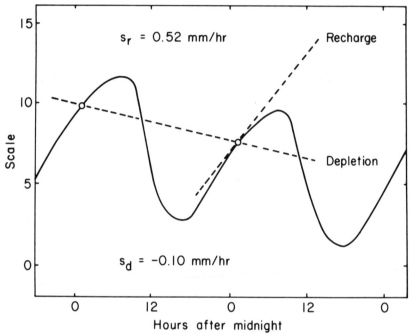

Figure 6.5. Diurnal cycle of shallow groundwater level caused by evapotranspiration.

negligible during the first few hours after midnight,

$$E \text{ (mm/day)} = 24 \, S_y \, (s_r - s_d) \qquad (6.34)$$

where $S_y$ is the specific yield of the underlying aquifer, $s_r$ (in mm/hr) is the slope of the recharge segment (early morning), and $s_d$ the corresponding slope of interdiurnal groundwater depletion.

## 6.3.b. Potential Evaporation

The *potential evaporation* $(E_p)$ concept was introduced about 30 years ago, and has been discussed in almost every hydrology text and major evaporation treatise published in English during the ensuing decades. Penman (1956) defined $E_p$ as "the amount of water transpired in unit time by a short green crop, completely shading the ground, of uniform height and never short of water," but his definition has been revised many times. Potential evaporation (or potential evapotranspiration) is usually said to be independent of plant or soil type (qualified only with respect to albedo differences), determined primarily or exclusively by prevailing weather, and limited by (cannot exceed) evaporation from an open water surface under the same atmospheric conditions.

The early definitions of $E_p$ were altogether incapable of being interpreted in a physical or quantitative sense, but this did not deter enterprising scientists from developing theoretical-empirical formulations to quantify $E_p$—in fact to redefine it according to individual preference. Unfortunately such formulations, especially the more sophisticated or complicated ones, were adopted almost universally by hydrologists and others, and applied with surprising credulity in violation of even the superficial restrictions that were originally intended. The broad generalizations that the $E_p$ concept was thought to support have proven faulty, and yet these continue to appear either implicitly or explicitly in textbooks and other scientific reports; an excellent treatment of some major misconceptions was given by Pruitt (1971).

Some of the early definitions of $E_p$ did not specify any minimum area to which the concept could be applied, and since it is known, for example, that evapotranspiration is greater at the windward edge of an irrigated plot or local moist area (because advection increases the energy supply relative to downwind positions), the definition was modified to require "adequate fetch" or "an extended area of uniform vegetation" to exclude oasis effects. It soon became evident, however, as demonstrated by Pruitt (1971) and others, that advective effects could extend hundreds of kilometers downwind, and Miller (1977) concluded that uniform vegetation must be "infinite in extent." Other hydrologists tended toward the opposite extreme, removing all area limitations and concluding with Van Bavel (1966) that "when the surface is wet and imposes no restrictions upon the flow of water vapor, the potential value is reached"; this definition permits $E_p$ to vary widely with variations in local microclimate—and thus robs the concept of its generality.

Any definition of $E_p$ for a "short green" crop of "uniform height" is not meaningful unless these terms are given some quantitative interpretation; unfortunately this restriction did not deter hydrologists and others from applying $E_p$ formulas derived for short-cropped grass to irregular forest canopies. Moreover, since a regenerating forest generally uses more water as it grows taller, "short" is not a useful qualification unless $E_p$ is defined to vary with forest age. Van Bavel's (1966) equation, in the form of equation 6.16, accounted for the aerodynamic properties of the canopy and was "by no means restricted to a short grass surface"; this definition required $E_p$ to vary continuously with both atmospheric conditions and natural changes in plant cover (assuming only a continuously "wet" canopy)—and further reduced the generality of the concept.

It is impossible to attach a consistent meaning to the intuitive language "never short of water"; in practice this is usually taken to describe the situation in which soil moisture content is near field capacity, or in some instances simply where there are no obvious signs of leaf wilting. But a canopy that is wet externally, after rain for example, loses water much more rapidly than by transpiration in the same weather, and it is worth noting that the $E_p$ concept has gained considerable leverage based on results of tests conducted over low crops which have much smaller minimum leaf resistances than trees. Again, according to the least restrictive $E_p$ concept, the "fundamental condition that defines potential evaporation is that the surface vapor pressure can be found from the surface temperature" (Van Bavel, 1966), which means that either the canopy is wet with intercepted water, or that canopy resistance is known, so that equation 6.27 can be applied.

The most consistent feature of the $E_p$ concept is that it attempts to define an upper limit to evapotranspiration as a function of local weather; the upper limit is attained only when the surface (i.e., the canopy) is wet, but in practice this is usually interpreted to mean only that the soil rooting zone is wet. Even for free water surfaces, however, whether in films or deeper pools, the rate of evaporation varies significantly with surface conditions; an extreme example (fig. 6.6) is that of a deep pool of free water that warms

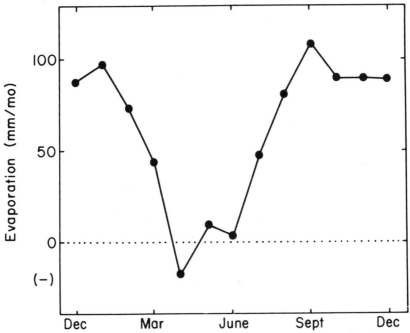

**Figure 6.6.** Monthly evaporation rates for Lake Ontario (after Richards and Irbe, 1969).

so slowly during summer that its annual evaporation cycle is completely out of phase with normal evapotranspiration. In the same sense, if not to the same extent, transpiration is more than an atmospheric phenomenon; it is a biospheric phenomenon with atmospheric, surface, subsurface, and biological controls.

Potential evaporation has no definition that is useful, either theoretically or practically, beyond the simple idea that, when a surface is wet, evaporation will occur at a rate determined by local weather and the characteristics of the surface; but this is true even if the surface is not wet. Formal evaporation equations may be solved for a range of atmospheric and surface conditions, alternately assuming that surface or canopy resistance is zero and some positive number, and if one prefers to call the former solutions "potential evapotranspiration" and the latter "actual evapotranspiration," the results may be instructive with regard to the relative or absolute effects of surface resistance in various situations. At the same time the exercise should help to dispense with, once and for all, any broad generalizations that the $E_p$ concept was thought to support.

### 6.3.c. Empirical Estimates

The superficial attractiveness of assuming that

$$E_p = E \text{ (moist land)} \tag{6.35}$$

and that evapotranspiration from moist land (irrespective of its cover) is determined by prevailing weather, has led to the development of numerous hypothetical and loosely empirical models for estimating $E_p$. Since many of the models were derived from correlations of weather elements (usually mean temperature) with evaporation data from lysimeters, plot studies on irrigated land, or catchment water budgets $(P - Q)$ in humid regions, their relative accuracy increases with the time interval over which weather elements and evaporation are averaged, and with the size of the region to which they are applied (accuracy of ± 20% for monthly averages is frequently described as "good"). Unfortunately the inherent limitations of such models have not deterred some hydrologists from applying the estimates to small catchments and short time periods.

Thornthwaite (1948) developed a complicated expression for $E_p$ in terms of mean air temperature:

$$E_p = 16 \left[ \frac{10T}{I} \right]^a \tag{6.36}$$

where $I$ is a local heat index roughly proportional to annual mean temperature, $a$ is a cubic function of $I$, and $E_p$ is in mm/month for mean monthly temperature $(T)$ in °C. This model has been widely used with little regard for Thornthwaite's admonition that whereas "the computed values . . . are of the right order of magnitude . . . they are . . . only approximate." Since there is no reason to expect the Thornthwaite formulation to be superior to any other, and since less complicated models yield about the same estimates, its current use has no logical justification.

Holdridge (1962) and Hamon (1963) developed simple expressions for $E_p$ that have been used by foresters and engineers. The Holdridge formula, based on "ecological life zones," for $E_p$ in mm/30-day month is

$$E_p = 4.8 \, T_b \qquad (6.37)$$

where $T_b$ is the daily mean "biotemperature" (i.e., air temperature above 0°C); Hamon's equation in the same units (assuming 12-hr daylight periods) is

$$E_p = 5.0 \, \rho_s \qquad (6.38)$$

where $\rho_s$ (in g/m³) is the saturation vapor density at mean air temperature. Equations (6.37) and (6.38) give almost the same answers because the numerical values of $T$(°C) and $\rho_s$ (g/m³) are about the same over the common range of growing season temperatures (see table 2.4).

It is frequently assumed that $E_p$ is a useful guide to $E$ when the soil moisture content is known. Based on the assumption of equation 6.35, it is intuitively attractive to generalize that

$$E = mE_p \qquad (6.39)$$

under any condition, where $m$ is the volume fraction of available mositure in the rooting zone. This relationship has been "tested" on numerous occasions using the data from plot or catchment water budget studies and, by circular reasoning, the $E_p$ model that yields best agreement is said to be most "accurate."

Normal annual evapotranspiration for geographic provinces can be estimated using Budyko's (1974) "radiative index" equation:

$$E = P - P \exp\left(-R/L_v P\right) = P(1 - e^{-I}) \qquad (6.40)$$

where the index $(I)$ is the ratio of net radiation $(R)$ to the latent heat of precipitation $(L_v P)$, and $e$ is the natural logarithm base. In the eastern United States where $I$ varies between about 0.5 and 1.5, evapotranspiration varies between about 40 and 80% of precipitation (for $I = 1.0$, $E/P = 0.63$). This is a type of "combination" (mass transfer-energy budget) equation in which normal annual discharge in the water budget $E = P - Q$ is expressed as a function of both mass $(P)$ and energy $(I)$.

Forest evapotranspiration is essentially a physical process of mass and energy exchange with atmospheric, edaphic, and biological control mechanisms, and as such it is amenable to physical interpretation in terms of relevant physical laws. There is no reliable method of estimating evapotranspiration rates based on simple weather-element data or potential evapotranspiration. The correlation of $E$ with "weather" is useful in some instances, but only as a first approximation; such correlations tend to obscure causal relationships, especially when combined with the debilitating $E_p$ concept.

## LITERATURE CITED

Budyko, M. I. 1974. *Climate and Life*. New York: Academic Press.

Federer, C. A. 1977. Leaf resistance and xylem potential differ among broadleaved trees. *Forest Science* 23:411–19.

Hamon, W. R. 1963. Computation of direct runoff amounts from storm rainfall. *Bulletin International Association of Scientific Hydrology* 63:52–62.

Holdridge, L. R. 1962. The determination of atmospheric water movements. *Ecology* 43:1–9.

Jarvis, P. G., G. B. James, and J. J. Landsberg. 1976. Coniferous forest. In J. L. Monteith, ed., *Vegetation and the Atmosphere*, 2:171–240. New York: Academic Press.

Kanemasu, E. T., G. W. Thurtell, and C. B. Tanner. 1969. The design, calibration, and field use of a stomatal diffusion porometer. *Plant Physiology* 44:881–85.

Miller, D. H. 1977. *Water at the Surface of the Earth*. New York: Academic Press.

Penman, H. L. 1948. Natural evaporation from open water, bare soil, and grass. *Proceedings of the Royal Society (London)* 193:120–45.

Penman, H. L. 1956. Evaporation: an introductory survey. *Netherlands Journal of Agricultural Science* 4:9–29.

Pruitt, W. O. 1971. Factors affecting potential evapotranspiration. In E. J. Monke, ed., *Biological Effects in the Hydrological Cycle*. West Lafayette, Ind.: Purdue University.

Richards, T. L. and J. L. Irbe. 1969. Estimates of monthly evaporation losses from the Great Lakes 1950 to 1958 based on the mass transfer technique. *Proceedings Conference Great Lakes Research* 12:469–87.

Rutter, A. J. 1967. Analysis of evaporation from a stand of Scots Pine. In W. E. Sopper and H. W. Lull, eds., *International Symposium on Forest Hydrology*. New York: Pergamon Press.

Thornthwaite, C. W. 1948. An approach toward a rational classification of climate. *Geographical Review* 38:55–95.
Van Bavel, C. H. M. 1966. Potential evaporation: The combination concept and its experimental verification. *Water Resources Research* 2:445–67.

## SELECTED READINGS

Eagleson, P. S. 1970. *Dynamic Hydrology*. New York: McGraw-Hill.
Fogg, G. E. 1965. *The State and Movement of Water in Living Organisms*. New York: Academic Press.
Monteith, J. L. 1975. *Vegetation and the Atmosphere*, vol. 1. London: Academic Press.
Munn, R. E. 1970. *Biometeorological Methods*. New York: Academic Press.
Penman, H. L. 1963. *Vegetation and Hydrology*. Farnham Royal, England: Commonwealth Agricultural Bureaux.

# 7 WATER YIELD

## 7.1. Discharge Processes

The net discharge ($Q$) of liquid water from a land area is the sum

$$Q = (Q_o - Q_i) + (L_o - L_i) \tag{7.1}$$

where $(Q_o - Q_i)$ and $(L_o - L_i)$ are net surface and subsurface flows, respectively (subscripts: $o$-outflow, $i$-inflow); for catchments, however, $Q_i = 0$, and if $L_o - L_i \simeq 0$, $Q \simeq Q_o$ can be taken as stream discharge. Ordinarily $Q$ is expressed as a mass flux in terms of equivalent volume per unit time (e.g., in $m^3$/sec), or as a rate per unit catchment area (e.g., in $m^3$/hr · ha, or mm/day) in units of velocity. Within a given catchment, streamflow is generated by a variety of discharge processes and flow accelerations (±) that determine the shape of the *streamflow hydrograph*—a plot of $Q$ over time.

### 7.1.a. Discharge Components

Streamflow, to the extent that it represents total catchment discharge, is ultimately that part of precipitation not lost to evaporation and transpiration; symbolically,

$$Q = P - E \tag{7.2}$$

from the long-term water balance (equation 2.8). Streamflow is generally classified as either *direct runoff* ($Q_d$, also called storm-flow and "quickflow") or *base flow* ($Q_b$, groundwater or "delayed" flow); in perennial streams $Q_b$ is continuous, but $Q_d$ is intermittent, occurring only in direct response to specific rainfall (or snowmelt) events. These definitions are somewhat artificial, based on the shape of the streamflow hydrograph (see fig. 7.1); clearly,

$$Q = Q_d + Q_b \qquad (7.3)$$

for any time interval, but the separation of flow components is arbitrary (see section 7.1.b).

Hydrologists are frequently concerned with quickflow ($Q_d$) because it is responsible for floods and other sharp rises in the streamflow hydrograph. The ratio

$$R_p = \frac{Q_d}{P} \qquad (7.4)$$

is a measure of the amount of rainfall or snowmelt that appears promptly as streamflow, and

$$R_q = \frac{Q_d}{Q} \qquad (7.5)$$

is the proportion of total discharge that occurs as quickflow; $R_p$ and $R_q$ are useful in characterizing the *hydrologic response* of small catchments. Table 7.1 gives the average annual response factors reported by Hewlett and Hibbert (1967) for 15 forested catchments in eastern United States; among these catchments quickflow varies from 4 to 18% of annual precipitation, and from 7 to 33% of total discharge.

Streamflow is generated by processes that may be identified in terms of the paths along which precipitation travels from its point of incidence to a catchment channel. *Channel precipitation* enters the stream directly, or as throughfall to a shaded stream, and reaches the catchment mouth very quickly; it is followed by *overland flow* that occurs along relatively impermeable surfaces, by *interflow* through more permeable upper soil horizons, and finally by *groundwater flow* in the zone of saturation. Channel precipitation and overland flow contribute to direct runoff, and groundwater flow is synonymous with base flow, but interflow is usually associated with both delayed and quickflow; the relative importance of any individual streamflow generating process depends on catchment physical parameters and cover characteristics.

**Table 7.1. Description and Hydrologic Response of Forested Catchments (Hewlett and Hibbert, 1967)**

| Catchment | Area (ha) | Mean elevation (m) | Mean slope (%) | Soil texture[a] | Forest type[b] | Hydrologic response | |
|---|---|---|---|---|---|---|---|
| | | | | | | $R_p$ | $R_q$ |
| Coweeta 2, N.C. | 13 | 850 | 30 | SL | OH | 0.04 | 0.07 |
| Coweeta 18, N.C. | 13 | 820 | 32 | SL | OH | 0.05 | 0.09 |
| Coweeta 14, N.C. | 62 | 880 | 21 | SL | OH | 0.05 | 0.09 |
| Coweeta 21, N.C. | 24 | 990 | 34 | SL | OH | 0.06 | 0.09 |
| Bent Ck 7, N.C. | 297 | 940 | 22 | SL | OH | 0.06 | 0.15 |
| Coweeta 8, N.C. | 760 | 950 | 22 | SL | MH | 0.07 | 0.12 |
| Union 3, S.C. | 9 | 170 | 7 | SC | P | 0.08 | 0.25 |
| Coweeta 28, N.C. | 146 | 1200 | 33 | SL | MH | 0.10 | 0.15 |
| Copper Basin 2, Tenn. | 36 | 580 | 27 | SL | OH | 0.10 | 0.22 |
| Leading Ridge 1, Pa. | 123 | 370 | 19 | TL | MH | 0.11 | 0.28 |
| Dilldown Ck, Pa. | 619 | 580 | 4 | SL | SO | 0.12 | 0.23 |
| Fernow 4, W. Va. | 39 | 820 | 18 | TL | MH | 0.14 | 0.23 |
| Coweeta 36, N.C. | 46 | 1300 | 47 | SL | MH | 0.15 | 0.22 |
| Burlington Bk, Conn. | 1067 | 270 | 3 | SS | NH | 0.17 | 0.30 |
| Hubbard Bk 4, N.H. | 36 | 600 | 26 | NL | NH | 0.18 | 0.33 |

[a]SL, sandy loam; SC, sandy clay; TL, silt loam; SS, stony sand; NL, stony loam.
[b]OH, oak hickory; MH, mixed hardwoods; NH, northern hardwoods; SO, scrub oak; P, pine.

Channel precipitation is usually said to contribute very little to discharge because stream surface area is only a small fraction of total catchment area; a quantitative estimate of the contribution can be derived in terms of channel geometry. From the continuity equation for steady flow, discharge in $m^3/sec$ is

$$Q = AV \simeq WRV \qquad (7.6)$$

where $A$ ($m^2$) is the area of stream cross-section at a point, and $V$ (m/sec) is the mean flow velocity in a stream of surface width ($W$, m) and hydraulic radius ($R$, m; $R$ is the ratio of $A$ to the wetted cross-section perimeter); combining $R$ and $V$ from the general hydraulic relationships (Albertson and Simons, 1964),

$$R = 0.47 \, Q^{0.33} \qquad (7.7)$$

and

$$V = 0.62 \, R^{0.5} \qquad (7.8)$$

yields

$$RV = 0.20 \, Q^{0.5} \qquad (7.9)$$

and by substitution in equation 7.6,

$$W = 5.0 \, Q^{0.5} \qquad (7.10)$$

relating stream width directly to mean discharge. Letting $W/2$ be an average stream width for the catchment ($W$ = width at catchment mouth), and drainage density ($D$, in $km/km^2$) a measure of total stream length, the ratio of stream surface area ($A_s$) to catchment area ($A_c$) is

$$Q_s = \frac{A_s}{A_c} = 2.5(10^{-3}) Q^{0.5} D \qquad (7.11)$$

and $Q_s$ is the fraction of catchment precipitation that falls directly into the stream; solutions to equation 7.11 for $A_c = 1$ $km^2$ show that for $5 < D < 10$ $km/km^2$ and $0.01 < Q < 0.10$ $m^3/sec$, $Q_s$ varies between about 0.1 and 0.8% of precipitation.

Although channel precipitation ($Q_s$) must be a very small part of total catchment precipitation, it may not be a negligible part of quickflow ($Q_d$); for example, where the hydrologic response ($R_p$, table 7.1) is less than 0.1, $Q_s$ may range from 1 to 20% of $Q_d$. Moreover, since stream channel dimensions (both length and width) increase during periods of quickflow, the relative effect on storm discharge may be even greater. The separate contributions of other flow components must be inferred from examination of the streamflow hydrograph.

### 7.1.b. Hydrograph Analysis

In natural catchments, "overland flow," "interflow," and "groundwater flow" are viable concepts only in a general descriptive sense. In the undisturbed forested catchments of humid regions, and in other heavily vegetated areas, overland flow is rare except as "surface runoff" in small ephemeral waterways; in less permeable catchments, hillside precipitation may begin its journey toward the stream as overland flow, later infiltrate and move laterally as interflow, percolate gradually to become part of a local groundwater stream, or surface again where a perched aquifer forms a spring. Traditionally, quantitative distinctions among the terms were based on the time of arrival of water in the stream channel, and this was inferred from its effect on the streamflow hydrograph.

A streamflow hydrograph illustrating the effects of short intense rainfall is shown in figure 7.1; it consists of an *approach segment* (*ab*), the *rising limb* (*bc*) and the *recession limb* (*ce*). Points *b*, *c*, and *d* projected to the time scale are called *time of rise* (*b'*), *peak point* (*c'*), and *end of quickflow* (*d'*); the interval *b'c'* is *lag time*, and *b'd'* is the *quickflow interval* or period of storm runoff. The dashed segment (*bd*) is known as the *hydrograph separation*; it supposedly separates quickflow (shaded area) from baseflow and defines the quickflow interval.

Hydrograph separation is useful in relating streamflow changes to discrete rainfall events, but all methods of separation are arbitrary and have little to do with the identification of discharge components: "Hydrograph separation appears to be little more than a convenient fiction" and "when we consider streamflow generated by subsurface stormflow, hydrograph separation becomes even

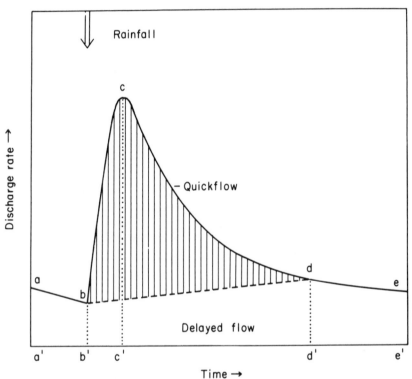

Figure 7.1. The streamflow hydrograph as influenced by a period of short intense rainfall.

more irrational" (Freeze, 1972). As a rule of thumb, the interval of time ($t$, hrs) from peak flow to the end of stormflow ($c'd'$ in fig. 7.1) can be estimated as

$$t = c'd' = 8A_c^{0.2} \qquad (7.12)$$

where $A_c$ is catchment area in hectares (adapted from Linsley, Kohler, and Paulhus, 1975). Hewlett and Hibbert (1967) suggested that a consistent rule be adopted such that the hydrograph separation line (segment $bd$ in fig. 7.1) would indicate a constant acceleration in base flow of 2 m$^3$/hr$^2 \cdot$ km$^2$ (in English units, 0.05 ft$^3$/sec $\cdot$ hr $\cdot$ mi$^2$).

Streamflow hydrographs rarely have the simple form illustrated in figure 7.1; rainfall may occur intermittently during the storm-

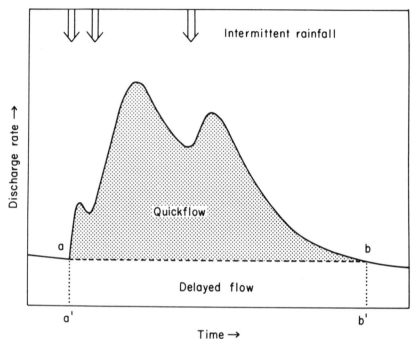

Figure 7.2. Complex hydrograph.

flow period, or continuously with intermittent bursts of high intensity, producing a hydrograph of complex form (fig. 7.2).
Complex hydrographs may be interpreted as a series of discrete
events, or as a single event for which Hewlett's separation slope
could be used. Otherwise the total volume of discharge (all sources)
attributable to the series of rainfall bursts can be estimated as the
total flow at rates greater than the initial (prerainfall) rate; in figure
7.2 this is the area above the horizontal segment (*ab*) connecting
points of equal discharge, and *a'b'* is the discharge interval.

If rainfall continues at uniform intensity for a longer period,
peak flow will be delayed at least as long as it takes channel flow
from the most remote point to reach the catchment mouth; this
interval is called *time of concentration* ($t_c$, min):

$$t_c \simeq 0.02 \, \frac{d^{1.2}}{z^{0.4}} \tag{7.13}$$

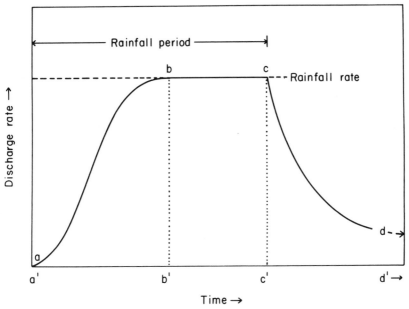

**Figure 7.3. Elemental hydrograph.**

where $d$ (m) and $z$ (m) are horizontal and vertical distances, respectively, to the most remote point. Long-continued rainfall of uniform intensity would produce a hydrograph of stormflow as idealized in figure 7.3 for a small impervious area; the discharge rate increases (segment $ab$) until it equals the rainfall rate, remains constant ($bc$) until the rain stops, and finally recesses exponentially ($cd$). In this *elemental hydrograph* the interval $a'b'$ is called the *time of equilibrium*; temporary storage (area above the rising limb)— the volume of water in transit during the interval $b'c'$—is discharged during the recession interval ($c'd'$).

Sherman (1932) formally introduced the idea that since many of the physical characteristics of a catchment are constant, similarity in streamflow hydrographs are to be expected from similar storms; the *unit hydrograph* is the typical hydrograph generated by a unit depth of rainfall excess (quickflow) distributed uniformly over the catchment, at a constant rate, during a specified period of time. The unit hydrograph theory means that the quickflow interval

($b'd'$ in fig. 7.1) is constant when the duration of rainfall excess is constant, and that quickflow rates within the interval are proportional to the total excess; for example, uniform storms that produce 10 and 20 mm/hr of rainfall excess will generate stormflow hydrographs of equal length but with ordinate values in the ratio 10:20. Unit hydrograph theory has been verified under a wide variety of conditions, and has been extended to the analysis of complex hydrographs; but atypical rainfall distributions, seasonal changes in catchment physical characteristics, and the problem of determining rainfall excess limit its predictive power even in the small catchments that are of primary concern in forest hydrology.

The recession limb of a streamflow hydrograph is a *depletion curve* with regard to catchment storage; the discharge rate ($Q_t$) at any time ($t$) is frequently given in the form,

$$Q_t = Q_o \, e^{-\alpha t} \tag{7.14}$$

where $Q_o$ is the initial rate at $t = 0$ (the equation is more accurate if $t_o$ is taken after the end of the quickflow period). If $Q_t$ is expressed in units of velocity (e.g., $m^3$/day·ha, or mm/day), integration of equation 7.14 between $t_o$ (at $Q_t = Q_o$) and $t_\infty$ (at $Q_t = 0$) gives the total discharge depth that can occur (without rain) before the stream becomes dry, or the total depth of water held in storage at time $t = 0$. In general form,

$$S_t \text{ (depth)} = \frac{Q_t}{\alpha} \tag{7.15}$$

where $S_t$ is storage depth at any time ($t$) during the recession period, and $\alpha$ is the recession constant.

### 7.1.c. Discharge Relations

Numerous models have been devised to express aspects of stream discharge in terms of hydrograph parameters, the hydraulic geometry of channels, and formal relationships drawn from fluid mechanics. Models may be based ultimately on the laws of physics, water- and energy-budget principles, and continuity relations, but in applied hydrology it is often necessary to develop approximations by interpreting physical laws and mathematical formulations in terms of more functional relationships. In practice, of course, the accuracy of discharge formulas is also limited by the accuracy with which critical parameters can be estimated or measured in the field.

The *hydraulic geometry* of a stream channel is a description of parameters in the continuity relationship for steady flow:

$$Q = AV = WDV \qquad (7.16)$$

from equation 7.6, where the cross-sectional area $(A)$ is the product of mean channel width $(W)$ and depth $(D)$. The basic equations are:

$$W = aQ^b \qquad (7.17)$$

$$D = cQ^f \qquad (7.18)$$

$$V = kQ^m \qquad (7.19)$$

in which the coefficients $(a, c, k)$ and exponents $(b, f, m)$ are empirical and

$$ack = b + f + m = 1 \qquad (7.20)$$

must be true to satisfy equation 7.16. The empirical values vary with catchment characteristics to some extent, but depend primarily on whether they are intended to describe changes at a particular cross-section, or differences among stations along a stream; table 7.2 lists some average values of the exponents derived from the classical study of Leopold and Maddock (1953), and other studies in the United States and Europe (note the agreement of the among-station "$b$" with the exponent in equation 7.10).

Table 7.2. Approximate Values of the Exponents
in Eqs. (7.17)–(7.20)

| Stream cross-section | Exponent | | |
|---|---|---|---|
| | $b$ | $f$ | $m$ |
| Single station | 0.2 | 0.4 | 0.4 |
| Among stations[a] | 0.5 | 0.4 | 0.1 |

[a]Defined for flows of the same frequency; values vary somewhat depending on whether median, mean, or bankfull flows are used.

The continuity equation is frequently expressed in a form that reflects the influences of channel slope and roughness; the well-known Chezy-Manning equation is

$$Q = AV = A \frac{R^{0.67} S^{0.5}}{n} \qquad (7.21)$$

in metric units ($Q$ in m$^3$/sec, for $A$ in m$^2$ and $R$ in m) where $S$ is the dimensionless slope of the energy gradient ($\simeq$ channel slope), and $n$ is a roughness coefficient. Equation 7.21 has also been used to express overland flow (sheet flow) in terms of the depth ($d$) of surface detention; sheet flow along a strip 1-m wide is

$$Q = \frac{d^{1.67} S^{0.5}}{n} \qquad (7.22)$$

since $A = d \simeq R$. Some typical values of the coefficient ($n$) for natural channels and other surfaces are given in table 7.3.

The Manning equation has been widely used for many purposes, including the extension of stage-discharge relations (see section

Table 7.3. Roughness Coefficients in the Manning Equation (adapted from Linsley, Kohler and Paulhus, 1975)

| Surface | Coefficient | |
|---|---|---|
| *Miscellaneous* | | |
| Smooth metal | 0.010 | |
| Ordinary concrete | 0.012 | |
| Unplaned timber | 0.014 | |
| Dressed stone | 0.016 | |
| Smooth earth | 0.018 | |
| Firm gravel | 0.020 | |
| *Natural channels* | High stage | Low stage |
| Straight: clean | 0.029 | – |
| weedy | 0.035 | – |
| Winding: clean | 0.039 | 0.047 |
| weedy | 0.042 | 0.052 |
| Sluggish: weedy | – | 0.065 |
| Very sluggish: weedy | – | 0.112 |

10.7) and the estimation of flood peaks from high water marks on ungaged streams; in the latter role it is sometimes referred to as the *slope-area* method of computation. The *rational formula* (so called only because the common English units are numerically consistent) has also been widely used, especially in engineering practice, for estimating flood peaks in urban areas and small catchments; for peak flow ($Q_p$) in m$^3$/sec,

$$Q_p = \frac{CiA_c}{360} \qquad (7.23)$$

where $C$ is a runoff coefficient ($0 < C < 1$), $i$ (mm/hr) is rainfall intensity, and $A_c$ (ha) is catchment area. The rational formula requires the assumption that rainfall continues at uniform intensity for a period at least as great as the time of concentration (equation 7.13), and that for such storms there is a simple proportionality between $Q_p$ and $i$ (i.e., $Q_p/i$ = constant for a given catchment); objections to these assumptions are serious, and the experimental data show that for natural catchments the coefficient ($C$) varies with both rainfall intensity and antecedent moisture conditions.

The difficulties involved in describing stream discharge as a deterministic (cause and effect) process, in which time variability is assumed to be entirely explained by other factors, have led to the development and use of probabilistic and stochastic methods. Probabilistic (statistical) methods are used to describe streamflow averages, extremes, and frequency distributions (in a manner analogous to the treatment of precipitation variability in section 3.2.b), and statistical relationships of discharge to atmospheric phenomena, catchment characteristics, and cover types (as applied to water yield in sections 7.2 and 7.3); probabilistic statements may, for example, allude to the fact that mean catchment discharge is exceeded only about 25% of the time in most catchments (low flows are predominant in streamflow frequency distributions), and the hydrologist can speak of a "50-year flood" (the one that is exceeded, on the average, only once in 50 years), or a "$Q_{7-10}$" (the 7-day mean low-flow that occurs, on the average, only once in 10 years). In contrast to deterministic and statistical analyses, which are based on finite data sets, stochastic methods make it possible to generate unlimited sets of synthetic streamflow and other sequential data that retain many of the mathematical properties of original series (e.g., the same probability of occurrence), but that differ in ways that are equally probable, as would be expected in a much longer series; in this way stochastic hydrology provides a much broader perspective for management and planning.

## 7.2. Yield Determinants

Catchment *water yield* is synonymous with total discharge, but "yield" is used more in the sense of "harvest" (analogous to timber yield), and usually is applied to total volumes, depths, or average flow rates for months, seasons, and years. Consequently, in the following discussion of yield determinants, focus is on typical or average influences of controlling factors, even when the reference is to instantaneous phenomena, e.g., peak discharge rates. Yield determinants are categorized here as atmospheric factors, catchment parameters, and forest influences, but it is important to recognize that there are numerous interactions, and that catchment responses occur as the result of unique combinations of factors.

### 7.2.a. Atmospheric Factors

From the long-term water budget (equation 7.2), catchment water yield must be a function of precipitation and other atmospheric factors that influence latent heat exchanges; the general relationship can be given in terms of Budyko's (1974) radiative index ($I$). From equation 6.40, normal annual discharge is

$$Q = Pe^{-I} = P \exp\left(-R/L_v P\right) \tag{7.24}$$

where $P$ and $R$ are normal (long-term average) precipitation and net radiation, respectively; net radiation is not strictly an atmospheric influence, and can be considered in this role only where surface properties are constant. In this restricted sense, water yield is simply the result of atmospheric inputs of water and energy; generally, however, surface differences are significant and equation

7.24 is useful in estimating the magnitude of cover-type influences on normal yield (see section 7.2.c).

In small catchments there is, of course, considerable variation in water yield from year to year (see table 6.6), but generally the correlation with annual precipitation is well-defined, as illustrated in figure 7.4. In this example, the standard error involved in estimating annual yield as a function of precipitation is 38 mm/yr, or only 6% of the mean ($\overline{Q}$ = 596 mm/yr); the regression should not be extrapolated beyond the range of the data (e.g., to $P$ = 613 and

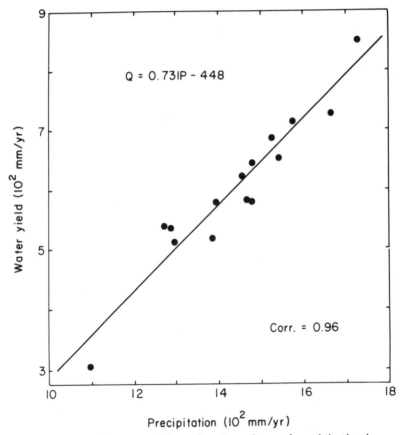

Figure 7.4. Annual water yield as a function of annual precipitation in a small catchment.

$Q = 0$ mm/yr!). Deviations about the regression line may reflect carry-over effects of alternating wet and dry years, differences in catchment storage at the beginning of a year, variations in precipitation timing, or other factors.

Seasonal variations in water yield usually conform to a distinct pattern, or *flow regime*, dominated by interactions of rainfall, snowmelt, and evaporation. Over much of the conterminous United States, flow rates are highest in spring, and lowest during late summer and autumn following the period of maximum evaporation; for record-keeping purposes the *water year*, 1 October–30 September, has been adopted by the Geological Survey and other agencies. A typical flow regime, resulting from relatively uniform precipitation (mainly rain) throughout the year, is shown in figure 7.5; in some areas, where streams are fed by melting snow, peak flows occur during late spring and early summer.

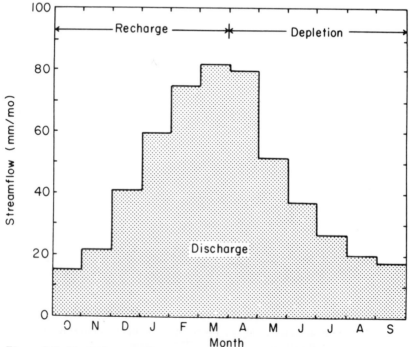

Figure 7.5. Typical streamflow regime in an area of relatively uniform seasonal rainfall.

The fraction of rainfall that appears as quickflow ($R_p$, table 7.1) is greater, as a rule, when individual storm rainfall depths are greater; $R_p > 0.5$ may occur during exceptionally large storms, even on heavily forested catchments (Hewlett and Hibbert, 1967). Hydrologic response is also greater when rainfall occurs more frequently, or when initial base flow is greater (in winter, for example), and when rain is unevenly distributed over the catchment so that a smaller fraction can be absorbed and held in storage. Peak flows are greater with higher rainfall intensities, even in catchments with exceptionally deep soils (see, e.g., comments by Lee and Tajchman, 1977, on the report by Hewlett, Fortson, and Cunningham, 1977); peaks are also greater when storms move along a catchment axis in the downstream direction, so that flood peaks from individual tributaries reach the gaging station at more nearly the same time.

Any atmospheric factor that tends to increase evaporative losses from an area will have an equal but opposite effect on total water yield. It follows that (from table 6.1) solar and net radiation, air and surface temperature, and windspeed will tend to be negatively correlated, and atmospheric humidity positively, with water yield among catchments having the same precipitation regime. Nevertheless, as demonstrated in chapter 6, evaporation is much more than an atmospheric phenomenon, and important differences in water yield can be traced directly to the influences of catchment physical parameters and forest cover.

### 7.2.b. Catchment Parameters

Catchment physical parameters, as given in section 2.3.b, include location, relief, area, shape, exposure, streams, and substrata; these have been discussed to some extent in previous sections, and only certain specific influences will be elaborated here. Geographic and elevation coordinates are indirect measures of climate that can be used to describe normal water yield in a statistical manner; for example, D. G. Boyer (personal communication), in an extension of his original work (Boyer, 1976), found that normal annual water yield ($Q$, mm/yr) from 44 basins in West Virginia could be described by

$$Q = 0.915P + 53.4Z + 112.4\phi - 5140 \qquad (7.25)$$

as a function of normal precipitation ($P$, mm/yr), latitude ($\phi$, degrees), and elevation ($Z$, $10^2$ m). The equation provides a useful approximation, showing that $Q$ increases by about 50 mm/yr per 100 m increase in elevation, and 100 mm/yr per degree of latitude; the correlation is 0.94, and standard error 67 mm/yr (12% of the mean).

Catchment exposure, which includes both steepness and aspect, is also an indirect climatic parameter; its usefulness in assessing water yield as an energy-budget factor is treated in greater detail in section 7.3.c. Catchment orientation is said to be instrumental in affecting peak streamflow rates (Wisler and Brater, 1959); if the major axis of a catchment is aligned in the direction of prevailing storm winds, flood peaks will be smaller if storms pass the outlet point first and move in an upstream direction. More commonly, however, aspect is discussed in relation to the microclimate of individual slope facets, and steepness is viewed with regard to its effects on the rapidity of surface and subsurface flows.

The description of drainage basin geometry for hydrologic purposes is based on concepts of quantitative geomorphology; surface features evolve gradually as an erosion process under the influence of flowing water and, under similar conditions of climate and lithology, evolving land forms attain a high degree of similarity. The evolutionary process is so slow that, at any given time, a steady state exists in which there is a fine adjustment between geometric properties and water flow. Similarity does not imply identity, of course, and land-form analysis is far from being an exact science; nevertheless, the general relationships are understood well enough to provide considerable leverage for the practicing hydrologist.

Under otherwise constant conditions, mean discharge must be directly proportional to catchment area ($A_c$), and average flow depths must be equal for all catchment sizes; conditions are not constant, of course, and smaller catchments (within a given drainage network) are restricted more to upland areas where both precipitation and discharge depths are usually greater. Flow rates per unit land area (m$^3$/sec · ha, or depth/time) generally follow the relationship

$$\frac{Q}{A_c} = kA_c^{\,x-1} \tag{7.26}$$

from equation 2.43 where $k$ is an empirical coefficient, and $x < 1$ for peak flows and $x > 1$ for low flows; figure 7.6 illustrates the typical effect of catchment size. In larger catchments the time of concentration is greater, and intense rainfall is less likely to occur over the entire area, so as area increases $Q/A_c$ decreases at high flows; but at low flow stages $Q/A_c$ increases with area as the result of delayed subsurface flow from tributary catchments.

In catchments of similar area, surface geometry is defined in terms of linear dimensions (length, width, perimeter, relief), dimensionless ratios (land and channel slope), numbers (streams, bifurcations), and other shape factors that are widely used in more comprehensive models of storm discharge volumes and peaks (e.g., the *Stanford Watershed Model*, in Crawford and Linsley, 1966,

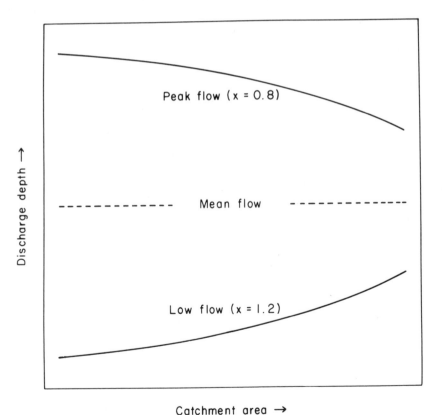

Figure 7.6. Relative discharge as related to catchment area.

Table 7.4.  Correlation Statistics Relating Water Yield to
Stream Length in Eastern United States
(adapted from Morisawa, 1967)

| Province | $a^a$ | $m$ | Correlation |
|---|---|---|---|
| Atlantic Coast | 0.11670 | 1.00 | 0.68 |
| New England | 0.01954 | 1.59 | 0.94 |
| Gulf Coast | 0.01450 | 1.51 | 0.81 |
| Glaciated Plateau | 0.00879 | 1.71 | 0.94 |
| Piedmont | 0.00637 | 1.84 | 0.80 |
| Unglaciated Plateau | 0.00583 | 1.95 | 0.99 |

[a]The coefficient was adjusted to give mean discharge ($Q$, equation 7.27) in $m^3$/sec for length ($L$) in km.

and the *SCS Method*, Kent, 1973); ordinarily these are used as weighting factors, or statistical parameters, where parameter choice depends on the "goodness of fit" in estimating flow. The assumption of geometric similarity implies that any linear measurement should be equally effective, and Morisawa (1967) suggested that mean annual discharge could be estimated simply as a function of longest stream length ($L$, source to mouth), or

$$Q = aL^m \tag{7.27}$$

where the coefficient ($a$) and exponent ($m$) vary with physiographic province; her statistical results are summarized in table 7.4. Total water yield and its flow regime are also strongly influenced by the hydrologic nature of catchment substrata (as discussed in ch. 5), and by vegetation—particularly forest cover.

### 7.2.c.  Forest Influences

It is a basic tenet of forest hydrology that water yield and streamflow regimen are distinctly and importantly influenced by the presence of forest cover; this principle has been verified by practical experience and scientific experimentation in every major forest zone of earth. But since forest cover can have little (if any) effect on gross precipitation (see section 3.3.a), its influence on the water budget must be related entirely to energy-budget effects, specifically latent heat exchanges, and short-term or seasonal modifications of discharge phenomena. Many aspects of the forest influence on water yield are treated in section 7.3 in terms of changes that have been observed to follow forest cutting and other management practices; here it may be sufficient to develop perspective with regard to some operative principles that underlie observed effects.

Forests of the earth thrive where water is plentiful relative to energy; in terms of Budyko's (1974) radiative index ($I$), where

$$I = \frac{R}{L_v P} \qquad (7.28)$$

from equation 6.40, forests are restricted to zones where $I$ does not greatly exceed unity. In a given climate, with fixed normal precipitation, any difference in net radiation ($R$) can be related directly to the difference in $I$, and to normal water yield ($Q$); specifically,

$$\frac{dQ}{dI} = - Pe^{-I} = - P \exp (-R/L_v P) \qquad (7.29)$$

or by substitution,

$$dQ = - QdI \qquad (7.30)$$

from equation 7.24. Figure 7.7 illustrates the relationship of the yield coefficient ($Q/P$) to $I$ over the range of interest.

For any finite difference in $R$ (i.e., $\Delta R$), the corresponding difference in $Q$ is given by

$$\Delta Q = Q_1 \frac{e^{-I_2} - e^{-I_1}}{e^{-I_1}} \qquad (7.31)$$

where $I_1$ is the base of reference ($\Delta Q > 0$ if $I_1 > I_2$), and

$$\frac{\Delta Q}{Q_1} = e^{-\Delta I} - 1 \qquad (7.32)$$

gives the relative change in yield for a given change in $I$ ($\Delta I = I_2 - I_1$). In a given climate with normal global radiation ($S_t$), a conservative estimate of $\Delta R$ is

$$\Delta R = - \Delta r S_t \qquad (7.33)$$

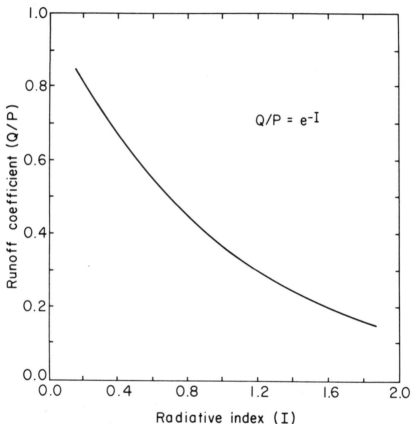

**Figure 7.7.** Relationship of the yield coefficient to the radiative index.

where $r$ is the surface reflectivity to shortwave radiation; also,

$$\Delta I = -\Delta r \, \frac{S_t}{L_v P} \tag{7.34}$$

and

$$\frac{\Delta Q}{Q_1} = 1 - \exp\left[(-\Delta r S_t)/L_v P\right] \tag{7.35}$$

by substitution in equation 7.32. In reduced form

$$\Delta Q = Q_1 \left(1 - e^{-k\Delta r}\right) \tag{7.36}$$

letting $k = S_t/L_v P$, and

$$\Delta Q \simeq Q_1 \, k\Delta r \qquad\qquad (7.37)$$

for small values of $\Delta r$; in the eastern United States $k \simeq 2$ ($1.8 < k < 2.2$) for most regions, so a difference in reflectivity of one percentage point ($\Delta r = 0.01$) denotes a 2% difference in water yield.

Differences in normal annual water yield between forests and other vegetation (range and cropland) in eastern United States were estimated by Lee (1977) using equation 7.35 and regional averages of $S_t$, $P$, and $Q$, and average reflectivities for cover types. Canopy reflectivities vary considerably as a function of forest type, time of day, season, and latitude; estimated average growing season albedoes for the ten major timber types of this region are listed in table 7.5 (range and cropland albedo was assumed to be 0.20, but with greater seasonal and latitudinal variability). The expected differences in annual water yield (table 7.5) are directly proportional

Table 7.5. Estimated Growing Season Albedoes and
Annual Water Yield Differences, Forest
versus Range and Cropland (Lee, 1977)

| Forest type | Albedo | Yield difference (mm/yr)[a] | |
|---|---|---|---|
| | | Mean | Range |
| *Coniferous* | | | |
| Spruce–fir | 0.10 | 167 | 86–196 |
| White–red–jack pine | 0.12 | 124 | 77–161 |
| Loblolly–shortleaf pine | 0.12 | 90 | 59–140 |
| Longleaf–slash pine | 0.12 | 74 | 59–112 |
| *Deciduous* | | | |
| Oak–pine | 0.15 | 59 | 37–101 |
| Oak–gum cypress | 0.15 | 52 | 37–76 |
| Elm–ash–cottonwood | 0.17 | 49 | 24–79 |
| Oak–hickory | 0.18 | 34 | 17–62 |
| Maple–beech–birch | 0.19 | 33 | 17–47 |
| Aspen–birch | 0.20 | 18 | 10–33 |

[a]Range and cropland yield greater than forest yield by the indicated amount.

to $Q$ and also vary, but to a lesser extent, with differences in $S_t$ and $P$ among regions where the forest types occur.

The foregoing analysis excludes any appraisal of catchment exposure to solar radiation, local climate eccentricities, energy advection, edaphic variability, and differences in tree physiology and phenology; these and other influences on forest water yield and the flow regime introduce a complexity that is poorly defined in the context of contemporary theory. Considerable understanding has been achieved through studies of individual hydrologic processes, and by development of comprehensive computerized models that attempt to integrate the effects and interactions of a wide range of ecosystem components. But the natural integrator is, of course, the catchment itself; carefully controlled studies on experimental catchments have "produced much of our present knowledge about the land phase of the hydrologic cycle" (Hewlett, Lull, and Reinhart, 1969), and have produced the most reliable information available with regard to forest management effects on water yield.

## 7.3. Management Effects

The presence of forest cover is associated with reduced annual water yield; this has been demonstrated repeatedly by comparisons of adjacent forested and nonforested catchment discharges, and by noting the effects of deforestation, reforestation, and afforestation. Forest cover also modifies the annual flow regime of streams; the seasonal pattern compared to nonforested, partially cut, and denuded areas depends on forest type and climate. Deforestation increases the volume of both quickflow and delayed flow, but the effect is proportionately larger during periods of delayed flow when a large fraction of the total yield volume occurs—which means that the forest influence on yield is predominately a delayed-flow influence.

### 7.3.a. Total Yield

In order to quantify the forest influence on water yield it is necessary to develop an adequate reference or basis for comparison;

this is accomplished by either of two basic methods of *catchment calibration*. A single catchment may be calibrated using climatological data, in effect calibrating the catchment upon itself, as in figure 7.4 for example, where the relationship between yield and precipitation is developed during a pre-treatment or *calibration period*; in this case (from fig. 7.4),

$$Q = 0.731P - 448 \tag{7.38}$$

is the *calibration equation* ($Q$ and $P$ in mm/yr). If the forest is cut following the calibration period, the change in yield ($\Delta Q$) is

$$\Delta Q = Q_i - Q = Q_i - 0.731P_i + 448 \tag{7.39}$$

where $Q_i$ and $P_i$ are the total yield and precipitation during any postcalibration year ($i$); this method can be extended using the procedure of double-mass analysis (section 3.2.c, fig. 3.10), or by developing more complicated expressions for assumed climatological effects (Reigner, 1964).

More commonly, and with greater precision, the catchment to be treated is calibrated against an adjacent undisturbed control catchment by plotting a series of annual yields $Q_t$ (test) over $Q_c$ (control) as in figure 7.8; in this example,

$$Q_t = 1.124Q_c - 7.7 \tag{7.40}$$

with a standard error of 19 mm/yr (3% of the mean). The reliability of the calibration in estimating subsequent deviations is determined statistically and, in analogy with equation 7.39, the treatment effect is

$$\Delta Q = Q_{ti} - Q_t = Q_{ti} - 1.124Q_{ci} + 7.7 \tag{7.41}$$

during any posttreatment year ($i$); the tacit assumption is that annual variations in precipitation, and other climatological variables, affect both catchments equally. It is particularly important to note that since only the *change* in yield is estimated subsurface flows (leakage) are canceled by subtraction,

$$\Delta Q = -\Delta E \tag{7.42}$$

can be assumed, and $\Delta Q$ is conservative (i.e., would be greater than estimated if, as expected, catchment storage increases after cutting).

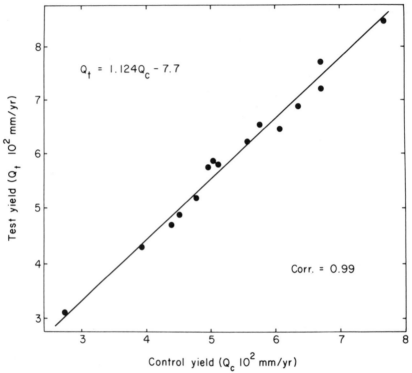

**Figure 7.8. Annual yield relationship between test and control catchments during a calibration period.**

Annual water yield increases following forest removal have been obtained from numerous catchment experiments under a wide variety of conditions; a selected list of results is given in table 7.6 based on a summary by Anderson, Hoover, and Reinhart (1976). Yield increases tend to be greater from areas where normal yield is greater, and from north- versus south-facing catchments in the same general climate. Complete deforestation generally increases the annual yield by between 20 and 40% of normal (last column, table 7.6), but maximum increases rarely exceed 400 mm/yr.

The data from these and other studies tend to confirm the general rules that 1) forest removal increases total water yield, 2) yield increases are greater when a greater fraction of the catchment

Table 7.6. Annual Water Yield Increases Following Forest Removal (Anderson et al., 1976)

| Location | Forest type[a] | Removal Fraction (f) | Method | Normal yield (Q, mm/yr) | Yield increase by years (mm/yr) $\Delta Q_1$ | $\Delta Q_2$ | $\Delta Q_3$ | $\Delta Q_1/Q_f$ (%) |
|---|---|---|---|---|---|---|---|---|
| North Carolina | MH[b] | 1.00 | Clearcut | 792 | 370 | 283 | 279 | 47 |
| | MH[c] | 1.00 | Clearcut | 607 | 127 | 95 | 59 | 21 |
| | MH | 0.50 | Strips | 1275 | 198 | 155 | 130 | 31 |
| | MH | 0.22 | Selection | 1222 | 99 | 56 | 71 | 37 |
| West Virginia | MH | 0.85 | Clearcut | 584 | 130 | 86 | 89 | 26 |
| | MH | 0.36 | Selection | 660 | 64 | 36 | — | 27 |
| | MH | 0.22 | Selection | 762 | 36 | — | — | 21 |
| | MH | 0.14 | Selection | 635 | 8 | — | — | 9 |
| Colorado | AC | 1.00 | Clearcut | 157 | 34 | 47 | 25 | 22 |
| | PSF | 0.40 | Clearcut | 283 | 86 | 53 | 79 | 76 |
| Oregon | DF | 1.00 | Clearcut | 1448 | 462 | 457 | — | 32 |
| | DF | 0.30 | Clearcut | 1448 | 150 | 163 | 150 | 35 |
| Arizona | PP | 1.00 | Clearcut | 153[d] | 96 | 23 | 46 | — |
| | PP | 0.32 | Strips | 170[d] | 50 | 15 | 9 | — |
| | PP | 0.75 | Thinning | 194[d] | 22 | 37 | 38 | — |

[a]MH, mixed hardwoods; AC, aspen-conifer; PSF, pine-spruce-fir; DF, Douglas fir; PP, Ponderosa pine.
[b]Northeast aspect.
[c]Southeast aspect.
[d]Winter discharge.

is deforested, 3) maximum increases occur the first year after cutting, 4) cutting effects decrease logarithmically with time, and 5) the effects persist longer when the initial effect is greater. Douglass and Swank (1975) attempted to quantify these statements as they apply to hardwood forest regions of eastern United States; the first-year change in yield ($\Delta Q_1$, mm/yr) can be estimated as

$$\Delta Q_1 = 44(f/S_p)^{1.45} \tag{7.43}$$

where $f$ is the fraction of catchment area deforested, and $S_p$ (in $10^6$ ly/yr) is potential solar radiation (see table A.4). Solutions to equation 7.43 for selected values of $f$ and $S_p$ are given in table 7.7.

The effects of cutting diminish logarithmically with time as the forest is regenerated. The increase in yield ($\Delta Q_i$) for any year ($i$) after treatment can be estimated using a modified form of the Douglass and Swank (1975) equation:

$$\Delta Q_i = \Delta Q_1 - \Delta Q_1 \frac{\ln i}{\ln n} \tag{7.44}$$

where $n$ is the persistence period. The influence of cutting persists until $i$ approaches its limiting value ($n$) defined by

$$n = i(\text{maximum}) = \frac{\Delta Q_1}{16} \tag{7.45}$$

where $n$ is an integer (rounded from equation 7.45).

For many practical purposes the total yield increase ($\Delta Q_t$, mm) integrated over the persistence period from $i = 1$ to $i = n$ is of special interest. The sum of effects for individual years is

$$\Delta Q_t = \sum_i^n \Delta Q_i = \sum_i^n \Delta Q_1 - \Delta Q_1 \frac{\ln i}{\ln n} \tag{7.46}$$

but since, for consecutive integers,

$$\sum_i^n \ln i = \ln n! \tag{7.47}$$

(Stirling's formula), the summation is

$$\Delta Q_t = n \, \Delta Q_1 - \Delta Q_1 \frac{\ln n!}{\ln n} \tag{7.48}$$

Table 7.7. First-Year Increase in Water Yield (mm/yr) Based on Equation 7.43 (after Douglass and Swank, 1975)

| $S_p$ | Fraction of forest removed ($f$) | | | | |
|---|---|---|---|---|---|
| ($10^6$ ly/yr) | 0.2 | 0.4 | 0.6 | 0.8 | 1.0 |
| 0.18 | 51 | 140 | 252 | 383 | 529 |
| 0.20 | 44 | 120 | 216 | 328 | 454 |
| 0.22 | 38 | 105 | 188 | 286 | 395 |
| 0.24 | 34 | 92 | 166 | 252 | 348 |
| 0.26 | 30 | 82 | 148 | 225 | 310 |
| 0.28 | 27 | 74 | 133 | 202 | 279 |
| 0.30 | 24 | 67 | 120 | 182 | 252 |
| 0.32 | 22 | 61 | 109 | 166 | 230 |
| 0.34 | 20 | 56 | 100 | 152 | 210 |

and this reduces to the approximation,

$$\Delta Q_t \simeq \Delta Q_1 \, (0.25 \, n + 0.85) \tag{7.49}$$

which is accurate to about 2% over the common range. Solutions to equations 7.45 and 7.48 are given in table 7.8 for selected values of $\Delta Q_1$; also listed are the average yield increases for persistence periods, and for an assumed 80-year rotation.

Considerable evidence has accumulated in support of the idea that coniferous forests yield less water to streamflow than do hardwood types in the same climate; the conservative data of table

Table 7.8. Persistence Period and Total Yield Increase as a Function of First-Year Increase

| Item | First-year yield increase (mm/yr) | | | | |
|---|---|---|---|---|---|
| | 50 | 100 | 200 | 300 | 400 |
| Persistence period $n$ (yrs) | 3 | 6 | 12 | 18 | 25 |
| Total increase $\Delta Q_t$ (mm) | 80 | 235 | 770 | 1605 | 2840 |
| Average increase $\Delta Q_t / n$ (mm/yr) | 27 | 39 | 64 | 89 | 114 |
| Average increase $\Delta Q_t / 80$ (mm/yr) | 1 | 3 | 10 | 20 | 36 |

7.5 imply that the difference may be of the order of 50 to 100 mm/yr, but other estimates range from zero to more than 300 mm/yr (Anderson, Hoover, and Reinhart, 1976). In the most carefully controlled experiment, Swank and Douglass (1974) found that when two catchments in North Carolina were completely converted from mixed hardwoods to white pine, annual water yields decreased rapidly; after 15 years the pine cover yielded 200 mm/yr less than the original hardwood cover. Greater water use by conifers is attributed to 1) greater canopy storage capacity and interception loss (see section 4.1), 2) greater total leaf area and transpiration, or at least 3) a longer transpiration season; conifers also influence the timing of snowmelt and modify the seasonal discharge regime.

### 7.3.b. Seasonal Variations

Seasonal patterns of streamflow are fixed to a large extent by regional climate; forest cover influences are secondary, being superimposed upon the general flow regime. The topic of streamflow "regulation" by forests, in the sense of control of unfavorable extremes, has been overemphasized; for example, despite abundant evidence to the contrary, it is still a matter of "common knowledge" that forest cover can both prevent great floods and maintain streamflow during long periods of drought. The forest influence is real nonetheless, and significant, and though its role may be less dramatic than sometimes supposed, objective knowledge of its workings can yet be put to beneficial use.

A forest is an ecosystem in which interception prevents some precipitation from reaching the soil, and where plant roots extract moisture from deeper soil layers; as a result, when rainfall or snowmelt occur, the moisture storage opportunity is greater and a smaller proportion of the total supply is discharged to streams. It is not surprising, therefore, that the forest influence on streamflow is greater following periods of greater evapotranspiration. Douglass and Swank (1972) found that when a hardwood forest was cut, about 60% of the streamflow increase came during the low-flow period, July–November; the pattern illustrated in figure 7.9 is typical in the eastern United States where most precipitation occurs as rain.

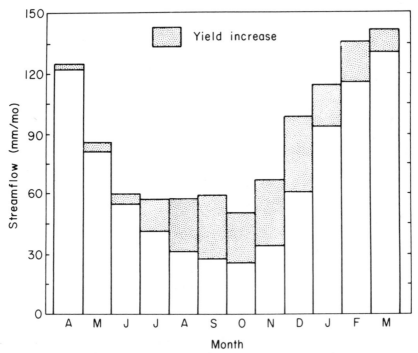

Figure 7.9. Seasonal distribution of streamflow increases following forest cutting (adapted from Douglass and Swank, 1972).

In areas where streams are fed predominately by snowmelt, the seasonal hydrograph peaks in spring or early summer; forest cover that shades the snowpack can delay snowmelt and shift the period of maximum discharge toward the warmer months. Under these conditions, water yield increases following forest removal appear predominantly during the snowmelt season, and maximum discharges occur earlier. Snowmelt discharge is treated in greater detail in section 9.4.

Forest type also plays a significant role in the modification of seasonal flow regimes. The general rule (for rainfall areas) is that any change in forest cover that results in a water yield change will have a greater effect during low-flow periods, but this may not be true for forest type changes. When hardwood forests are converted to pine, for example, the reduction in water yield occurs primarily during the dormant season, evidently as the result of greater interception by the coniferous type (Swank and Miner, 1968).

Clearcutting coniferous stands usually produces greater total yield increases, and the increases occur more uniformly by seasons because reductions in both summer transpiration and winter interception are reflected in the flow regime. None of the forest influences on streamflow timing is independent of climate, of course, and both precipitation type (rain versus snow) and seasonal distribution must be considered. In western Oregon, for example, where most precipitation occurs during the winter half-year, forest removal may cause especially high flows during fall months when soils on cutover areas become saturated earlier than those in the forest (Harr, 1976).

### 7.3.c. Flow Extremes

The popular notion that forests tend "to retard and lower flood crests and prolong increased flow in low-water periods" (Kittredge, 1948) was still in vogue among foresters until the middle of the current century. It is true, to a degree, that forests "lower flood crests," but the statement requires careful interpretation; some of the largest floods on record have occurred in forested drainages (see section 9.3). The attractive notion that the existence of forest cover will "prolong increased flow in low-water periods" is clearly false.

In evaluating the effects of forest cutting on peak stream discharges it is necessary to distinguish among 1) effects caused simply by tree felling with a minimum of soil disturbance, 2) those produced when exceptional care is taken in harvesting the tree crop, and 3) the more common effects that occur when poor harvesting practices are used (effects produced when forest cutting is followed by fire, site destruction, or alternative land uses are considered separately in section 9.1). Hoover (1944) demonstrated that tree felling alone, on a steep mountain catchment, had no significant effect on maximum discharges; in order to prevent soil disturbance "trees were left where they fell and no material was removed." In sharp contrast, Reinhart, Eschner, and Trimble

(1963) employed the common method of "commercial clearcutting," and even though there was no "serious disturbance of the forest floor except on limited areas of skidroads," maximum storm discharge increased by an order of magnitude.

Forest cutting effects on peak flow vary with catchment conditions, season, climate, and storm size, as well as with harvesting procedures, so it is difficult to generalize. Peak flows account for only a small part of the total yield increase, and frequently occur during seasons when the forest influence is small; since total yield increases commonly vary between 20 and 40% during the first

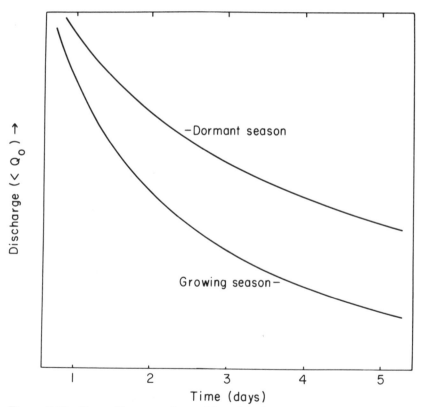

Figure 7.10. Streamflow recessions with and without transpiration (after Federer, 1973).

year (see table 7.6), typical peak flow increases during the same period are probably less than 20%. This assumption applies, of course, only to situations where cutting and harvesting operations follow the high standards that are used on most experimental catchments.

The influence of forest cutting on low flows is of great practical importance because the increases occur when streamflow is in greatest demand; average low-flow increases must be of the same order as total yield increases, and seasonal variations follow the same trends (see fig. 7.9). The transition from high to low flow, the recession limb of the hydrograph, is also influenced by cutting; Federer (1973) used the equation

$$Q = Q_o \left( e^{-1.7t} + e^{-0.35t} \right) \tag{7.50}$$

to describe the recession limb with transpiration occurring in a hardwood forest, where $Q_o$ is the initial flow rate at $t = 0$, $Q$ is the flow $t$ days later, and

$$Q = Q_o \left( e^{-1.7t} + e^{-0.16t} \right) \tag{7.51}$$

applies in the absence of transpiration. The difference in stream-flow recession (fig. 7.10) explains the fact that, during the growing season, transpiration removes water that would otherwise contribute to low flow.

## LITERATURE CITED

Albertson, M. L. and D. B. Simons. 1964. Fluid mechanics. In V. T. Chow, ed., *Handbook of Applied Hydrology*. New York: McGraw-Hill.

Anderson, H. W., M. D. Hoover, and K. G. Reinhart. 1976. *Forests and Water: Effects of Forest Managment on Floods, Sedimentation, and Water Supply*. Forest Service Technical Report PSW-18. Berkeley, Calif.: U.S. Department of Agriculture.

Boyer, D. G. 1976. "The Climatological Water Balance in a Mountainous Terrain." Master's thesis, West Virginia University, Morgantown.

Budyko, M. I. 1974. *Climate and Life*. New York: Academic Press.

Crawford, N. H. and R. K. Linsley. 1966. *Digital Simulation in Hydrology*. Civil Engineering Technical Report 39. Palo Alto, Calif.: Stanford University.

Douglass, J. E. and W. T. Swank. 1972. *Streamflow Modification Through Management of Eastern Forests*. Forest Service Research Paper SE-94. Asheville, N.C.: U.S. Department of Agriculture.

——. 1975. Effects of management practices on water quality and quantity: Coweeta Hydrologic Laboratory, North Carolina. In *Proceedings Municipal Watershed Symposium*, Forest Service Technical Report NE-13. Upper Darby, Pa.: U.S. Department of Agriculture.

Federer, C. A. 1973. Forest transpiration greatly speeds streamflow recesion. *Water Resources Research* 9:1599–1604.

Freeze, R. A. 1972. Role of subsurface flow in generating surface runoff. 1: Base flow contributions to channel flow. *Water Resources Research* 8:609–23.

Haar, R. D. 1976. *Forest Practices and Streamflow in Western Oregon*. Forest Service Technical Report PNW-49. Portland, Ore.: U.S. Department of Agriculture.

Hewlett, J. D. and A. R. Hibbert. 1967. Factors afffecting the response of small watersheds to precipitation in humid areas. In W. E. Sopper and H. W. Lull, eds., *International Symposium on Forest Hydrology*. New York: Pergamon Press.

Hewlett, J. D., H. W. Lull, and K. G. Reinhart. 1969. In defense of experimental watersheds. *Water Resources Research* 5:306–16.

Hewlett, J. D., J. C. Fortson, and G. B. Cunningham. 1977. The effect of rainfall intensity on storm flow and peak discharge from forest land. *Water Resources Research* 13:259–66.

Hoover, M. D. 1944. Effect of removal of forest vegetation upon water yields. *Transactions American Geophysical Union* 25:969–75.

Kent, K. M. 1973. *A Method for Estimating Volume and Rate of Runoff in Small Watersheds*. Soil Conservation Service Technical Paper 149. Washington, D.C.: U.S. Department of Agriculture.

Kittredge, J. 1948. *Forest Influences*. New York: McGraw-Hill.

Lee, R. 1977. Opportunities for increasing Water Supplies in the eastern United States by vegetation management. Report to the Forest Service, Contract OM-40-0452-7-1008. Wenatchee, Wash.: U.S. Department of Agriculture.

Lee, R. and S. Tajchman. 1977. Comment on "The effect of rainfall intensity on storm flow and peak discharge from forest land" by J. D. Hewlett, J. C. Fortson, and G. B. Cunningham. *Water Resources Research* 13:1025.

Leopold, L. B. and T. Maddock. 1953. *The Hydraulic Geometry of Stream Channels*, Geological Survey Professional Paper 252. Washington, D.C.: U.S. Department of Interior.

Linsley, R. K., M. A. Kohler, and J. L. H. Paulhus. 1975. *Hydrology for Engineers*. New York: McGraw-Hill.

Morisawa, M. E. 1967. Relation of discharge and stream length in eastern United States. In *Proceedings International Hydrology Symposium*, vol. I. Fort Collins, Colo.: Colorado State University.

Reigner, I. C. 1964. *Calibrating a Watershed by Using Climatological Data*. Forest Service Research Paper NE-15. Upper Darby, Pa.: U.S. Department of Agriculture.

Reinhart, K. G., A. R. Eschner, and G. R. Trimble. 1963. *Effect on Streamflow of Four Forest Practices*. Forest Service Research Paper NE-1. Upper Darby, Pa.: U.S. Department of Agriculture.

Sherman, L. K. 1932. Stream flow from rainfall by the unit-graph method. *Engineering News Record* 108:501–05.

Swank, W. T. and J. E. Douglass, 1974. Streamflow greatly reduced by converting deciduous hardwood stands to pine. *Science* 185:857–59.

Swank, W. T. and N. H. Miner. 1968. Conversion of hardwood covered watersheds to white pine reduces water yield. *Water Resources Research* 4:947–54.

Wisler, C. O. and E. F. Brater. 1959. *Hydrology*. New York: Wiley.

## SELECTED READINGS

Bruce, J. P. and R. H. Clark. 1966. *Hydrometeorology*. New York: Pergamon Press.

Chow, V. T. 1964. Runoff. In V. T. Chow, ed., *Handbook of Applied Hydrology*. New York: McGraw-Hill.

Davis, S. N. and R. J. M. De Wiest. 1966. *Hydrogeology*. New York: Wiley.

Hjelmfelt, A. T. and J. J. Casidy. *Hydrology for Engineers and Planners*. Ames: Iowa State University Press.

Miller, D. H. 1977. *Water at the Surface of the Earth*. New York: Academic Press.

Monke, E. J., ed. 1971. *Biological Effects in the Hydrological Cycle*. West Lafayette, Ind.: Purdue University.

# 8 WATER QUALITY

## by
## W. E. Sharpe and D. R. DeWalle

### 8.1. Quality Parameters

Forest hydrology, as the "science of water-related phenomena that are influenced by forest cover" (section 1.5.c), must include the study of forest influences on water quality. In fact, much of the current interest in forest hydrologic processes is related to their effects on erosion and sedimentation, water temperature, and water chemistry; forest water quality has become a major area of specialization. The conditions, processes, and human actions that ultimately determine the quality of water yield are the subject of this chapter.

### 8.1.a. Quality Definition

Pure water never occurs in a forested ecosystem. Water vapor that condenses on nuclei or other surfaces is "contaminated" on contact, so even fresh rainwater, which comes as close to being pure as any natural form, invariably contains at least minute amounts of dissolved minerals and salts. When rain strikes a tree canopy, a series of dynamic processes begins that may greatly alter the water's constituents and properties; accordingly, at any point in its movement through the ecosystem, *water quality* is defined in terms of its physical, chemical, and biological characteristics.

## 8.1.b. Pollution Definition

Since all natural waters are "contaminated" (impure), it is important to differentiate between "natural" or "normal" contamination and other levels that can be traced directly or indirectly to human activities. It should be clear, however, that any such distinction cannot be precise; some natural water is contaminated to such an extent that it is unfit for certain designated purposes (e.g., naturally brackish water is unfit for drinking, and "pure" water from a deep well may serve poorly as a cleansing agent). As a practical expedient, sources of human-caused pollution are usually identified by comparing water quality with the average or *background* contamination in the same area, but unaffected by the suspected source.

One state government defined *pollution* as "contamination of any waters . . . such as will create or is likely to create a nuisance or to render such water harmful, detrimental or injurious to public health, safety or welfare, or to domestic, municipal, commercial, industrial, agricultural, recreational, or other legitimate beneficial uses, or to livestock, wild animals, birds, fish or other aquatic life, including but not limited to such contamination by alteration of the physical, chemical or biological properties of such waters or change in temperature, taste, color or odor thereof, or the discharge of any liquid, gaseous, radioactive, solid or other substances into such waters" (Commonwealth of Pennsylvania, 1937). According to a simpler definition, free of legalese, water pollution is "any impairment of the suitability of water for any of its beneficial uses, actual or potential, by man-caused changes in the quality of water" (Warren, 1971); here the keywords are "impairment" and "beneficial use." Identification of impairments that might result from forest management activities, or the beneficial uses that such activities might preempt, requires the adoption of specific water quality standards.

## 8.1.c. Quality Standards

Water quality standards are extreme values (usually minima) used to indicate levels of constituents or properties at which water becomes either aesthetically offensive, economically unsuitable, or hygienically unfit for some intended use. Such standards are frequently adopted by industry, or by governments either as recommended criteria or regulatory instruments designed to safeguard public health. Some drinking water standards in the United States are given in table 8.1.

Water discharged from undisturbed forested catchments is generally suitable for a wide range of beneficial uses, but human

Table 8.1. Drinking Water Standards in the United States, EPA (1975, 1977)

| Mandatory | mg/l | Recommended | mg/l |
|---|---|---|---|
| *Chemical–inorganics* | | *Chemical* | |
| Arsenic | 0.05 | Chloride | 250 |
| Barium | 1.0 | Copper | 1 |
| Cadmium | 0.01 | Hydrogen sulfide | 0.05 |
| Chromium | 0.05 | Manganese | 0.05 |
| Fluoride | 1.4–2.4[a] | pH | 6.5–8.5 |
| Lead | 0.05 | Sulfate | 250 |
| Nitrate–nitrogen | 10.0 | Total dissolved solids | 500 |
| Selenium | 0.01 | Corrosivity | (non- |
| Silver | 0.05 | | corrosive) |
| *Chemical–organics* | | Foaming agents | 0.5 |
| Endrin | 0.0002 | | |
| Lindane | 0.004 | | |
| Methoxychlor | 0.1 | | |
| Toxaphene | 0.005 | | |
| 2, 4-D | 0.1 | | |
| 2, 4, 5 TP Silvex | 0.01 | | |
| Trihalomethanes (THM) | 0.10 | | |
| *Physical* (surface water supplies only) | | | |
| Turbidity | 1 NTU monthly average[b] | Odor | 3 threshold odor number |
| | 5 NTU average for two consecutive days | Color | 15 color units |
| *Biological* | | | |
| Coliform bacteria | 1 per 100 ml[c] | | |
| | 4 per 100 ml[d] | | |

[a] Depending on air temperature.
[b] NTU = nephelometric turbidity unit.
[c] As monthly mean.
[d] In one sample with <20 samples per month.

**Table 8.2. Water Quality Standards Relevant to Specific Forest Activities**

| Activity; uses potentially affected | Possible pollutants | Observations and analyses | Water quality standards[a] |
|---|---|---|---|
| *Timber Harvesting* | | | |
| Cold water fishery, trout stocking, public water supply, anadromous fishery | Thermal | Temperature | >18°C, or >BL |
| | Sediment | Turbidity | T |
| | Nutrient outflow | Nitrates, phosphates | >BL |
| | Logging debris | Dissolved oxygen; visual inspection | <BL |
| | | Biological sampling | BI <6 |
| *Camping* | | | |
| Cold and warm water fishery, water contact sports, public water supply | Sewage | Coliform bacteria | T; 10/ml for swimming |
| | | Nitrates | >BL |
| | | Specific conductance | >500 $\mu$mho/cm |
| | | Dissolved oxygen | <BL |
| | | Odor | Noticeable |
| | | Biological sampling | BI <6 |
| | | Dye trace | Positive dye test |
| | Sediment | Turbidity | T |
| *Forest Fertilization* | | | |
| Public water supply | Nitrates | Nitrates | T; >BL |

*Herbicides* (silvicultural)

| | | | |
|---|---|---|---|
| All water supplies and fisheries | Toxic herbicides and carriers | Herbicide used | 2, 4, D >0.1 mg/l<br>2, 4, 5 TP (Silvex) >0.01 mg/l |
| | | Biological sampling | Unexplained changes in benthic community structure |

*Pesticides*

| | | | |
|---|---|---|---|
| All water supplies and fisheries | Toxic pesticides and carriers | Pesticide used | Endrin >0.0002 mg/l<br>Lindane >0.004 mg/l<br>Toxaphene >0.005 mg/l<br>Methoxychlor >0.1 mg/l |
| | | Biological sampling | Unexplained changes in benthic community structure |

*Acid Rainfall*

| | | | |
|---|---|---|---|
| Public water supplies and fisheries | Low pH | pH<br>Biological sampling | <BL or historical level<br>Same as for pesticides |

*Oil-Gas Exploitation*

| | | | |
|---|---|---|---|
| All water supplies and fisheries | Salt brines<br>Oil<br>Low pH | Sodium, chloride, iron<br>Oil<br>pH<br>Biological sampling | >BL<br>Presence<br><BL<br>Same as for pesticides |

**Table 8.2.** (*Continued*)

| Activity; uses potentially affected | Possible pollutants | Observations and analysis | Water quality standards[a] |
|---|---|---|---|
| *Coal exploitation* | | | |
| All water supplies and fisheries | Acidity | Acidity | >BL |
| | Iron | Iron | >BL |
| | Manganese | Manganese | >BL |
| | Sulfates | Sulfates | >BL |
| | Dissolved solids | Specific conductance | >BL |
| | Low pH | pH | <BL |
| | Ferric hydroxide | Visual inspection | Presence |
| | | Biological sampling | Same as for pesticides |
| *Wildlife* (concentrations) | | | |
| Public water supply and water contact sports | Bacteria | Coliform bacteria | T; >10/ml for swimming |
| *Livestock Grazing* | | | |
| Public water supply and water contact sports | Bacteria | Bacteria | Same as for wildlife |
| | Sediment | Turbidity | T |
| *Highway Deicing Salts* | | | |
| Public water supply and water contact sports | Sodium | Sodium | >BL, or >20 mg/l |
| | Chlorides | Chlorides | >BL, or >250 mg/l |

[a]BL, background level; BI, biotic index (see section 8.5.c); mho, reciprocal ohms; T, see table 8.1 for drinking water standards.

activities within the forested ecosystem can have profound effects on the quality of water yield. Of primary concern are timber harvesting and other ecosystem disturbances; these are discussed in greater detail in sections 8.3 and 8.4. Table 8.2 summarizes key activities, potential water uses affected, potential pollutants, required observations and analyses, and applicable water quality standards.

## 8.2. Natural Quality

The characteristics of water are affected by both natural and human factors; where the human influence is small, water quality can be viewed as a product of climatological, geochemical, physiographic, edaphic, and forest influences. Natural water quality varies considerably from place to place, depending on local combinations of controlling factors, and also fluctuates in response to seasonal and aperiodic events. When considering the effects of specific ecosystem phenomena, it is important to recognize that causal agents are interdependent, and act in concert, so that any single-factor analysis of environmental influences on water quality is apt to be misleading.

### 8.2.a. Climatological Influences

The atmosphere influences water quality directly because it is the source of both water and impurities. Significant amounts of nitrogen, sulphur, chlorides, phosphorus, hydrogen ions, aerosols, and gases are brought to the surface by precipitation, dry fallout, and diffusion; an example of dissolved substance concentrations in precipitation is given in table 8.3 along with simultaneous concentrations in local streamflow. The acidity of precipitation is treated separately, in the context of an ecosystem disturbance, in section 8.4.f.

Climate also affects the quality of water yield by determining the absolute amount of water input (diluting influence) as well as regulating losses to evapotranspiration (concentrating effect); if,

Table 8.3. Average Concentrations of Dissolved
Substances in Precipitation and
Streamflow from Undisturbed Forest
Catchments in New Hampshire
(Likens et al., 1977)

| | Concentration (mg/l) | |
|---|---|---|
| Substance | Precipitation | Streamflow |
| $H^+$ | 0.073 | 0.012 |
| $Ca^{2+}$ | 0.16 | 1.65 |
| $Na^+$ | 0.12 | 0.87 |
| $Mg^{2+}$ | 0.04 | 0.38 |
| $K^+$ | 0.07 | 0.23 |
| $NH_4^+$ | 0.22 | 0.04 |
| $NO_3^-$ | 1.47 | 2.01 |
| $SO_4^{2-}$ | $2.9^a$ | 6.3 |
| $PO_4^{3-}$ | 0.008 | $0.002^b$ |
| $Cl^-$ | 0.47 | 0.55 |

[a] Does not include aerosols or gases.
[b] Does not include suspended or bedload discharges.

for example, streamflow volume were 50% of precipitation volume,
then, in the absence of additions or losses of pollutants within the
ecosystem, streamflow concentrations would be doubled. The data
of Likens et al. (1977), given in table 8.3, show that average ionic
concentrations in streamwater were more than twice as great as that
found in precipitation, even though 62% of precipitation appeared
as stream discharge (concentrating effect 1.6). Obviously there are
changes in concentrations of dissolved and suspended substances
as water moves through a forest ecosystem, but many of these are
also climate-related.

Climate affects water quality indirectly through its influences
on rock weathering, soil development, organic matter decomposition, soil chemical reactions, and biological processes; rainfall
characteristics help to determine surface and channel erosion
potential, mass wasting, and sediment production. Groundwater
temperature, which largely determines the temperatures of springs
and effluent streams under forest cover, varies only within a few

Table 8.4. Oxygen Solubility as a Function of Temperature and Pressure

| Temperature (°C) | Atmospheric pressure (mb) | | | | |
|---|---|---|---|---|---|
| | 1000 | 900 | 800 | 700 | 600 |
| 0 | 14.6 | 13.2 | 11.7 | 10.3 | 8.8 |
| 5 | 12.8 | 11.5 | 10.2 | 9.0 | 7.7 |
| 10 | 11.3 | 10.1 | 9.0 | 7.9 | 6.8 |
| 15 | 10.0 | 9.0 | 8.0 | 7.0 | 6.0 |
| 20 | 9.0 | 8.1 | 7.2 | 6.3 | 5.4 |
| 25 | 8.2 | 7.4 | 6.5 | 5.7 | 4.9 |

degrees of mean annual air temperature; water temperature determines the solubility of oxygen, and indirectly the composition and productivity of aquatic ecosystems. Oxygen solubility in water ($O_2$ in mg/l) is given approximately by

$$O_2 = 14.6 \frac{p}{1000} e^{-0.024T} \tag{8.1}$$

where atmospheric pressure ($p$) is in mb and temperature ($T$) in °C (accurate to within 2% for $0 < T < 25°C$); table 8.4 shows that the values range from about 5 to 15 mg/l under ordinary conditions.

## 8.2.b. Geochemical Influences

The quality of water yield from catchments is strongly influenced by the mineral composition and solubility of underlying rocks. Water that percolates through catchment soil and substrata en route to the stream may be greatly "enriched" in terms of dissolved solids; whereas precipitation usually contains 10 ppm or less of dissolved material, it is not uncommon to find from $10^2$ to $10^3$ ppm in groundwater, and values greater than $10^5$ ppm have been reported in extreme cases. Some of the major and secondary constituents of groundwater are listed in table 8.5; Davis and DeWiest (1966) also listed 23 minor and 21 trace constituents.

It seems reasonable to expect correlation between the mineral composition of water and that of the geologic formation with which the water has been in contact; table 8.6 is a summary of some

Table 8.5. Classification of Dissolved Solids in
Groundwater (Davis and DeWiest,
1966)

| Major constituents ($10^0$–$10^3$ ppm) | Secondary constituents ($10^{-2}$–$10^1$ ppm) |
|---|---|
| Sodium | Iron |
| Calcium | Strontium |
| Magnesium | Potassium |
| Bicarbonate | Carbonate |
| Sulphate | Nitrate |
| Chloride | Fluoride |
| Silica | Boron |

Minor constituents ($10^{-4}$ – $10^{-1}$ ppm): 23
Trace constituents ($<10^{-3}$ ppm): 21

general relationships reported by Davis and DeWiest (1966). It is important to recognize, however, that other influences may have an overshadowing effect; according to Hem (1970), "differences in climate or other influences on the weathering process can produce very different types of water from essentially similar source rocks" so that "it is not likely that a completely satisfactory system of classifying water could ever be developed that was based entirely on composition of source rocks." Certainly in assaying the geochemical influence in small catchments there is no substitute for direct observation.

Streams with high alkalinity due to a continuous source of carbonate, bicarbonate, phosphate, or hydroxide ions are well buffered against pH changes; hydrogen ions from any added acid combine chemically with alkalinity-causing ions. On the other hand, streams flowing from areas where rocks are resistant to weathering (usually rocks high in quartz such as sandstone), and poor in alkalinity-causing ions, will be poorly buffered; additions of acid to such streams (following coal mining, for example) can cause serious reductions in pH and degradation of aquatic ecosystems. Most natural waters are buffered by a carbon dioxide-carbonate buffer system that serves to stabilize pH in the 6.5–8.5

Table 8.6. Some General Relationships Between Rock Types and Water Quality (Davis and DeWiest, 1966)

| Rock type | Water quality |
|---|---|
| *Metamorphic and plutonic igneous* | Almost always excellent; exceptions in arid regions and coastal areas; generally high silica content; low total dissolved solids |
| Dolomite, marble | Moderate to high hardness (calcium, magnesium) |
| Serpentine, dolomite, gabbro, and amphibolite | Hardness due more to magnesium than to calcium concentrations |
| Diorite, syenite | Dissolved silica 25–55 ppm |
| Quartzite, marble, slate | Dissolved silica <30 ppm |
| Granite, gneiss, rhyolite, and mica schist | Slightly acid, lower total dissolved solids and hardness |
| Gabbro, diorite, andesite, and hornblende gneiss | Slightly alkaline, higher total dissolved solids and hardness |
| *Volcanic* | Good to excellent; exceptions near hot springs; tends to be "calcium-magnesium-bicarbonate" water, or when acidic "sodium-bicarbonate" with high silica content |
| *Sedimentary* | Variable; salinity increases with depth |
| Shale | High amounts of iron and fluoride; pH 5.5–7.0 |
| Limestone | Low silica; high calcium and magnesium; pH >7.0 |
| Sandstone | Variable; deep aquifers may yield soft water with high sodium and bicarbonate contents |

range; carbonic acid, formed by the reaction of carbon dioxde with water, promotes the dissolution of carbonate rocks, but in turn reacts with carbonate to produce the bicarbonate that ionizes to form a weak base.

## 8.2.c. Physiographic Influences

Land form affects erosion and sedimentation, water movement, and local climate, all of which bear directly or indirectly on water discharge quality. Sediment yield $(Y)$ per unit area generally decreases with catchment size $(A_c)$, as indicated by the data of table 8.7; the relationship can be given in a form similar to equation 7.26 (as applied to peak discharge rates):

$$\frac{Y}{A_c} = kA_c^{x-1} \qquad (8.2)$$

where $x < 1$. The correlation with size may be purely fortuitious, however, since in general smaller headwater catchments are steeper, and Schumm (1954) found the depth of sediment yield to be closely correlated with average basin slope.

Slope steepness $(S)$ influences mass soil movements and overland transport of eroded soil particles. Steep slopes contribute to shear stress forces acting on a soil mass, and landslides may occur when the resistance to downslope movement is reduced, for example by high soil moisture content following heavy rain. Where overland flow occurs, the velocity of running water is proportional to $S^{0.5}$ (from equation 7.22), the size of sediments carried is proportional to $S$, and their mass to $S^3$.

Topography also may cause accumulations of water in localized depressions, bogs, or swamps. This increases the residence time of water in the catchment, and may lead to increased concentrations of dissolved solids, or chemical changes. Water emanating from bogs often contains dissolved organic acids, and may be highly colored by virtue of its prolonged contact with decomposing organic matter.

Table 8.7. Mean Sediment Production as a Function
of Watershed Area in the United States
(adapted from Gottschalk, 1964)

| Watershed area (km$^2$) | Mean sediment yield | |
|---|---|---|
| | (mm/yr) | (m$^3$/ha · yr) |
| $A_c < 25$ | 1.81 | 18.1 |
| $25 < A_c < 250$ | 0.76 | 7.6 |
| $250 < A_c < 2500$ | 0.48 | 4.8 |
| $2500 < A_c$ | 0.24 | 2.4 |

Land form also introduces significant variations in climate that affect water quality directly and interact with other controlling factors as indicated in section 8.2.a. Precipitation is generally greater at higher elevations but air, soil, and water temperatures are lower, as is atmospheric pressure and consequently the solubility of oxygen in water; factors affecting stream temperature and dissolved oxygen content may be more critical at higher elevations. Topographic exposure influences vegetation type, density, and phenology; the radiant energy exchange; drying rates; the frequencies of fires and freeze-thaw cycles; infiltration rates; and soil chemistry and microorganisms—all of which contribute directly or indirectly to *water yield quality*.

### 8.2.d. Edaphic Influences

The influence of forest soil on water yield quality depends on its ability to absorb, modify, and add to the leachate transmitted from the atmosphere, canopy, and litter. Edaphic influences, which depend on physical, chemical, and biological characteristics of soil, can be inferred to some extent from these properties and from an understanding of soil water movements and intrasystem nutrient cycling. In this case it is especially important to recognize the interdependence of various ecosystem control mechanisms.

The most important impurities in natural water are mineral and organic sediments eroded from soil. Soil *erodibility*, a measure of the tendency of soil to be detached and moved, is intuitively clear but difficult to quantify precisely; it is related to soil texture and degree of aggregation, or the difficulty with which individual soil particles can be dispersed in water. Smaller soil particles (clay and silt) are most easily transported by water, and generally constitute the bulk of sediment discharge, but are more resistant to dispersion; the larger particles (sand) are more easily detached, but are less likely to be suspended or transported.

Any circumstance that reduces the infiltration capacity of soil makes it susceptible to erosion by overland flow; in this case the intrinsic properties of soil are important but other factors (e.g., climate, physiography, and vegetation) may be overshadowing. Infiltrating water delivers dissolved substances to soil, but it also has a leaching effect, dissolving minerals released by chemical weathering and transporting organic acids produced by decomposing organic materials; the quality of soil effluent must depend, therefore, on the mineral composition, chemical reaction rates, and ionic exchange capacity of soil. In forest soils, nutrient losses in percolating water are reduced because organic matter provides additional adsorption sites, and plant nutrient uptake and recycling maintain an enriched rooting zone.

In general, factors affecting water movement and storage, or the ability of soil to adsorb cations, influence the quality of percolating water. Coarse-textured, rocky, and shallow soils facilitate rapid drainage of infiltrating water, but provide less opportunity for cation adsorption, uptake by plants, and other chemical interactions. Heavy-textured (clayey) soils usually have lower infiltration capacities, but their greater surface area per unit volume provides greater numbers of exchange sites for the adsorption of cations.

### 8.2.e. Forest Influences

Forest cover maintains very low erosion rates, and consequently low suspended sediment concentrations in streams; design curves for suspended load estimation developed by Fleming (1969) are useful in comparing relative efficiencies of various cover types:

Desert–scrub: $Y = 4.9(10^5)Q^{0.72}$ (8.3)

Scrub–grass: $Y = 2.0(10^5)Q^{0.65}$ (8.4)

Grass–conifer: $Y = 6.7(10^4)Q^{0.82}$ (8.5)

Conifer–hardwood: $Y = 4.5(10^3)Q^{1.02}$ (8.6)

where $Y$ is suspended load in m ton/yr, and $Q$ is mean discharge in $m^3$/sec. The general relationships are illustrated in figure 8.1 for the range of discharges typical of smaller watersheds. Forest litter protects the soil from raindrop impact and helps maintain high infiltration capacity, so surface erosion is seldom a serious problem in undisturbed forests; tree roots also help bind the soil mass, greatly reducing the hazard of mass soil movements even on steep slopes.

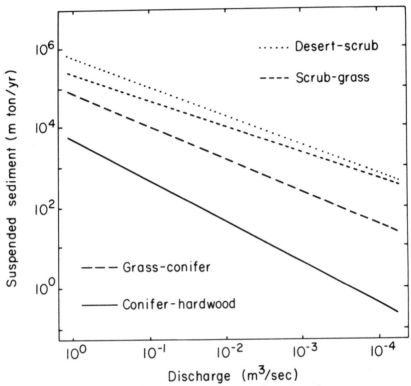

Figure 8.1. Suspended sediment production as a function of average stream discharge for various cover types (adapted from Fleming, 1969).

Trees affect the chemical quality of water both directly and indirectly; Likens et al. (1977) found that both throughfall and stemflow are considerably enriched, by contact with trees, in all the major cations and anions except hydrogen, which is reduced. Tarrant et al. (1968) reported increases in nitrogen, principally as organic nitrogen, in throughfall and especially in stemflow; the increase in organic nitrogen was markedly higher in stemflow from alder than from conifers. Alteration of the chemical composition of stemflow and throughfall has been attributed to 1) solution of material deposited on trees from the atmosphere during nonstorm periods, 2) leaching from plant tissues, and 3) action of nitrifying and ammonifying bacteria and other microorganisms.

Uptake of nutrients by trees and their eventual return to the soil in litterfall must be recognized for its role in influencing seasonal variations in the concentration of some streamflow nutrients. Nitrate nitrogen levels often rise appreciably when forest uptake of nutrients ceases during the dormant season. Litterfall, especially from deciduous species, added to water bodies with low flushing rates may increase true color, iron, bicarbonate, and manganese concentrations, and decrease dissolved oxygen levels and pH (Slack and Feltz, 1968).

The forest substantially modifies the heat balance at ground level, especially during periods of positive net radiation, and reduces soil temperature fluctuations. Closed forest stands limit the receipt of solar radiation by streams during daytime, thereby reducing stream temperature maxima (see section 8.3.b). Forest streams tend to have relatively stable temperature regimes with a daily range of only a few degrees Celsius.

## 8.3. Timber Harvesting

Timber harvesting is an ecosystem disturbance with potentially drastic impacts on the quality of water yield; accelerated erosion and sedimentation, thermal pollution, and changes in water chemistry and the normal nutrient cycle are common hazards. Greatest damage usually occurs where skidtrails, logging roads, and heavy machinery remove or compact forest floor organic layers, or where riparian zones are disturbed. The extent of the impact of timber harvesting on water quality depends on the degree of vegetational change, logging methods used, the proportion of watershed area disturbed, and the rate of natural or manipulated rehabilitation.

### 8.3.a. Sediment Yield

Erosion and sedimentation are of particular concern in forest water management because "erosion is reported to cause 80 percent of the deterioration of water quality . . . products of erosion interact strongly with other components, and . . . erosion is directly affected by forest management" (Anderson, Hoover, and Reinhart, 1976). Increases in erosion and sedimentation following deforestation have been reported for centuries, but only the more recent studies permit detailed analysis of specific causes; the data of table 8.8 illustrate several important aspects of the clearcutting effect. Kochenderfer and Aubertin (1975) found that 1) when exceptional care was used in the location, construction, and maintenance of skidtrails, roads, and landings, stream turbidity increases were relatively small compared with the effects produced by commercial harvesting methods, 2) in undisturbed and carefully harvested catchments, maximum stormflow turbidities were an order of magnitude greater than base flow averages, but where commercial harvesting was practiced the ratio was two orders of magnitude, and 3) the greater initial disturbance persisted longer, but in a humid climate natural rehabilitation invariably occurred within a few years.

Increases in all three major types of erosion, i.e., surface erosion, mass-wasting, and channel scour, can be induced by timber harvesting. Surface erosion is increased because mineral soil is exposed to raindrop impact, and the detached particles are trans-

Table 8.8. Effects of Timber Harvesting on Stream Turbidity in a
Humid Region (Kochenderfer and Aubertin, 1975)

| Treatment | Stream turbidity (JTU) | |
|---|---|---|
| | Base flow mean | Stormflow maximum |
| Commercial clearcut[a] | | |
| During logging | 490 | 56000 |
| First year after cut | 38 | 5000 |
| Second year after cut | 2 | 170 |
| Silvicultural clearcut[b] | | |
| During logging | 6 | 90 |
| First year after cut | 5 | 35 |
| Second year after cut | 2 | 23 |
| Undisturbed control | 2 | 25 |

[a] Logger's choice; water values not considered.
[b] Exceptional care to protect water values.

Table 8.9. Relative Disturbance from Roads in Logged Areas
(Rice, Rothacher, and Megahan, 1972)

| Logging technique | Cutting method | Location | Area disturbed (%) | | |
|---|---|---|---|---|---|
| | | | Roads | Other | Total |
| Jammer | Group selection | Idaho | 25–30 | – | 25–30 |
| High lead | Clearcut | Oregon | 6.2 | 3.6 | 9.8 |
| Tractor | Selection | California | 2.7 | 5.7 | 8.4 |
| Tractor | Selection | Idaho | 2.2 | 6.8 | 9.0 |
| Tractor | Group selection | Idaho | 1.0 | 6.7 | 7.7 |
| Skyline | Clearcut | Oregon | 2.0 | – | 2.0 |
| Helicopter | Clearcut | (Estimated) | 1.2 | – | 1.2 |

ported by surface runoff from compacted areas; the most critical zones are skidtrails, log landings, and haul roads used to transport felled timber. The fraction of catchment area disturbed by the transport system is determined by the care used in its location, construction, and maintenance, and by the choice of logging technique; some reported values, as summarized by Rice, Rothacher, and Megahan (1972), are given in table 8.9.

Where slopes are steep and vegetation is difficult to establish, mass-wasting may be the dominant erosional type associated with timber harvesting. Road cuts remove support for the upslope soil mass, and reduced evapotranspiration following deforestation increases the frequency of soil saturation and mass soil movements; gradual loss of soil-shear strength following root decay may also be a contributing factor. The data of table 8.10 (Rice, 1977) illustrate the effect of vegetation type (presumably correlated with the depth and density of roots systems) on mass movements.

Stream discharge increases following deforestation may lead to accelerated channel erosion. Heede (1972) has shown that large debris added to stream channels following natural mortality reduces the number of gravel bars and amount of bed load movement. On the other hand, excessive debris from logging may effectively dam a stream and create devastating effects when the dams fail during high flows; other effects of channel debris on water quality are discussed in section 8.3.c.

Table 8.10. Disturbance by Mass Soil
Movement on Steep Slopes
(Rice, 1977)

| Vegetation type | Area disturbed (%) |
|---|---|
| Sage and barren | 23.9 |
| Perennial grass | 11.9 |
| Annual grass | 6.5 |
| Riparian woodland | 5.3 |
| Chamise chaparral | 3.3 |
| Oak chaparral | 2.6 |
| Broadleaf chaparral | 1.2 |

## 8.3.b. Thermal Pollution

Deforestation exposes forest streams to direct solar radiation, causes significant increases in stream temperatures during clear days, and leads to important physical and biological changes in the aquatic ecosystem; maximum temperature increases of 5 to 10°C are commonly reported (Lee and Samuel, 1976). As water temperature increases, its oxygen-holding capacity decreases (see section 8.2.a, table 8.4), rates of chemical processes are accelerated, and biological oxygen demand levels increase. Temperature plays a major role in promoting algal growth and eutrophic processes, and its effect on all organisms is important because the species in an aquatic environment are interdependent; in particular, microorganisms at the base of the food chain are directly affected.

The energy budget as applied to forest stream temperature changes can be given in the form

$$\frac{\Delta T}{\Delta t} = \frac{E_n}{\rho c D} \tag{8.7}$$

where $\Delta T$ (°C) is the change in water temperature over the time interval $\Delta t$, $E_n$ is the net energy exchange rate per unit of surface area ($E_n$ is energy absorbed in heating or released in cooling), $\rho c$ is the thermal capacity of water (1 cal/cm$^3$ · °C), and $D$ is mean stream depth. As the stream flows through a clearcut area, it will be exposed over some length ($L$); the period of exposure ($\Delta t$) is given by

$$\Delta t = \frac{L}{V} \tag{8.8}$$

where $V$ is the mean stream velocity, and the temperature increase caused by deforestation is

$$\Delta T = \frac{E_n}{\rho c V} \frac{L}{D} \tag{8.9}$$

from the combination of equations 8.7 and 8.8, or

$$\Delta T = \frac{E_n}{\rho c} \frac{A}{Q} \tag{8.10}$$

where $A$ is the exposed area of stream surface and $Q$ is the discharge rate. This analysis assumes that groundwater inflow is negligible along the exposed segment, and that isothermal conditions (complete mixing) exist at any stream cross-section.

Equations 8.9 and 8.10 show that $\Delta T$ is directly proportional to $E_n$, $L$, and $A$, and inversely proportional to $V$, $D$, and $Q$. In equation 8.9, $L/D$ is a dimensionless parameter (length/depth) that can be used to show the relative magnitudes of temperature changes to be expected for typical ranges of environmental conditions. Solutions to equation 8.9 for $L = 10^3 D$ are given in table 8.11; if, under the forest canopy, $\Delta T/L$ is negligible for short stream segments, the tabled values are temperature increases that would be

Table 8.11. Temperature Increases (°C)
in Exposed Stream Segments
(Equation 8.9 for $L = 10^3 D$)

| $V$ (m/min) | $E_n$ (1y/min) | | |
|---|---|---|---|
| | 0.4 | 0.8 | 1.2 |
| 1 | 4.0 | 8.0 | 12.0 |
| 2 | 2.0 | 4.0 | 6.0 |
| 5 | 0.8 | 1.6 | 2.4 |
| 10 | 0.4 | 0.8 | 1.2 |
| 20 | 0.2 | 0.4 | 0.6 |

induced by clearcutting or exposure of the stream to the open atmosphere.

In any particular instance, the stream parameters $L$, $D$, $V$, $A$, and $Q$ can be obtained by direct observation, but $E_n$ is the residual in the energy-budget equation:

$$E_n = R + H + L_v E + B \qquad (8.11)$$

where $B$ is conduction into the streambed, and the individual terms may take either positive or negative values. During clear days $R$ is positive (delivering energy to the water), $H$ is positive when the air is warmer than water, and $B$ is usually zero or negative (heat loss from water to streambed); $L_v E$ may be either positive or negative, but its absolute value is relatively small for cool water. Research reported by Brown (1972), DeWalle and Kappel (1975), and Lee (1978) has shown that, for short exposed stream segments,

$$L + H + L_v E \simeq 0 \qquad (8.12)$$

where $L$ is longwave net radiation, so that

$$E_n \simeq S + B \qquad (8.13)$$

where $S$ is shortware net radiation; in some instances $B$ may be negligibly small (in clayey stream bottoms, for example) and

$$E_n \simeq S \qquad (8.14)$$

can be assumed as a first approximation.

Downstream of an exposed or deforested segment, stream temperature decreases in response to reduced energy input, groundwater inflow, or mixing with cooler tributary streams; the rate of decrease owing to reduced energy input is more gradual than the rate of increase during exposure. The general relationship was documented by Day (1976) who studied temperature changes in forest streams crossing areas cleared for power line corridors in New Hampshire, West Virginia, and Georgia; figure 8.2 shows a typical horizontal profile of stream temperature as influenced by clearing. Cooling caused by groundwater inflow or tributary mixing may be more abrupt; the temperature of the mixed flow is sim-

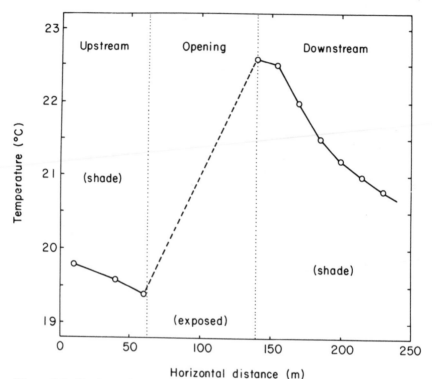

Figure 8.2. Horizontal profile of stream temperature showing the effect of an exposed segment (generalized after Day, 1976).

ply the weighted mean:

$$\overline{T} = \frac{QT + Q_i T_i}{Q + Q_i} \tag{8.15}$$

where $Q$ and $T$ are the stream discharge and temperature, and $Q_i$ and $T_i$ are corresponding inflow values.

Daily maximum temperatures are increased, but daily minima are affected very little by the removal of stream shade. Figure 8.3 shows a typical diurnal pattern of stream temperatures in forested and clearcut catchments as reported by Lee and Samuel (1976). The figure shows that maximum temperatures are not only much greater in exposed streams, but also that the maxima occur much earlier in the day.

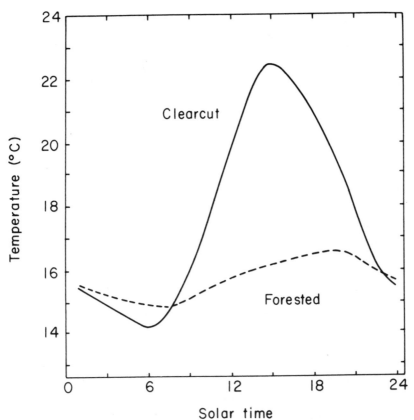

Figure 8.3. Typical diurnal pattern of stream temperatures during clear weather in forested and clearcut catchments (Lee and Samuel, 1976).

## 8.3.c. Nutrient Cycling

Timber harvesting alters the normal nutrient cycle in the forest, and may ultimately lead to changes in the nutrient content of discharge water; nutrient outflow occurs as dissolved or suspended solids, or as bed load discharge. The disruption occurs because of reduced nutrient uptake by the residual forest, and as the result of increased geochemical weathering and organic matter decomposition caused by changes in microclimate at the soil surface. The magnitude of the effect varies considerably with forest type and condition, climate, soil characteristics, and geology, and its longevity depends on the rapidity of reforestation.

Timber harvesting is usually accompanied by temporary increases in dissolved nitrate-nitrite concentrations; concentrations following cutting are usually below the drinking water standard, but may exceed 20 mg/l in some instances (Likens, Bormann, and Johnson, 1969). Both Likens, Bormann, and Johnson, and Fredrikson (1971) reported increased concentrations of Na, K, Ca, and Mg in streams following clearcutting; Lynch et al. (1975) found that "clearcutting had little if any apparent effect on the concentration" of these cations, but no pretreatment calibration data were available to justify the conclusion. Other than causing temporary increases in nitrate-nitrite concentrations, timber harvesting effects on nutrient discharges cannot be generalized or predicted on the basis of current knowledge.

Logging debris that enters stream channels either as finely-divided wood residue or large pieces of slash and tree bole may present serious problems for the aquatic ecosystem. Fine debris may be incorporated into the bottom sediments and interfere with the reaeration needed for successful development of salmon fry and benthic organisms; it may also serve as a substrate for decomposing organisms and exert a demand on dissolved oxygen, or decrease the thermal conductivity of rock streambeds and increase midday water temperatures. Large debris may form dams in stream channels, act as a barrier to fish movement, or lead to channel scour when dams fail during high flows; the damming effect, by reducing stream velocity, also tends to increase midday temperatures, and allows oxidizable and color-imparting substances to leach from the debris.

Timber harvesting that does not disturb the riparian zone will have a minimum impact on stream quality; sediment yield, thermal pollution, and logging debris problems can usually be solved by leaving buffer strips or no-cut zones along stream channels, including intermittent and ephemeral reaches. The width of buffer strip needed to control logging impact varies with site conditions (e.g., slope steepness, soil and erodibility, climate, and expected runoff) and the nature of the pollution problem to be avoided.

Narrow buffer strips may suffice on gentle slopes, where irregular surfaces form numerous natural debris basins, or where rapid revegetation can be anticipated; in steep terrain, without surface depressions, or where natural rehabilitation is slow, wider zones are required.

Buffer strips left for sedimentation and logging debris control do not require the existence of large trees, but if the riparian zone is selectively logged, exceptional care must be taken to avoid soil disturbance and logging debris pollution. Thermal pollution can only be avoided by maintaining adequate shade; no-cut strips of about 30-m width have proven adequate for temperature control, and for small streams shading by understory vegetation may be adequate. Buffer strips are also important in connection with other common ecosystem disturbances described in the following section.

## 8.4. Ecosystem Disturbance

Disturbances other than timber harvesting that affect the quality of water yield include those associated with silvicultural operations and the use of forest land for recreation, grazing, and wildlife production. Also, prescribed burning and wildfire can disrupt normal nutrient cycling, modify soil physical and chemical properties, and increase overland flow, erosion, and sedimentation. In recent times there has been an acceleration of disturbances caused by acid precipitation, the introduction of chemicals and wastes into forest ecosystems, and the extraction of mineral resources.

### 8.4.a. Silvicultural Manipulations

Silvicultural management operations that produce no detectable change in the gross water balance may nevertheless cause subtle changes in nutrient cycling, aquatic biota, and water quality. The effects of auxiliary activities, such as prescribed burning and chemical wastewater applications, have been most studied; these are treated separately in sections 8.4.e, g, and h, respectively. Little direct information is available with respect to other minor changes, many of which must be inferred from biological indicators in aquatic ecosystems.

Manipulation of the forest overstory to reduce heavy shade in the riparian zone can be beneficial to aquatic ecosystem production. At the same time, since many types of aquatic insect larvae feed preferentially on certain tree leaves, removal of the preferred species constitutes removal of food supply. Wallace (1974) found that stonefly larvae, a common inhabitant of Appalachian streams, prefer leaves of alder, dogwood, sourwood, and elm over those of white oaks, rhododendron, and white pine.

Wallace also compared populations of bottom-dwelling organisms in streams draining watersheds at the Coweeta Hydrologic Laboratory where silvicultural manipulations had produced different cover types from the original hardwood forest; his data are given in table 8.12. The total biomass of benthic organisms on the coppice hardwood watershed was significantly higher than on the others, whereas that on the pine forest catchment was lower. Wallace concluded that the type and amount of leaf detritus was a major factor in accounting for the differences.

Forest species also affect the quality of throughfall and stem-flow; Tarrant et al. (1968) reported a five-fold increase in throughfall nitrogen content beneath red alder, and Tarrant (1969) found annual inputs of 112 kg/ha of nitrogen under alder compared to 36 kg/ha beneath conifer overstory. Other studies have shown that throughfall is relatively rich in calcium, potassium, and magnesium (Ovington, 1968), and that the additional nutrients have definite effects on soil properties (Zinke, 1962); Voight (1960) showed

Table 8.12. Average Monthly Total Numbers and Biomass of Benthic Organisms (Wallace, 1974).

| Cover type | Number ($1/m^2$) | Biomass ($g/m^2$) |
|---|---|---|
| White pine forest | 716 | 0.59 |
| Hardwood forest | 804 | 1.07 |
| Coppice hardwoods | 783 | 2.75 |

that stemflow from beech did not contain as many nutrients as that from red pine and eastern hemlock. Despite the observed local effects, no one has yet determined the influence of species on the quality of catchment water yield.

### 8.4.b. Forest Recreation

Recreational activities in forests can have very serious water quality impacts, ranging from the erosion and sedimentation associated with off-road use of recreational vehicles to water pollution from sewage facilities. Nutrients, bacteria, and organic loadings from human waste disposal have much greater potential for damage to water quality than most other disturbances discussed in this chapter. Consequently, the provision of adequate sewage treatment facilities in remote areas, a service that most recreationists take for granted, has been the focus of much concern.

Even small amounts of untreated sewage can raise stream bacteria levels above allowable (health standard) limits and cause illness to those who use the water. The introduction of these oxygen-demanding wastes into the stream environment can also lead to a decline in fish food organisms, a loss of fish reproductive capability, and even direct fish mortality. Finally, the continuous addition of sewage nutrients (primarily phosphorus and nitrogen) to waterways may stimulate the growth of aquatic plants and weeds, which ultimately interfere with recreational activities, and can also lead to fish mortality.

Sewage treatment processes are designed to prevent water quality problems by processing wastes prior to discharge to streams or groundwater; commonly used treatment methods, and their relative efficiencies, are listed in table 8.13. The tabled data show that substantial nutrient removal is possible only where tertiary treatment or land application are employed. The costs involved in adequate treatment for remote recreational facilities are often prohibitive, although either an aerated lagoon, or package plants combined with land application, may be feasible for larger recreational developments.

In remote areas the vault privy remains one of the most effective nonpolluting methods of waste disposal. The vaults can be

Table 8.13. Sewage Treatment Methods and Some Typical Values
of Their Pollutant Removal Efficiency

| Method | Effluent quality (mg/l) | | | Bacteria $(10^7C/l)^b$ |
|---|---|---|---|---|
| | $BOD^a$ | N | P | |
| Raw sewage | 200 | 40 | 10 | 10.0 |
| Conventional: primary | 70 | 30 | 10 | — |
| secondary | 26 | 18 | 7 | 0.2 |
| tertiary | 5 | — | 0.5 | <0.2 |
| Ponds, aerated lagoons | 35 | 30 | 8 | <0.2 |
| Land application$^c$ | 1 | 3 | 0.1 | 0.0 |
| Package plants | 7.5 | $15^d$ | $22^e$ | — |
| Septic tanks (no drain field) | 158 | 38 | 14 | 11 |
| Vault privies | No effluent with toilet facilities only | | | |
| Composting toilets | No effluent with toilet facilities only | | | |
| Recycle systems | No effluent with toilet facilities only | | | |

$^a$Biochemical oxygen demand.
$^b$Total coliforms.
$^c$Assumes pretreatment in aerated lagoon.
$^d$As $NO_3$-N.
$^e$As phosphate.

emptied periodically with ultimate disposal at an accepted treatment facility, or a new vault can be installed after sealing the old one. If less primitive facilities are required a mineral oil recycling system, or a larger vault with minimum flush toilet fixtures, may be used; in the latter case the vault or holding tank must be emptied more frequently.

Composting toilets are being tested for use in remote area sewage disposal, but how well they will function is still uncertain. These systems require careful management and a source of heat to prevent condensation. They are advantageous in that, when operated properly, the compost is relatively pathogen-free, eliminating the problem of treatment before disposal.

Land application sites must be chosen carefully to avoid secondary pollution problems, and such systems must be closely managed. Winter operation of these systems in cold climates is not advisable, nor is continuous operation at a site for more than one year. Problems associated with forest irrigation using treated sewage effluent are treated in greater detail in section 8.4.h.

Other recreation-related pollution problems include erosion and sedimentation from access roads, hiking trails, and off-road compactions caused by horseback riding and recreational vehicles. Heavily used camping facilities also suffer from vegetation disturbance and soil compaction that contribute to the erosion problem. Motorized boating in lakes and other surface impoundments adds directly to the pollution of waterways as the result of engine emissions and the indiscriminate use of the water bodies as convenient dumps for general wastes.

## 8.4.c. Forest Grazing

Foresters have generally opposed the practice of grazing domestic livestock on forest land because the animals may damage young trees, compact soil, and cause erosion and site deterioration. Nevertheless about 100 million hectares of forest land are still used as rangeland for livestock in the conterminous United States (Anderson, Hoover, and Reinhart, 1976). Research has shown that, in the mountainous eastern deciduous forests, grazing results in serious disturbance to watershed stability, and the practice is now confined largely to regions of southern pines and the more open parks and subalpine meadows of western forests.

Numerous studies have supported the idea that "overgrazing" (a much-used but poorly defined term) causes range deterioration, soil compaction, reduced infiltration, and increased overland flow, erosion, and sedimentation. Since "overgrazing" can only be interpreted in the sense that, from some particular perspective, the effects are undesirable, it is not surprising that there has been a long history of grazing controversy. The current consensus among foresters appears to be that "properly managed forest grazing has little adverse effect on surface hydrology or erosion . . . [but] it can have much greater effects on . . . water quality" (Anderson, Hoover, and Reinhart, 1976).

The data of Kunkle and Meiman (1967) appear to confirm the consensus: grazing of an irrigated mountain meadow in Colorado did not affect the suspended sediment load of stream discharge. But fecal coliform were much higher in the grazed area discharge than in that of an ungrazed control, as illustrated in figure 8.4.

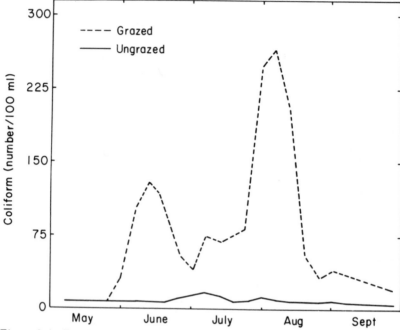

**Figure 8.4.** Fecal coliform concentrations in streams draining grazed and ungrazed watersheds (smoothed means as adapted from Kunkle and Meiman, 1967).

This study and others indicate that, with a high degree of probability, grazing increases stream bacteria levels to the point of creating a health hazard; the effects are greatest during periods of high streamflow, and where grazing animals are in close proximity to the stream.

### 8.4.d. Wildlife Influences

Wildlife is a part of the undisturbed forest ecosystem but, since it is controlled to some degree by human regulations, an unnatural situation exists that can be viewed as an ecosystem disturbance. Information on the impact of wildlife on water quality is relatively meager; apparently this is because, until recently, the impact was thought to be of little significance. As we scrutinize the quality of water more closely, however, wildlife influences become more prominent.

Walter and Jezeski (1973) measured coliform bacteria in two public water supply catchments in Montana; one watershed, closed to public recreation, contained a concentration of elk that raised the water's bacteria count above that of the adjacent area that was open to the public. Moreover, after the closed watershed was opened to the public, bacteria counts abruptly declined; figure 8.5 shows the average numbers of coliform observed before and after the area was opened to recreation in 1970. Shortly after the opening, the large resident elk herd was dispersed by increased human activity, and the authors concluded that elk were responsible for earlier high bacteria counts.

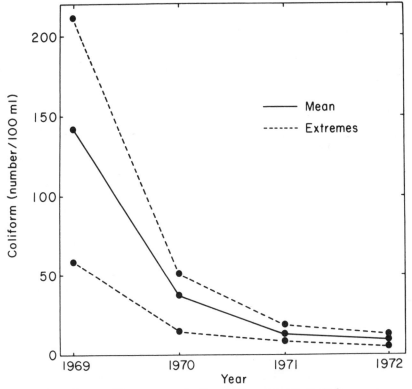

Figure 8.5. Mean coliform counts in the public water supply before and after a municipal watershed was opened to public recreation in 1970 (adapted from Walter and Jezeski, 1973).

Large concentrations of waterfowl and beaver have also been implicated as agents in water quality deterioration. Beaver dams reportedly increase the color and lower the pH and dissolved oxygen content of impounded water; beaver have also been implicated as a carrier of the cysts of *Giardia lamblia*, an infectious organism that causes severe gastroenteritis (giardiasis) in humans. Although studies of the influence of wildlife on water quality have shown relatively small impacts, it is worth noting that detrimental effects do occur, and that evidence of their number and relative importance probably will increase as research continues.

### 8.4.e. Forest Fire

Wildfire is a common occurrence in some forest ecosystems; it can destroy both trees and forest floor organic materials with attendant impacts on surface hydrologic processes as described in section 9.1.c. The effects of fire on catchment water quality depend on the frequency, extent, and severity of burning, watershed physical conditions, postfire weather, and the rapidity of reforestation. Light wildfire or prescribed burning may have no detectable effect on discharge quality, but frequent or severe wildfire can cause changes similar to the effects that accompany careless harvesting operations.

Numerous investigators have studied the effects of forest fire on nutrient cycling and water chemistry. Generalization of the results is difficult because of confounding variables, but apparently the overall impacts on water chemistry are negligible. It is worth noting, however, that where burning is severe and trees are killed, the total export of nutrients may be increased without any increase in concentration levels, simply because discharge volume is increased.

Severe forest fire causes serious acceleration of erosion and sedimentation, especially when heavy rains follow burning, or in semiarid regions where complete revegetation may be delayed for many years. Also, if the forest canopy is destroyed, streams exposed to direct solar radiation will experience temperature changes comparable to the effects produced by clearcutting. Helvey (1972) measured stream temperature increases after wildfire had completely killed the ponderosa pine and Douglas fir forest on a 560-ha

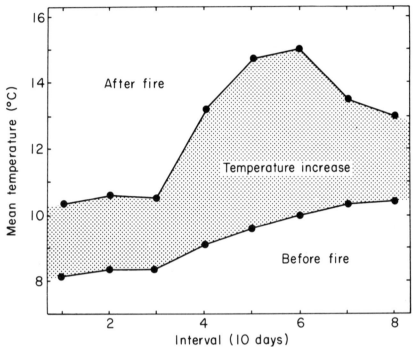

Figure 8.6. Average maximum stream temperatures for 10-day intervals from 10 June to 30 August before (1970) and after (1971) severe fire (adapted from Helvey, 1972).

watershed in Washington; figure 8.6 shows that average 10-day maximum stream temperatures increased by more than 5°C during the summer following fire.

## 8.4.f. Acid Precipitation

Acid precipitation is a relatively recent and potentially serious disturbance of forest ecosystems; it occurs when sulfuric and nitric acids are formed in the atmosphere from oxides emitted by the combustion of fossil fuels. Normal precipitation is slightly acidic as a consequence of the combination of atmospheric carbon dioxide and water that forms carbonic acid, but this process cannot produce rain with pH $<$ 5.7. In the northeastern United States, the average pH of rainfall varies between 4 and 5, and values of pH $<$ 4 have been recorded.

In Scandinavian countries the pH of precipitation has been monitored for more than 20 years. Figure 8.7 illustrates the trend of mean annual values at Lista, Norway, for the 1956–1973 period; the annual means appear to be correlated (inversely) with the rate of fossil fuel consumption in Europe, and with the number of barren lakes in an adjacent Norwegian watershed. No attempt has been made at rigorous scientific analysis, but the correlation is credible from both meteorological and ecological viewpoints.

The problem of acid rainfall is more critical in areas where streams and lakes are poorly buffered (see section 8.2.b). Recent surveys in New York show values of pH < 5 in about half of Adirondack lakes at elevations above 600 m, and of these 90% contain

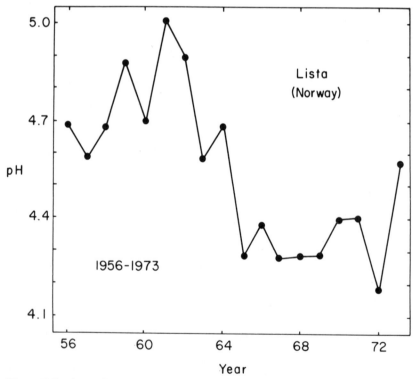

Figure 8.7. Annual mean pH of precipitation at Lista, Norway, 1956–1973 (adapted from Braekke, 1976).

no fish; data for the same lakes during the 1929–1937 period show only 4% with no fish and pH < 5. Apparently fossil fuel combustion, acid precipitation, and surface water quality are related, and the effects on terrestrial ecosystems are widespread and accelerating.

*8.4.g. Forest Chemicals*

The introduction of insecticides, herbicides, fertilizers, and salt into the forest ecosystem poses a hazard to the chemical quality of stream discharge, and to unintended victims of chemical agents and their carriers. The extent of the hazard depends on the amount of chemical applied, its toxicity or other potential for damage, persistence in the environment, and the method and care exercised in application. Recent environmental concern has limited the use of forest chemicals; Tarrant, Gratkowski, and Waters (1973) discussed their future role in forestry, and emphasized the importance of other methods of forest protection and treatment of unhealthful ecological conditions.

Chemicals that are introduced into catchments as aerial sprays or pellets by low-flying aircraft may reach streams directly, by drift in atmospheric currents, or as part of overland flow. In some instances less than half the volume of aerial sprays reaches intended target areas; inputs to streams from drift or direct application often result in temporary lethal concentrations of pesticides in water, and have resulted in fish kills. These problems are greatly reduced where chemical applications are restricted to nonriparian zones; many chemicals are readily absorbed, filtered, and degraded by soil so that, in the forest where overland flow is infrequent, stream pollution protection is largely a matter of careful application.

Common insecticides pose the greatest potential hazard to wildlife and humans, and their widespread use in forestry has been largely discontinued. Herbicides are generally less toxic and less persistent; most observers agree that their use in limited quantities and restricted zones can prevent most serious instances of stream contamination. The effects of chemical fertilizers are least problematic; their use is relatively widespread and increasing, especially in southeastern and northwestern coniferous regions of the United States.

Nitrogen fertilizer is usually applied aerially in the form of urea pellets; the pellets have less tendency to drift than do pesticides, but leaching from the forest floor is an additional method of movement to surface streams. Concentrations of the various forms of nitrogen in streams can be increased significantly following fertilization; concentrations usually do not exceed drinking water standards, except in eastern hardwood forests. The data of Aubertin, Smith, and Patric (1973) for a West Virginia catchment with hardwood cover showed that increased stream nitrogen concentrations persisted for a year after application, with frequent peaks (following major storms) in excess of the safe drinking water limit; in general, however, problems are minor, and some authors have even suggested that small nitrogen increases may be beneficial to aquatic life in mountain watersheds (Werner, 1973; Sharpe, 1975).

The widespread use of highway deicing salts has resulted in considerable environmental damage, particularly in areas adjacent to roadways and salt storage facilities. Ordinary rock salt (sodium chloride) or calcium chloride is usually applied at the rate of from 20 to 40 tons/yr per lane mile of highway in northeastern United States; sodium concentrations in excess of 20 mg/l (the standard recommended by the American Heart Association), and chlorides exceeding 250 mg/l (safe drinking water standard), have been reported in water supplies polluted by deicing salt runoff. Although direct salt toxicity to aquatic life has been reported, it appears to be rare; water density changes, which alter annual cycles of lake overturn, have potentially more significant impacts on aquatic biota.

### 8.4.h. Wastewater Application

The practice of applying wastewater from municipal sewage treatment plants to forest land is gaining increased acceptance in the United States; the wastewater is disinfected and does *not* contain the high levels of heavy metals that are often found in sewage *sludge*. Land application is actually a method of tertiary sewage treatment designed to prevent the eutrophication of waterways; however, its use does result in disruption of the terrestrial forest ecosystem. Generally speaking, the trade-off between the terres-

trial disturbance and potentially severe aquatic ecosystem disturbances that might otherwise result favors the use of land application to meet tertiary sewage treatment requirements.

In the land application process, nutrients and other impurities
in sewage effluent are physically removed by soil filtration, chemically altered in the soil, acted upon by soil microorganisms, and
utilized by forest vegetation for growth and development. Equally
important in terms of forest vegetation responses is the amount of
additional moisture added to the ecosystem. The end result of
these complex processes is an effluent that is much improved in
quality by the time it reaches the groundwater table beneath the
irrigation site.

Climatic conditions are important in the use of land application
for tertiary treatment; winter operation presents special problems
both in the operation of the system and in the nature of its effects
on the forest. Continuous applications of effluent to forest land
is no longer recommended because of nitrate breakthroughs to the
groundwater table; after six months to a year of repeated applications nitrogen additions are more or less balanced by nitrogen
outflows and little of the added nitrogen is retained. New management recommendations call for resting the site periodically, for
example by irrigating only during the growing season.

### 8.4.i. Mineral Extraction

Forest land is frequently underlain by rich mineral deposits, the
extraction of which can cause exceptionally severe impacts on the
quality of water yield. Coal mining, for example, has had a particularly devastating effect in Appalachia where acid drainage from
abandoned mines degrades some 5000 km of streams. In this case
acid is commonly formed by the oxidation of exposed pyrite:

$$2Fe\,S_2 + 2H_2O + 7O_2 \longrightarrow 2Fe\,SO_4 + 2H_2\,SO_4 \qquad (8.16)$$

and further oxidation of the ferrous sulphate (certain autotrophic
bacteria may hasten the reaction); some typical properties of
stream water affected by coal mine drainage are given in table
8.14.

Acid drainage from deep coal mines can be prevented by treat-

Table 8.14. Typical Water Analysis for a
Stream Polluted by Coal Mine
Drainage

| Quality parameter | Value |
|---|---|
| pH | 3.3 |
| Total alkalinity | 0 mg/l |
| Total acidity | 180 mg/l |
| Total iron | 46 mg/l |
| Sulphate | 265 mg/l |

ment at discharge points, but the problem is not so simply handled in the case of surface mines where drainage to groundwater and streams is likely to be a source of acid for many years; surface mining also accelerates erosion and sedimentation, especially in steep topography or where revegetation is difficult. Sand and gravel mines in close proximity to streams often lead to channel instability and realignment, and the disturbed area may become a major long-term sediment source. Other mining activities are of great local significance; for example, placer gold mining is a serious problem on affected streams, resulting in acid conditions and heavy loadings of metals such as iron and aluminum.

## 8.5. Quality Sampling

Determination of forest water quality requires some form of sampling and analysis. Where highly accurate results are required, sampling and analysis are better left to practicing chemists and experienced aquatic biologists. The forest hydrologist should have some knowledge of these techniques, however, at least to the extent of being able to collect and transport water samples properly, and to make rough-cut field determinations of water quality.

### 8.5.a. Sample Collection

Water quality sampling usually consists of extracting a sample volume from a stream, lake, or other source; there are three basic methods of collecting water samples: grab sampling, composite sampling, and integrated sampling. The *grab sample* is taken at a specific time and place, and can represent only the composition of water at that time and place. Since the composition of natural water varies in space and time, grab sampling must be repeated in order to obtain information with regard to water quality variability, or mean quality.

A series of grab samples taken at different times, but at the same location, can be combined to form a *composite sample*. The quality of a composite sample represents the average water quality, at one location, for the interval of time over which the series of grab samples was taken. Composite sampling may be useful, for example, in determining the average quality of stream discharge for a month, week, day, or single storm event.

A series of grab samples taken at different places in a water body, but at the same time, can be combined to form an *integrated sample*. The quality of an integrated sample represents the average quality of the water body at a given time. Integrated sampling is useful in lake or reservoir work where a sample representative of the entire body of water is desired; both composite and integrated sampling reduce the amount of required analytical work.

Containers used to extract sample volumes of water should be uncontaminated; sterile collection vessels are necessary for bacteriological sampling. The container should be rinsed two or three times with the water being sampled just prior to taking the sample; during the actual sampling the container should be opened and closed under water to insure sampling only at the desired point. A single grab sample from a stream should ordinarily be taken at midpoint in the stream cross-section and at middepth.

Recommended procedures for handling water samples prior to analysis are given in table 8.15; it is impossible to prevent changes in the characteristics of water samples during transport and storage, but the recommended procedures help to minimize undesirable changes. Laboratory analysis of field samples should always be accomplished as soon as possible after the samples have been

Table 8.15. Sample Handling Recommendations for Commonly Measured
Forest Water Quality Parameters (Environmental Protection
Agency, 1974)

| Parameter | Volume[a] (ml) | Preservative measure | Holding time (maximum) |
|---|---|---|---|
| Acidity | 100 | Cool to 4°C | 24 hours |
| Alkalinity | 100 | Cool to 4°C | 24 hours |
| Ammonia | 400 | Cool to 4°C; add sulfuric acid to pH < 2 | 24 hours |
| BOD | 1000 | Cool to 4°C | 6 hours |
| Chloride | 50 | None required | 7 days |
| Chlorine residual | 50 | Determine on site | – |
| Color | 50 | Cool to 4°C | 24 hours |
| Dissolved oxygen: | | | |
| Meter | 300[b] | Determine on site | – |
| Winkler | 300[b] | Fix on site | 8 hours |
| Hardness | 100 | Cool to 4°C | 7 days |
| MBAS (detergents) | 250 | Cool to 4°C | 24 hours |
| Metals | 200 | Add nitric acid to pH < 2 | 6 months |
| Nitrate | 100 | Cool to 4°C; add sulfuric acid to pH < 2 | 24 hours |
| pH | 25 | Cool to 4°C; determine on site if possible | 6 hours |
| Phosphorus: | | | |
| Ortho- | 50 | Cool to 4°C; filter on site | 24 hours |
| Total | 50 | Cool to 4°C | 7 days |
| Specific conductance | 100 | Cool to 4°C | 24 hours |
| Sulfate | 50 | Cool to 4°C | 7 days |
| Temperature | 1000 | Determine on site | – |
| Turbidity | 100 | Cool to 4°C | 7 days[c] |

[a]Minimum volume; plastic or glass containers recommended except for dissolved oxygen.
[b]Glass container recommended.
[c]Shake vigorously just prior to analysis.

collected. In some instances, for example in determinations of dissolved oxygen content, pH, and water temperature, analysis should (or must) be conducted in the field.

### 8.5.b. Field Analysis

Determinations of many water quality parameters can be accomplished in the field using portable test kits and apparatus that are relatively inexpensive and easy to operate. Field test kits normally contain required reagents in premeasured amounts, and simple directions that enable those unfamiliar with the intricacies of water chemistry to obtain reliable measurements. The accuracy of field determinations obtained by a forester using portable apparatus cannot, of course, be compared to that of laboratory determinations by a certified chemist; on the other hand, the accuracy is usually more than sufficient for practical management purposes.

The primary advantages of portable water analysis kits are that they 1) permit field analysis of parameters that must be determined on site, 2) are inexpensive and easy to use, 3) use premeasured reagents that eliminate possible errors in preparation, and 4) provide suitable accuracy for most survey and monitoring work. The disadvantages are that 1) the accuracy of results obtained is open to question (e.g., in court proceedings), 2) standard methods are sometimes abridged with resultant loss in reliability, 3) field analyses during inclement weather may be less carefully performed, and 4) many of the kits use color comparators which introduce an element of subjectivity in determining results. Where circumstances permit, laboratory analyses are to be preferred over field determinations.

### 8.5.c. Biological Sampling

Observations of aquatic biota are an important complement to any water quality survey. Just as the forest ecologist can often read the past in the subtle mix of forest vegetation, a skilled aquatic biologist can learn much about the water quality of a stream (present and recent past) by looking at the community of plants and animals residing therein. Foresters can acquire, with minimal effort, the basic skills necessary to fit aquatic biota into the rest of the water quality picture.

The mix of algae and other aquatic plants, invertebrate animals, and fish can be used to create a clear picture of water quality, but special taxonomic skills and considerable tedium of sampling and analysis are required; fortunately, simpler techniques can be employed to provide at least an approximate evaluation. The assessment of aquatic biota for nonaquatic biologists should be limited to macroinvertebrates, in particular to benthic organisms; of these, various larval forms of aquatic insects offer the greatest diagnostic potential and pose the least taxonomic challenge. Guides to the study of macroinvertebrates have been provided by Needham and Needham (1962) and Hilsenoff (1975).

Aquatic invertebrates are quite sensitive to water quality, and most have at least annual life cycles; consequently their presence and abundance can be used as indicators of both past and present water quality. The equipment needed to sample these organisms is simple: a kick screen can be constructed easily using ordinary window screening and two dowel rods. Although identification beyond orders is difficult, classification at the order level is not, and can be accomplished using simplified keys and handbooks.

A number of simple numerical indices have been developed to facilitate comparisons of the invertebrate populations of streams, and to relate these populations to water quality. One of the simplest of these was developed by Beck (1955); the Beck Index classifies invertebrates simply as "pollution intolerant," "moderately tolerant," and "tolerant." Kimmel and Sharpe (1975) modified this classification for Pennsylvania conditions, and organized orders into three classes as given in table 8.16.

Each Class I organism is assigned a numerical value of 2, each Class II organism a value of 1, and each Class III organism is discounted completely (value zero). The numerical or Biotic Index (BI) for a stream is determined as

$$BI = 2n(\text{Class I}) + n(\text{Class II}) \qquad (8.17)$$

where $n$ is the number of different orders of a given class found in the stream. A clean stream is defined as one with $BI \geqslant 10$,

Table 8.16. Classes of Aquatic Invertebrates (Kimmel and Sharpe, 1975)

| Class[a] | BI[b] Value | Order Latin name | Order Common name |
|---|---|---|---|
| I | 2 | Ephemeroptera | Mayflies |
| | | Plecoptera | Stoneflies |
| | | Trichoptera | Caddisflies (case-building) |
| | | Decapoda | Crayfish |
| | | Pelecypoda | Fingernail clams |
| II | 1 | Trichoptera | Caddisflies (without cases) |
| | | Coleoptera | Beetle larvae, riffle beetle |
| | | Isopoda | Aquatic sow bug |
| | | Amphipoda | Scud |
| | | Megaloptera | Hellgrammites |
| | | Odonata | Dragonflies |
| III | 0 | Diptera | True flies |
| | | Gastropoda | Snails |
| | | Trichadida | Flatworms |
| | | Oligochaeta | Aquatic earthworms |
| | | Hirudinea | Leeches |

[a]I, pollution intolerant; II, moderately tolerant; III, tolerant.
[b]Biotic index.

$1 \leq BI \leq 6$ indicates moderate pollution, and B = 0 indicates gross pollution; $7 \leq BI \leq 9$ is rarely encountered and generally indicates a clean stream with lack of habitat diversity.

Beck's index should not be strictly interpreted because there are significant variations in pollution tolerance within orders, and gross identifications of invertebrates will generally lead to underestimates of species diversity. The index does recognize the importance of community structure, however, rather than relying solely on indicator organisms, and it usually provides satisfactory results. Neither Beck's index, nor any other field survey technique, should be considered conclusive; for example, a "clean" stream (BI > 10) may contain a sublethal level of mercury that is not reflected in the macroinvertebrate community.

Collection of aquatic macroinvertebrates is relatively simple: an aquatic insect net or kick screen is held against the stream bottom in a riffle area, the stream bottom upstream of the net is disturbed, and benthic macroinvertebrates are dislodged from the bottom and carried into the net. If the sample is to be preserved for later use, it should be tightly sealed in a container of 70% ethanol. Sampling should be done in the spring to avoid natural fluctuations and life-cycle changes that may give artificially low values.

### 8.5.d. Sampling Strategy

In developing a strategy for water quality sampling there is no substitute for thorough reconnaisance of the watershed to be surveyed; since water quality analysis is both expensive and time-consuming, it is important to determine the location, time, and frequency of sampling that are most likely to provide maximum information per sample. Obviously all potential sources of pollution should be identified, and the likely points of discharge of pollutants thoroughly delineated; this may be a difficult task, especially where groundwater pollution has occurred and evidences itself as a diffuse input to surface streams. In general it is best to sample both above and below a suspected pollution source, such as a campground; sampling time will vary with the suspected pollution problem, stream stage, and weather conditions.

It is advisable to sample when water quality conditions are expected to be poorest: if an acid coal mine drainage problem is suspected, sampling should be at times of high flow from a surface mine, but during low flow periods when drainage is from an abandoned deep mine. Problems with forest chemicals, bacterial contamination from grazing, and turbidity from roads and logging operations are likely to be greatest during stormflow periods. Similarly, water temperatures should be measured on clear summer afternoons, and at low stages, when they are likely to be at a maximum and pose the greatest threat to fishery resources.

The frequency of sampling will depend on the suspected problem and related hydrologic and climatic conditions. If you must sample stormflows, then storm occurrence may determine sampling frequency; or if wildlife use a particular area of concern on a seasonal basis, the sampling schedule must be adjusted accordingly. Also, if precise quantification of water quality variables is required, or if the variability of sampled parameters is great, more frequent sampling will be necessary.

### 8.5.e. Dye Tracing

Diffuse or concealed point sources of pollution are difficult to detect. Sewage pollution from campgrounds, recreational developments, or small communities can cause significant water quality problems and go undetected in normal watershed reconnaisance. Dye tracing has been used successfully to pinpoint sources of pollution in these types of situations.

The most frequently used dye is fluorescein; it can be obtained in powdered, solid, or liquid form. Fluorescein breaks down rapidly in sunlight and in acid waters, so its use under these conditions is limited. Also, soil appears to be a very effective filter for fluorescein dye; consequently it is difficult to use in tracing water that flows through deep soil layers.

If the suspect pollution source is directly connected to the water body in question, and the distance between the two is small, direct observation of the emerging dye is possible. However, many situations involve dilution of the dye to the point of invisibility, or several days or weeks may elapse before the polluted water emerges; in such cases the dye is collected by placing charcoal packets in the waterway. Charcoal absorbs the dye, and even minute quantities can be detected in laboratory analysis.

The amount of dye to use in any situation depends on the volumes of water involved and other factors. One suggested formula is

$$M = 24.6 \left[\frac{DQ}{V}\right]^{0.5} \tag{8.18}$$

where $M(g)$ is the mass of dye, $D$ (km) the distance of flow, $Q$ (m$^3$/sec) the flow rate, and $V$ (m/sec) the velocity of flow. Equation 8.18 tends to be conservative; care should be exercised to avoid obvious visual discoloration of water, and local authorities should be consulted before using dyes to trace water movements.

Dye tracing is most effective in open conduit groundwater systems where minimal soil filtration is encountered; highly successful dye traces over long distances have been accomplished in such systems. W. E. Sharpe once traced the flow of turbid water from a sediment retention basin in the Ozark Mountains through 14 km of highly fractured and solutionalized limestone to a large spring;

dye injected into the pond following heavy rain appeared in the spring 11 days later. Dye tracing is often unsuccessful because it involves considerable uncertainty, so much so that a negative finding cannot be used to presume a lack of physical connection; on the other hand a positive finding is almost conclusive evidence that a connection exists between the tested pollution source and the receiving water body.

## LITERATURE CITED

Anderson, H. W., M. D. Hoover, and K. G. Reinhart. 1976. *Forests and Water: Effects of Forest Management on Floods, Sedimentation, and Water Supply*. Forest Service Technical Report PSW-18. Berkeley, Calif.: U.S. Department of Agriculture.

Aubertin, G. M., D. W. Smith, and J. H. Patric. 1973. Quantity and quality of streamflow after urea fertilization on a forested watershed: First-year results. In *Forest Fertilization Symposium Proceedings*, Forest Service General Technical Report NE-3. Upper Darby, Pa.: U.S. Department of Agriculture.

Beck, W. M. 1955. Suggested method for reporting biotic data. *Sewage and Industrial Wastes* 27:1193–97.

Braekke, F. H. 1976. *Importance of Acid Precipitation on Forests and Freshwater Ecosystems in Norway*. Research Report FR 6/76, SNSF Project. Oslo, Norway.

Brown, G. W. 1972. *An Improved Temperature Model for Small Streams*. Water Resources Research Institute Report 16. Corvallis: Oregon State University.

Commonwealth of Pennsylvania. 1937. *Clean Streams Law of 1937*. Public Law 1987. Harrisburg: Commonwealth of Pennsylvania.

Davis, S. N. and R. J. M. DeWiest. 1966. *Hydrogeology*. New York: Wiley.

Day, C. G. 1976. "Effects of Power Line Corridor Clearance and Maintenance on Stream Habitat." Master's thesis, West Virginia University, Morgantown.

DeWalle, D. R. and W. M. Kappel. 1974. Estimating effects of clearcutting on summer water temperatures of small streams. In *Proceedings of the National Convention*. Washington, D.C.: Society of American Foresters.

Environmental Protection Agency. 1974. *Manual of Methods for Chemical Analysis of Water and Wastes*. Methods Development and Quality Assurance Research Laboratory Report EPA-625-6-74-003. Washington, D.C.: Environmental Protection Agency.

Fleming, G. 1969. Design curves for suspended load estimation. *Institution of Civil Engineers* 43:1-9.

Fredrickson, R. L. 1971. Comparative chemical water quality: natural and disturbed streams following logging and slash burning. In *Proceedings, Symposium on Land Uses and Stream Environment*. Corvallis: Oregon State University.

Gottschalk, L. C. 1964. Reservoir sedimentation. In *Handbook of Applied Hydrology*, ed. V. T. Chow. New York: McGraw-Hill.

Heede, B. H. 1972. Influences of a forest on the hydraulic geometry of two mountain streams. *Water Resources Bulletin* 8:523–29.

Helvey, J. D. 1972. First-year effects of wildfire on water yield and stream temperature in north-central Washington. In S. C. Csallany, T. G. McLaughlin, and W. D. Striffler, eds., *Watersheds in Transition*. Urbana, Ill.: American Water Resources Association.

Hem, J. D. 1970. *Study and Interpretation of the Chemical Characteristics of Natural Water*. Geological Survey Water Supply Paper 1473. Washington, D.C.: U.S. Department of the Interior.

Hilsenhoff, W. L. 1975. *Aquatic Insects of Wisconsin*. Technical Bulletin 89. Madison, Wisc.: Department of Natural Resources.

Kimmel, W. G. and W. E. Sharpe. 1975. *Biological Indicators of Water Quality*. University Park, Pa.: Forest Resources Extension, Pennsylvania State University.

Kochenderfer, J. N. and G. M. Aubertin. 1975. Effects of management practices on water quality and quantity. In *Municipal Watershed Management Symposium Proceedings*, Forest Service General Technical Report NE-13. Upper Darby, Pa.: U.S. Department of Agriculture.

Kunkle, S. H. and J. R. Meiman. 1967. *Water Quality of Mountain Watersheds*. Hydrology Paper No. 21. Fort Collins, Colo.: Colorado State University.

Lee, R. 1978. *Forest Microclimatology*. New York: Columbia University Press.

Lee, R. and D. E. Samuel. 1976. Some thermal and biological effects of forest cutting in West Virginia. *Journal of Environmental Quality* 5:362–66.

Likens, G. E., F. H. Bormann, and N. M. Johnson. 1969. Nitrification: Importance to nutrient losses from a cutover forest ecosystem. *Science* 163:1205–6.

Likens, G. E., F. H. Bormann, R. S. Pierce, J. S. Eaton, and N. M. Johnson. 1977. *Biogeochemistry of a Forested Ecosystem*. New York: Springer.

Lynch, J. A., W. E. Sopper, E. S. Corbett, and D. W. Aurand. 1975. Effects of management practices on water quality and quantity. In *Municipal Watershed Management Symposium Proceedings*, Forest Service Technical Report NE-13. Upper Darby, Pa.: U.S. Department of Agriculture.

Needham, J. G. and P. R. Needham. 1962. *A Guide to the Study of Freshwater Biology*. San Francisco: Golden-Day.

Ovington, J. D. 1968. Some factors affecting nutrient distribution within ecosystems. In F. E. Eckhardt, ed., *Functioning of Terrestrial Ecosystems at the Primary Productivity Level.* Paris: United Nations Educational, Scientific, and Cultural Organization.

Public Health Service. 1962. *Drinking Water Standards.* Publication 956. Washington, D.C.: Public Health Service.

Rice, R. M., J. S. Rothacher, and W. F. Megahan. 1972. Erosional consequences of timber harvesting: An appraisal. In S. C. Csallany, T. G. McLaughlin, and W. D. Striffler, eds., *Watersheds in Transition.* Urbana, Ill.: American Water Resources Association.

Rice, R. M. 1977. Forest management to minimize landslide risk. In *Guidelines for Watershed Management,* Food and Agricultural Organization Conservation Guide No. 1. Rome: United Nations.

Schumm, S. 1954. The relation of drainage basis relief to sediment loss. *International Association of Scientific Hydrology Publication* 36:216-19.

Sharpe, W. E. 1975. Timber management influences on aquatic ecosystems and recommendations for future research. *Water Resources Bulletin* 11:546-50.

Slack, K. V. and H. R. Feltz. 1968. Tree leaf control on low flow water quality in a small Virginia stream. *Environmental Science and Technology* 2:126-31.

Tarrant, R. F., K. C. Lu, W. B. Bollen, and C. S. Chen. 1968. *Nutrient Cycling by Throughfall and Stemflow Precipitation in Three Coastal Oregon Forest Types.* Forest Service Research Paper PNW-54. Portland, Ore.: U.S. Department of Agriculture.

Tarrant, R. F., K. C. Lu, W. B. Bollen, and J. F. Franklin. 1969. *Nitrogen Enrichment of Two Forest Ecosystems by Red Alder.* Forest Service Research Paper PNW-76. Portland, Ore.: U.S. Department of Agriculture.

Tarrant, R. F., H. J. Gratkowski, and W. E. Waters. 1973. *The Future Role of Chemicals in Forestry.* Forest Service Technical Report PNW-6. Portland, Ore.: U.S. Department of Agriculture.

Voight, G. K. 1960. Alteration of the composition of rainwater by trees. *The American Midland Naturalist* 63:321-26.

Wallace, J. B. 1974. *Studies on Southeastern Aquatic Insects.* Washington, D.C.: Environmental Protection Agency.

Walter, W. G., and J. J. Jezeski. 1973. *Microbial and Chemical Studies in a Watershed Used for Municipal Supply and Waste Disposal.* Water Resources Research Center Report No. 41. Bozeman: Montana State University.

Warren, C. E. 1971. *Biology and Water Pollution Control.* Philadelphia, Pa.: Saunders Company.

Werner, R. G. 1973. Water quality-limnological concerns about forest fertilization. In *Forest Fertilization Symposium Proceedings,* Forest Service General Technical Report NE-3. Upper Darby, Pa.: U.S. Department of Agriculture.

Zinke, P. J. 1962. The pattern of influence of individual forest trees on soil properties. *Ecology* 43:130-33.

## SELECTED READINGS

American Public Health Association. 1971. *Standard Methods for the Examination of Water and Wastewater*. Washington, D.C.: American Public Health Association.

Brown, G. W. 1974. *Forestry and Water Quality*. Corvallis: Oregon State University Bookstore.

Carroll, D. 1962. *Rainwater as a Chemical Agent of Geologic Processes— A Review*. Geological Survey Water Supply Paper 1535-G. Washington, D.C.: U.S. Government Printing Office.

National Academy of Sciences. 1977. *Drinking Water and Health*. Washington, D.C.: National Academy of Sciences.

Pearson, F. J. and D. W. Fisher. 1971. *Chemical Composition of Atmospheric Precipitation in the Northeastern United States*. Geological Survey Water Supply Paper 1535-P. Washington, D.C.: U.S. Government Printing Office.

# 9 SPECIAL TOPICS

## 9.1. Water Management

Application of hydrologic principles to forest land mangement is complicated by the diversity of both ecosystem conditions and human objectives; additional problems arise when wildfire, insect and disease attacks, violent weather, and human folly cause disturbances of normal ecosystem functioning. Intelligent use of the societal resource, land, requires comprehensive planning to "harmonize," insofar as possible, the complexity of natural forces and human aspirations. From the hydrologist's point of view, and as a continuing theme in all forest management plans, harmonious use focuses on the need for watershed protection.

### 9.1.a. Watershed Management

Foresters have traditionally described their craft as a combination of science and art, stressing the "how-to-do-it" approach as opposed to basic understanding; accordingly, the branch that deals specifically with water-related phenomena has been called "watershed management." But "watershed management" is a tenuous concept, implying the existence of a vocation for which there can be no general practitioners; it is widely used with reference to water husbandry and soil site protection, or as a vague synonym for the field of soil and water conservation. Intelligent land management must be interdisciplinary, so there are no "watershed managers," and those who deal with forest-water relationships can contribute only to the extent that they have been trained as forest hydrologists.

Watershed management (as applied forest hydrology) is the overall endeavor to take advantage of known forest influences on streamflow; as such it is obviously concerned with the volume, timing, and quality of forest water yield. In practice the hydrologist is faced with three major groups of limitations: 1) intrinsic limitations—those dictated by the normal nature of ecosystem responses, 2) conflicting-use limitations, and 3) limitations that arise as a result of natural disturbances—these two latter are considered separately in sections 9.1.b and c. Another category, societal limitations, might also be cited, but it is important to recognize that the hydrologist's public role is advisory and, as befits a professional, strictly objective; soical, political, and so-called "moral" roles are a matter of personal choice.

The extent to which watershed practices or forest-cover manipulations can influence water yields is limited by climate, catchment characteristics, and forest type and condition, i.e., by the innate nature of particular ecosystems. Volumetric and regimen limitations (section 7.3), and influences on water quality (sections 8.3 and 8.4), can be estimated approximately for typical situations, but single-parameter limitations are interdependent; for example, manipulated increases in flow volume are almost invariably associated with greater peak flows and additional erosion and sedimentation. This interdependence means that even single-use management entails decisions with regard to parameter optimization; in multiple-use management the decisions are far more complicated.

### 9.1.b. Conflicting Uses

Forest land is used for a variety of purposes; its wealth of timber, wildlife, forage, and minerals is harvested along with water, while simultaneously the land is used for recreation and aesthetic appreciation. Inevitably the uses conflict, and "wise use" can be defined only by reference to some tautology concerning "the greatest good for the greatest number in the long run." "Integrated forest management," "multiple-use management," and other modern clichés recognize that conflicts exist and, in the public mind at least, may help promote the image of professional forestry wisdom when conflicts are resolved, as they must be, by some arbitrary decision.

Timber and water management are compatible to the extent that when increases or decreases in total water yield are called for, forest cutting or reforestation may produce the desired effect; moreover, forest protection from fire, insects, disease, and weather, erosion control, and grazing, mining, wildlife, and recreation restrictions frequently produce mutually desirable results. In recent years there has been a general increase in demand for both timber products and water, and much has been written with regard to an alleged "harmony" of uses; but timber management and harvesting almost invariably produce some unwanted hydrologic effects: forest thinning, pruning, cleaning, prescribed burning, and other minor silvicultural operations usually produce marginal effects on water supply, forest fertilization may accelerate forest growth but would tend to reduce water yield, chemicals used for insect and brush control pose a hazard to water quality, and clearcutting, logging, and road systems cause accelerated erosion and sedimentation, increase peak flows and flood damages, and expose streams to thermal pollution (buffer strips required for erosion control and shading along streams can be accommodated only at the expense of more valuable cove timber). In general, also, there is no guarantee that timber management operations can be synchronized to produce desirable effects at a mutually desirable time.

Grazing of domestic livestock on forest land is common; in the conterminous United States, 40 to 50% of the forest is grazed, and in eastern forests 20% is overgrazed to the extent that undesirable hydrologic effects have been reported (Anderson, Hoover, and Reinhart, 1976). Overgrazing reduces infiltration capacity, increases overland flow, erosion, and stormflow volumes and peaks, and has deleterious effects on water quality (see section 8.4.c); the only effective watershed control is "properly managed grazing," meaning essentially to reduce herd sizes to the point where undesirable effects can be tolerated. Less information is available with regard to the influences of big game concentrations (see section 8.4.d), but similar effects and controls are suggested.

The use of forest land by humans for recreation and aesthetic appreciation poses special hazards, and imposes limitations on water management activities. Bacterial pollution is usually of greatest concern (see section 8.4.b), but access roads and trails, and vehicular recreation, can also create important hydrologic disturbances; special provisions for human waste disposal, and the setting aside of parks, historic sites, and wilderness areas to restrict the human influence to controlled sites, are usually recommended. Silvicultural practices are frequently modified in high-use areas to make sylvan vistas more appealing to the public eye.

Forest land is being denuded and otherwise disturbed with increasing frequency in the extraction of mineral resources; surface coal mining alone accounts for more than 500 $km^2$/yr of forest land disturbance in the United States. The hydrologic effects of surface mining have not been throughly evaluated; undoubtedly it causes an increase in total water yield similar to the effect of clearcutting, but changes in flow extremes and water quality (see section 8.4.i) are much greater, and all of the effects persist longer. Accelerated erosion and sedimentation from surface-mined lands create serious problems and, when acid substrata are exposed, the effects on aquatic ecosystems and discharge quality are extreme.

Curtis (1972) found that average peak flow rates increased by a factor of from 3 to 5 after surface mining had disturbed about half of two small catchment areas in eastern Kentucky; apparently peak flow increases are common, but Curtis (1977) called attention to conflicting evidence from both Kentucky and West Virginia. Where original soils are thin, the spoil banks, fractured substrata, and additional surface detention caused by mining may effectively increase catchment storage capacity and reduce peak flows. Figure 9.1 illustrates the effect as recorded during the exceptional flood of April 1977; in the mined area, 56% of the surface had been disturbed, yet total stormflow and peak discharge were 18% below that of the forested catchment.

## 9.1.c. Natural Disturbances

Any natural (unplanned) disturbance that significantly modifies forest density, structure, or composition can cause detectable changes in the water balance. Earthquakes and massive earth movements, volcanic eruptions, severe ice storms, and other catastrophic events can effectively deforest an area, reduce

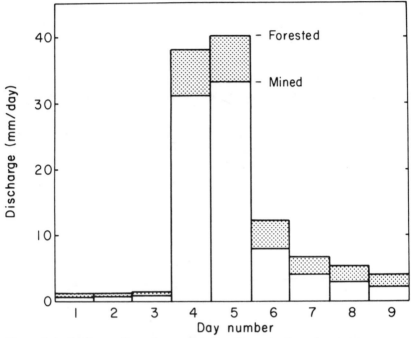

Figure 9.1. Discharge from forested and surface-mined catchments in southern West Virginia as affected by an extreme rainfall event (adapted from Curtis, 1977).

evapotranspiration, and increase total runoff. Several natural disturbances that cause hydrologic changes are common enough to be of concern in water management and planning.

Fire is a relatively common natural occurrence in the forest, and some forest types owe their very existence to occasional wildfires that destroy competitive species; other forest fires occur as the result of human negligence, or when burning is prescribed for silvicultural purposes. The hydrologic effects of fire range from negligible to extreme depending on the severity and frequency of occurrence, the character of forest cover and soil, sequences of weather conditions following fire, and climate-soil-forest interactions that determine the rate of forest recovery. Fire may destroy the intercepting and transpiring forest canopy directly (crown fires), or indirectly by the destruction of stem conductive tissues at ground level (ground fires); severe ground fires can reduce catchment infiltration capacity, and increase overland flow, debris discharge, and other forms of erosion and sedimentation.

Water yield increases following severe wildfire are probably about the same as those caused by clearcutting and, calculated on a catchment area basis, should be roughly proportional to the fraction of forest cover that is destroyed. The effect on peak discharge may be greater than that of timber harvesting if litter and organic soil layers are extensively burned; even the intentional burning of logging slash has been found to increase overland flow and erosion. Intense fires frequently cause drastic increases in the amount of debris discharge that occurs during floods (see section 8.4.e for a discussion of other influences on yield quality).

Insects, disease, and violent weather destroy the equivalent of about 8,000 km$^2$ of standing timber each year in the United States and, when damages are concentrated, their hydrologic effects are similar to those of planned deforestation; in this case, however, soil disturbance may be negligible, and the effects are manifested mainly as changes in annual or seasonal water yields. Bethlahmy (1974) evaluated annual yield increases following a severe bark-beetle epidemic in northwestern Colorado where much of the Engelmann spruce–subalpine fir forest was killed; after 25 years, basal area averaged only 10 m$^2$/ha compared with the original 34 m$^2$/ha. Figure 9.2 shows average yield increases from two large basins by 5-year intervals between 1940 and 1965; the epidemic started following wind damage in 1939, and it struck first in the White River watershed.

Eschner and Satterlund (1966) studied the hydrologic effects of steadily increasing forest cover in the Sacandaga River watershed (Adirondack Mountains, northern New York). Annual, dormant season, and April water yields decreased gradually over a period of more than 30 years during which the forest basal area increased from about 17 to 30 m$^2$/ha. In 1950 a violent storm caused extensive blowdown, and abruptly reversed the long-term trends; the results are illustrated in figure 9.3.

Trees and shrubs that grow below the forest zone adjacent to streams in arid and semiarid regions are called phreatophytes; they

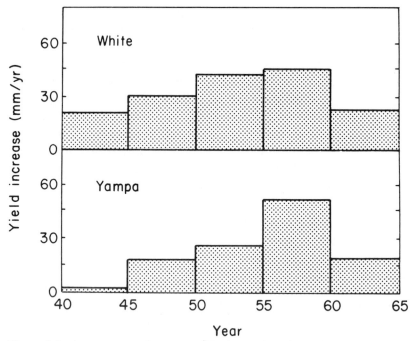

Figure 9.2. Average annual water yield increases from the White and Yampa River watersheds following a bark-beetle epidemic (Bethlahmy, 1974).

are said to consume some 30 km$^3$ of water each year, or twice the average annual discharge of the Colorado River. The principal species (saltcedar, mesquite, and others) have little or no commercial value, and serious attempts have been made to eradicate the plants and save water. In one instance, when an area greater than 20 km$^2$ was cleared, the saving was estimated to be 800 mm/yr, or $1.7(10^7)$m$^3$ (Anderson, Hoover, and Reinhart, 1976).

## 9.2. Watershed Rehabilitation

Forest land that has been seriously disturbed by the actions of natural or human agents may require special management to prevent further deterioration and to restore desired surface characteristics.

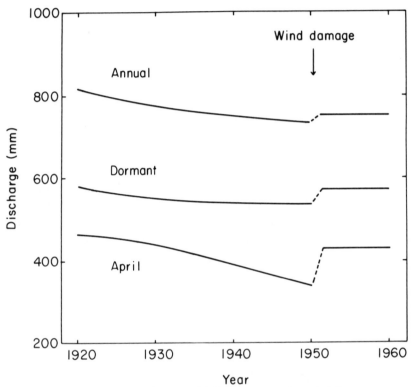

Figure 9.3. Water yield trend reversal following extensive wind damage (Eschner and Satterlund, 1966).

Flow regime, water quality, and erosion control are most important hydrologically, but forest productivity, wildlife habitat, recreation potential, aesthetic appeal, and other land-use values must also be considered. Land "healing" occurs naturally, of course, but sometimes decades or even centuries may be required for complete natural restoration.

### 9.2.a. Disturbed Land

The environment of disturbed land is basically unlike that of the forest; extreme difficulty may be encountered in revegetation attempts, especially if the soil mantle has been removed and unweathered material exposed. Newly exposed parent material and mining spoil tend to be physically unstable, chemically inferior, and microclimatologically unfavorable for forest regeneration. Understanding the environment of disturbed land is the key to its successful reclamation.

Barren land is physically unstable because it is subject to the full force of raindrop impact, sheet, rill, and gully erosion, and massive gravity-caused movements including soil creep, slumps, landslides, and mud flows. The erosion potential is especially great in rugged topography where road-cut material or the overburden from contour surface mining is sidecast downhill to create a flat surface or mining bench above. If the sloping spoil contains soil, plants may be established readily in some instances, only to be uprooted from time to time when rainfall or concentrated discharge from the bench cause saturation and mass slumpages or landslides.

Water that occurs in the interstices of "soil" on disturbed areas may be highly acidic or contain toxic concentrations of various chemicals, especially the heavy metals. Acid soils inhibit plant growth, retard the absorption of water and nutrients, and restrict the development of microogranisms required for physiological processes by vascular plants. In addition, spoil materials are frequently deficient in the plant nutrients, nitrogen, phosphorus, and potassium, and the availability of nutrients to plant roots is reduced by interactions with heavy metals and other chemicals.

The surface layers of barren soils dry rapidly following rain; direct exposure to solar radiation favors higher maximum surface temperatures, and the lack of any wind protection leads to initially high evaporation rates. Moreover, coarse spoil fragments can hold little water against the force of gravity, so the rooting zone for seedlings may be uncommonly droughty. If spoil salt concentrations are very high, seedling establishment may be difficult because the water potential is reduced to the point where "physiological drought" limits the availability of water to plants.

Temperature extremes severely restrict survival rates of tree seedlings which are closely coupled to energetic processes at the surface; Deely (1970) observed that maximum surface temperatures on clear summer days were 50 to 55°C on dry, light-colored spoils, and 65 to 70°C on dark spoils. From energy-budget considerations

Table 9.1. Albedo and Thermal Conductivity of Some
Common Spoil Materials (Deely, 1970)

| Material | Albedo (%) | Conductivity (mcal/cm · min · °C) | |
|---|---|---|---|
| | | Dry | Moist |
| Light sandstone | 33 | 34 | 202 |
| Light mineral shale | 24 | 39 | 226 |
| Dark mineral shale | 12 | 57 | 189 |
| Dark organic shale | 10 | 47 | 86 |
| Bituminous coal | 06 | 11 | 63 |

(section 2.2.c), net radiation must vary inversely with surface albedo, so the darker (less reflective) spoils tend to be warmer; albedoes for some typical spoil materials are listed in table 9.1. Temperature maxima are greater when spoils are dry because a smaller fraction of net radiation is dissipated as latent heat; also, thermal conductivity decreases as spoil dries (see table 9.1), and less of the available energy is conducted to deeper layers.

## 9.2.b. Engineering Controls

Severely disturbed lands are rehabilitated using a combination of engineering controls and vegetative measures; as a rule the former must precede the latter in order to provide and maintain a stable rooting zone for plants. Returning the land to its original contour, regrading, terracing, or reshaping the surface in various ways by pitting or furrowing may be required to reduce surface runoff velocity and provide for normal drainage; culverts, diversion ditches, and paved or riprapped waterways give additional protection during initial stages of revegetation, and channel improvements (removal of logging debris), check dams, and sediment basins are used to inhibit streambank and channel erosion, sediment discharge, and gully formation. The *Engineering Field Manual for Conservation Practices* (Soil Conservation Service, 1969), and publications by Kochenderfer (1970) and Heede (1977a) provide detailed information with regard to design, application, and effectiveness of the various structures and practices; a valuable case study is given in the report by Heede (1977b).

### 9.2.c. Vegetative Measures

Forest watershed rehabilitation, for hydrologic purposes, usually implies the eventual reforestation of a disturbed area; initially, however, revegetation may be most important from the standpoint of soil stabilization and erosion control, and minor vegetation types are frequently relied upon to provide quick cover. If some of the original soil remains in place, and if engineering controls have been effective, natural revegetation or seeding and planting operations ordinarily succeed within a year or two in humid regions, but under semiarid conditions the same recovery may require a decade or more. In more difficult situations, vegetation establishment must be based on consideration of both specific site conditions and species adaptability.

Revegetation problems have been studied in the past primarily on an empirical basis and, as a rule, disturbed site conditions are still described simply in terms of average weather, or spoil pH and nutrient conditions, and species are selected based on the results of survival tests and growth experiments. In view of the severity and geographical extent of projected disturbances, more basic approaches will be required: "It is no longer practical to rely only upon . . . trial-and-error empiricism" (Van Haveren and Brown, 1975). It is surprising that, in the modern scientific era, foresters still know so little about the basic physical conditions that govern tree growth and survival.

Table 9.2. Radiation Components and Maximum Surface Temperatures on Natural and Treated Coal Spoils (Lee, Hutson, and Hill, 1975)

|  | Surface (dry) | |
| --- | --- | --- |
| Parameter | Natural | Whitened |
| *Net radiation* (ly/min) | | |
| Shortwave | 1.25 | 0.88 |
| Longwave | -0.31 | -0.21 |
| Allwave | 0.94 | 0.67 |
| *Albedo* (%) | 5 | 33 |
| *Maximum temperature* ($^\circ$C) | 66 | 53 |

The value of a biophysical approach to reclamation problems was demonstrated by Lee, Hutson, and Hill (1975); it was found that both black locust (a preferred species in the eastern United States) and Virginia pine could survive and grow rapidly in West Virginia on a highly acidic ($3.1 < pH < 3.6$) black coal spoil where only the reflectivity of the surface was modified. Table 9.2 lists the radiation components and maximum surface temperatures on the treated and natural spoils. On natural coal spoils the black locust survival rate is higher than that of many other species, not because it is "acid-tolerant," but probably because the radiative absorptivity ($a = 0.39$) of its foliage is exceptionally low.

## 9.3. Flood Mitigation

A *flood* may be defined as any relatively high flow rate that causes a stream to overtop its banks; according to this definition a stream channel that is bankfull is said to be at *flood stage*. The magnitude of a flood may be expressed in terms of height above flood stage; as a flow rate (volume/time, e.g., $m^3$/sec); or in units of velocity as a flow rate per unit of land area (volume/time · area, e.g., mm/hr). Table 9.3 characterizes the magnitudes of flood discharges from small watersheds in humid regions (it is important to recall, from section 7.2.b, that peak flows per unit area are generally greater for smaller catchments); note that record flood

Table 9.3. Order of Magnitude of Stream Discharge Rates per Unit Area for Small Watersheds in Humid Regions

| Flow parameter | Flow rate per unit area | |
|---|---|---|
| | ($m^3$/sec · $km^2$) | (mm/time) |
| Normal base flow | $10^{-2}$ | 1 mm/day |
| Average stormflow | $10^{-1}$ | 10 mm/day |
| Annual flood peak | $10^0$ | 4 mm/hr |
| Extreme flood peak | $10^1$ | 40 mm/hr |
| Record flood peak | $10^2$ | 400 mm/hr |

peaks are of the same order as maximum recorded rainfall intensities (equation 3.13).

In upstream forested areas the riparian zones are not much used by people, and even major floods may cause little damage. Downstream, however, flood plains are prime agricultural lands, and cities, highways, and railroads are built to take advantage of level land and the waterway's usefulness for water supply, sewage disposal, and navigation; as a result, floods are the most damaging of all natural catastrophies. Most floods can be "controlled" (i.e., damages greatly reduced) by the use of engineering structures and careful management of upstream land and vegetation; it has been estimated that flood-control reservoirs alone reduce economic losses by about 60% (Hoyt and Langbein, 1955).

The forest influence on floods was a matter of considerable controversy for many years; to foresters it was an article of faith on which they based a crusade for the setting aside of vast forest reserves, and public acceptance of their position led to far-reaching legislation. Fortunately the weight of evidence could not forever be denied, and although public opinion changes slowly, it is now generally recognized by professional foresters that some of the most devastating floods on record have occurred in undisturbed forest watersheds; a list of record peak flows and percentages of forest cover, as adapted from Anderson, Hoover, and Reinhart (1976), is given in table 9.4. More detailed treatment of the controversy, the evidence, and recent forest policy recommendations were given by Lull and Reinhart (1972) in their monograph *Forests and Floods*.

Frye and Runner (1970) evaluated the influence of watershed physical features, soils, climatic variables, and forest cover on the magnitudes of flood peaks ($Q_p$) in West Virginia tributaries of the Ohio River; multiple regression analysis was used to derive predictive equations that reduce to the form

$$Q_p = aKf^b \qquad (9.1)$$

where $f$ is the percentage of forest cover, $K$ is the influence of all other significant parameters, and $a$ and $b$ are constant for a given flood frequency. The equations were based on peak flows with av-

Table 9.4.  Some Record Peak Flows from Larger Forested Watersheds
(adapted from Anderson, Hoover, and Reinhart, 1976)

| Watershed | Area $(km^2)$ | Peak flow $(m^3/sec \cdot km^2)$ | Forest cover $(\%)$ |
|---|---|---|---|
| *North Atlantic* | | | |
| Ellis River, N.H. | 73 | 5.78 | 100 |
| Rondout Creek, N.Y. | 259 | 2.92 | 80 |
| Rapidan River, Va. | 1204 | 1.37 | 53 |
| *South Atlantic* | | | |
| Morgan Creek, N.C. | 70 | 12.14 | 61 |
| Henry Fork, N.C. | 207 | 4.27 | 88 |
| Yadkin River, N.C. | 1277 | 3.54 | 90 |
| *Ohio Basin* | | | |
| Elk Creek, N.C. | 109 | 7.16 | 67 |
| Watauga River, N.C. | 236 | 6.12 | 62 |
| Watauga River, Tenn. | 1106 | 1.84 | 64 |
| *Pacific Slope (South)* | | | |
| San Antonio Creek, Ca. | 44 | 13.85 | 63 |
| San Gabriel River, Ca. | 264 | 3.65 | 100 |
| Los Angeles River, Ca. | 1326 | 1.43 | 28 |
| *Pacific Slope (North)* | | | |
| Skokomish River, Wa. | 155 | 4.24 | 75 |
| Wynooche River, Wa. | 272 | 2.60 | 90 |
| Skykomish River, Wa. | 1386 | 1.62 | 78 |

erage recurrence intervals between 2 and 50 years as shown in table 9.5; the exponent $b$ was positive and generally decreased as the interval increased. Most of the 75 basins were at least 50% forested, but the analysis confirmed the general rule that peak flow increases as the percentage of forest cover increases.

Higher peak flows frequently occur in forested basins, *not* because of a forest influence, of course, but because forests are typically situated in local uplands where precipitation is greater, soils are shallower, and topography is steeper. *In the regions where forests occur*, total discharge, stormflow volume, and peak discharge are generally smaller than from adjacent nonforested land; but "smaller" is not a very significant qualification in the case of rec-

Table 9.5. Relative Values of Peak Discharge as a Function
of Forest Cover Percentage (Frye and Runner,
1970)

| Recurrence interval (yrs) | Exponent $b$ (equation 9.1) | Forest cover (%) | | |
|---|---|---|---|---|
| | | 50 | 75 | 100 |
| 2 | 0.43 | 1.00 | 1.19 | 1.35 |
| 5 | 0.40 | 1.00 | 1.18 | 1.32 |
| 10 | 0.38 | 1.00 | 1.17 | 1.30 |
| 25 | 0.39 | 1.00 | 1.17 | 1.31 |
| 50 | 0.33 | 1.00 | 1.14 | 1.26 |

ord peak flows and damaging floods. The forest influence becomes less important as the storm size, or flood size, increases; the chief mechanisms, interception and greater diversion to soil moisture storage, become relatively ineffective when these capacities are greatly exceeded by the volume of storm rainfall.

The most important influence of forest cover on floods, and flood damages, has more to do with sedimentation and debris discharge than with the absolute volume or rate of flow. Organic and inorganic sediments obviously increase the flood volume, and when deposited in a stream channel will reduce its carrying capacity and increase the likelihood of overbank flooding; the sedimentation of reservoirs decreases their usefulness for flood control and other purposes. In general, "dirty flood water is more damaging than relatively clean water, and sediment left by a flood can cause a substantial part of its total damage" (Anderson, Hoover, and Reinhart, 1976); it follows that "as forest cover inhibits erosion, it significantly contributes to preventing flood damage."

The forest provides the best possible cover for preventing flood damages, especially those that occur as the result of erosion and sedimentation (see section 8.3.a); other land with complete vegetative cover may perform with comparable efficiency if undisturbed by human activity, fire, and overgrazing. Clearcutting, roadbuilding, and other forest management activities, even surface mining, *can* be accomplished without increasing erosion or peak flows substantially, but too frequently the additional care and cost involved have discouraged the use of recommended procedures. Forest fire prevention, grazing restrictions, reforestation of abandoned land, and more strict control of clearcutting and other watershed disturbances are ways in which forest management can contribute to the reduction of flood damage.

## 9.4. Snow Hydrology

Snowfall is common throughout the middle and higher latitudes where it may constitute 25% or more of the annual precipitation mass (5 to 25% in the northeastern United States). Snow is sometimes referred to as "delayed precipitation" for hydrologic purposes because it is relatively immobile and cannot contribute significantly to streamflow until melted. In some regions streamflow consists mainly of snowmelt water, and the seasonal flow regime is dominated by peak discharges following spring melting of the winter's snow accumulation.

Record snowfall depths have been observed to exceed 25 m in a single season, and 1 m in a day, but in terms of equivalent liquid water these intensities are small by comparison with maximum observed rainfall (see equation 3.13). The density of new snow generally varies between 0.07 and 0.15 g/cm$^3$, but the sharp crystalline structure changes rapidly as the result of vapor metamorphism and regelation to'form a coarse-textured snowpack through the process of *ripening;* ripe snow has a density of from 0.45 to 0.50 g/cm$^3$. Coarse snow, like coarse soil, can hold little liquid water against the force of gravity, so as ripe snow begins to melt it can contain no more than 3 to 5% (by mass) of liquid water, and the energy required for melting ($E_m$, ly) is

$$E_m = L_f \rho_p zq \qquad (9.2)$$

where $L_f$(cal/g) is the latent heat of fusion (see table 2.1), and $\rho_p$ (g/cm$^3$), $z$ (cm), and $q$ (dimensionless) are snowpack density, depth, and *thermal quality*, respectively; thermal quality is the fraction of solid phase water ($0.95 < q < 1.0$).

Energy for snowmelt is delivered to a snowpack by radiation

$(R)$, conduction $(B)$, convection $(H)$, and latent heat exchange $(L_s E$, condensation) or in some instances by raindrops $(D)$; symbolically.

$$E_m = R + B + H + L_s E + D \qquad (9.3)$$

for which most of the basic equations are given in section 2.2.c. It is helpful to evaluate the magnitudes of the energy components under typical conditions of melting in order to determine their relative importance. In the following analysis it is assumed that $L_f = 80$ cal/g (constant), and the depth (in cm/day) of meltwater $(M = z\rho_p)$ is expressed as a function of energy input and other appropriate variables.

Net radiation $(R)$ consists of both shortwave (solar) and longwave (thermal) radiation; the former is most important in open areas or on the exposed forest canopy, and the latter under a dense forest canopy. If shortwave net radiation is utilized entirely for melting, the corresponding depth $(M_s)$ is

$$M_s = \frac{E_s}{L_f} = \frac{(1 - r)S_t}{80} \qquad (9.4)$$

where $S_t$ is incoming solar (global) radiation, $r$ the snowpack albedo, and $E_s = (1 - r)S_t$; considering the normal range of $S_t$ during the snowmelt season (i.e., $100 < S_t < 500$ ly/day during clear days), and letting $r = 0.5$, $6 < M_s < 30$ mm/day are the approximate upper limits. Longwave radiation exchange is usually negative and counteracts the shortwave effect, but under a relatively warm forest canopy, the depth $(M_l)$ of longwave-induced melting is

$$M_l = \frac{E_l}{L_f} \simeq \frac{10T_c}{80} \qquad (9.5)$$

where $T_c$ (°C) is canopy temperature (snow temperature = 0°C), and for $0 < T_c < 20$°C, $0 < M_l < 25$ mm/day.

When the snowpack is at the melting point (0°C) and cooler than the ambient air, the heat transfer equation for convection $(H)$ is

$$H = h_c T_a \qquad (9.6)$$

Table 9.6. Snowmelt (mm/day) by
Convection under Typical
Conditions in Open Areas

| Windspeed | Air temperature (°C) | | | | |
|-----------|----|----|----|----|----|
| (m/sec) | 2 | 4 | 6 | 8 | 10 |
| 1 | 3 | 7 | 10 | 14 | 17 |
| 2 | 5 | 10 | 15 | 20 | 25 |
| 5 | 8 | 16 | 24 | 31 | 39 |

where $h_c$ is the transfer coefficient (from equation 2.32, for example) and $T_a$ (°C) is air temperature. Accordingly, an estimate of the daily melting depth ($M_c$) by convection in open areas is given by

$$M_c = \frac{E_c}{L_f} = \frac{1.4 u^{0.5} T_a}{80} \qquad (9.7)$$

where $u$ (cm/sec) is mean windspeed, and $T_a$ is mean air temperature. Solutions to equation 9.7 for a range of typical conditions are given in table 9.6; under a forest canopy both $u$ and $T_a$ would generally be smaller than in an open area, and the melting rate greatly reduced.

Vapor pressure over snow is 6.1 mb at 0°C (see table 2.4), so if the ambient vapor pressure ($e_a$) is greater than 6.1 mb, condensation will occur and release 677 cal/g of energy for melting (if $e_a <$ 6.1 mb, energy is absorbed in the process of sublimation). In this instance the appropriate heat transfer equation (a modified form of equation 6.7) is

$$L_s E = 1.8 h_c (e_a - 6.1) \qquad (9.8)$$

where $L_s$ is the latent heat of sublimation, and the daily melt ($M_v$) caused by vapor condensation is given by

$$M_v = \frac{E_v}{L_f} = \frac{2.6 u^{0.5} (e_a - 6.1)}{80} \qquad (9.9)$$

where $e_a$ is mean ambient vapor pressure; some solutions to equation 9.9 are given in table 9.7. According to the Corps of Engi-

Table 9.7. Snowmelt (mm/day) by Vapor Condensation
under Typical Conditions in Open Areas

| Windspeed (m/sec) | Vapor pressure difference, $e_a$ - 6.1 (mb) | | | | |
|---|---|---|---|---|---|
| | 1 | 2 | 3 | 4 | 5 |
| 1 | 3 | 6 | 10 | 13 | 16 |
| 2 | 5 | 9 | 14 | 18 | 23 |
| 5 | 7 | 14 | 22 | 29 | 36 |

neers (1956), both $M_c$ and $M_v$ should be reduced to about half for heavily forested areas.

When rain occurs on snow, energy is absorbed and some additional melting $(M_r)$ occurs; for rain at temperature $T_r$ (°C),

$$M_r = \frac{E_r}{L_f} = \frac{T_r P}{80} \qquad \text{9.10)}$$

where $P$(cm) is rainfall depth. Even for a very heavy warm rain, e.g., $T_r = 10°C$ and $P = 100$ mm/day, the effect ($M_r = 12$ mm/day) may be small compared with that caused by other factors. Heat may also be delivered to the snowpack by conduction ($B$) from the ground, but ordinarily during late winter and early spring $B$ is quite small, and the corresponding melting rate $M_b < 1$ mm/day.

Snow accumulation, melting, and associated discharge events are affected by forest cover; accumulations are reduced by interception, and melting and snowmelt discharge are delayed, especially under coniferous forest types. Table 9.8 summarizes the effects of forest cutting on snow accumulation as adapted from the literature survey data of Anderson, Hoover, and Reinhart (1976). Forest cutting not only reduces interception, but also changes the aerodynamic properties of the landscape; as a result, greater snow accumulations in openings may be partly balanced by decreases under the adjacent forest.

Forest cutting alters the flow regime of snowmelt runoff; in cut-over areas more snow accumulates, but it begins to melt earlier in the season and produces an earlier peak in the streamflow hydrograph. Figure 9.4 (adapted from Leaf, 1975) illustrates the effect

Table 9.8. Increase in Snow Accumulation after Cutting Coniferous Forests
(adapted from Anderson, Hoover, and Reinhart, 1976)

| Forest | Treatment | | Increase (mm)[a] | (%) |
|---|---|---|---|---|
| Lodgepole pine, Colo. | Percent cut: | 50 | 21 | 12 |
| | | 66 | 26 | 15 |
| | | 83 | 38 | 21 |
| | | 100 | 51 | 29 |
| Ponderosa pine and Douglas fir, Colo. | Selection cut | | 11 | 6 |
| | Clearcut | | 31 | 29 |
| Hemlock–fir, Ore. | Strip cut | | 127 | 15 |
| Red fir, Calif. | Selection cut | | 178 | 14 |
| | Clearcut | | 279 | 23 |
| | East-west strip | | 305 | 26 |
| | Block cut | | 381 | 34 |
| | Wall-and-step | | 483 | 25 |
| Black spruce, Minn. | Selection cut | | 3 | 4 |
| | Shelterwood | | 18 | 28 |
| | Strip cut | | 38 | 60 |
| | Patch cut | | 51 | 80 |

[a]Increase in equivalent depth of liquid water.

on streamflow timing caused by forest strip cutting in the Rocky Mountains; in this instance peak flow was not significantly affected even though the total volume of yield increased (average increase of 89 mm/yr for 17 years). Snowmelt and associated discharge peaks naturally occur earlier at lower elevations and on southfacing aspects in mountainous terrain; this desynchronization of flow, which is useful in reducing flood damages, can be manipulated to some extent by alternating forest and cutover plots in selected areas of the landscape.

Snowpack management for water supply augmentation has received most attention in areas where snowmelt is the major source of streamflow, and where delayed melt and runoff are desirable so that more water will be available during the period of greater demand for agricultural and municipal use. The dual objectives,

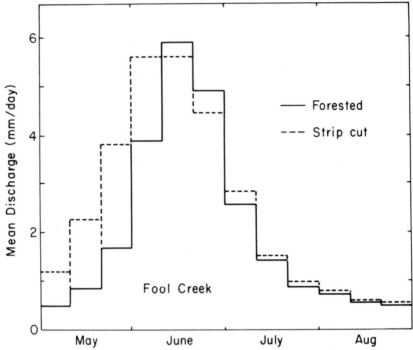

Figure 9.4. Average discharge rates during the snowmelt season before (solid bars) and after (dashed bars) strip-cutting Rocky Mountain conifers (adapted from Leaf, 1975).

greater snowfall accumulation and delayed melt, appear to be antagonistic, but forest cutting methods can be adapted to some extent to optimize the effects; the accumulating snowpack in a forest opening is partially shaded by the residual stand, and the shading effect is greatest in small openings, or in narrow strip openings that are judiciously oriented to maximize shading on any given topographic facet (e.g., east-west strips on level land and south- and north-facing slopes). Engineering controls-used in snowpack management include the use of snowfences upwind of natural snowfields to increase both the depth and melting period, and snow albedo modifications to accelerate the melting of mountain glaciers during periods of drought.

## 9.5. Municipal Watersheds

Municipal watersheds are areas managed primarily for the regulated production of high quality water. Water shortages, and the increasing pollution of natural waterways, are continuing threats to municipal life; seasonal and drought-year shortages occur even in humid regions, and the rapidly increasing demands of growing cities suggest that more general shortages are imminent. The existence of municipal watersheds is evidence of the recognition that intensive watershed management and forest manipulation can play a vital role in solving local water problems.

Numerous reports on the effectiveness of municipal watershed management have appeared during the past two decades. Results of a general survey in the northeastern United States were reported by Corbett (1970); they revealed that more than 8000 km$^2$ of land were controlled by 750 local agencies as water-source areas or protection lands for municipal water supplies. About two-thirds of the watersheds were smaller than 25 km$^2$; also, about two-thirds were owned by municipalities, one-fifth were in other public ownership, and one-sixth were privately owned.

Timber harvesting was permitted on more than half of the municipal watersheds surveyed by Corbett; the primary reasons given for cutting were to improve water yield and to derive income from timber sales. Recreational activity was permitted on three-fifths of the watersheds, whereas two-fifths had complete restriction on recreational use. Interestingly, water quality control was also listed as a major area of concern on three-fifths of the watersheds, and water yield improvement was somewhat less frequently cited as a major problem area.

Action programs on municipal watersheds in eastern United States are concerned primarily with water quality. One obvious reason for this is that, as a rule, water supplies have been adequate; precipitation averages about $3(10^6)$ liters/day · km$^2$, with a fairly even seasonal distribution, so less than 2% of the total supply is required to satisfy all domestic and municipal needs. Also, per-capita streamflow in the East averages about 20,000 liters per day, or 25 times the normal requirement, so it is understandable that other problems (e.g., reservior storage and water quality) are given higher priority than water supply augmentation.

Where water supplies are limited, "water harvesting," or "precipitation harvesting," provide maximum efficiency in water supply procurement. If an impermeable surface is created on a watershed, almost all precipitation becomes discharge, and the supply problem is reduced to that of providing sufficient reservoir storage capacity. Lull (1967) estimated that water harvesting in New Jersey would yield $9.2(10^8)$ liters/yr $\cdot$ km$^2$, and that treatment costs would easily be competitive with current municipal water costs.

The practice of water harvesting is not widespread; it may not be an aesthetically appealing alternative, and it precludes using the land to attain other economic objectives, e.g., timber production. Some studies have shown that total economic returns and social benefits may be greater when water management is combined with timber management and other activities. For example, according to Spencer (1975), the Metropolitan District Commission of Boston combined timber and water management operations on 4000 hectares of forested watershed, and over a 10-year period water yield was valued at only 30% of timber production.

Municipal land is valuable, of course, for many purposes. It is important to recognize that water yield augmentation and water quality protection are only two of the many considerations. But it is equally important to recognize that the "wise use" of municipal or other land, economically interpreted, may be foolhardy.

## LITERATURE CITED

Anderson, H. W., M. D. Hoover, and K. G. Reinhart. 1976. *Forests and Water: Effects of Forest Management on Floods, Sedimentation, and Water Supply.* Forest Service Technical Report PSW-18. Berkeley, Calif.: U.S. Department of Agriculture.

Bethlahmy, N. 1974. More streamflow after a bark beetle epidemic. *Journal of Hydrology* 23:185–89.

Corbett, E. S. 1970. The management of forested watersheds for domestic water supply. In *Proceedings Georgia Forest Resource Council.* Atlanta, Ga.: Georgia Forest Resource Council.

Corps of Engineers, 1956. *Snow Hydrology*. Portland, Ore.: U.S. Army.

Curtis, W. R. 1972. Strip-mined mountain watersheds have greater flood potential. In S. C. Csallany, T. G. McLaughlin, and W. D. Striffler, eds., *Watersheds in Transition*. Urbana, Ill.: American Water Resources Association.

Curtis, W. R. 1977. *Surface Mining and the Flood of 1977*. Forest Service Research Note NE-248. Berea, Ky.: U.S. Department of Agriculture.

Deely, J. D. 1970. "High Surface Temperatures on Sunlit Strip-Mine Spoils in Central Pennsylvania." Master's thesis, Pennsylvania State University, University Park, Pa.

Eschner, A. R. and D. R. Satterlund. 1966. Forest protection and streamflow from an Adirondack watershed. *Water Resources Research* 2:765–83.

Frye, P. M. and G. S. Runner. 1970. *A Proposed Streamflow Data Program for West Virginia*. Geological Survey. Charleston, W.Va.: U.S. Department of Interior.

Heede, B. H. 1977a. Gully control structures and systems. In S. H. Kunkle and J. L. Thames, eds., *Guidelines for Watershed Management*. Rome: Food and Agriculture Organization of the United Nations.

Heede, B. H. 1977b. *Case Study of a Watershed Rehabilitation Project: Alkali Creek, Colorado*. Forest Service Research Paper RM-189. Fort Collins, Colo.: U.S. Department of Agriculture.

Hoyt, W. G. and W. B. Langbein. 1955. *Floods*. Princeton, N.J.: Princeton University Press.

Kochenderfer, J. N. 1970. *Erosion Control on Logging Roads in the Appalachians*. Forest Service Research Paper NE-158. Upper Darby, Pa.: U.S. Department of Agriculture.

Leaf, C. F. 1975. *Watershed Management in the Rocky Mountain Subalpine Zone: The Status of Our Knowledge*. Forest Service Research Paper RM-137. Fort Collins, Colo.: U.S. Department of Agriculture.

Lee, R., W. G. Hutson, and S. C. Hill. 1975. Energy exchange and plant survival on disturbed land. In D. M. Gates and R. B. Schmerl, eds., *Perspectives of Biophysical Ecology*. New York: Springer.

Lull, H. W. 1967. Management for water production on municipal watersheds. In *Proceedings Fifth World Forestry Congress* 5:1686–90.

Lull, H. W., and K. G. Reinhart. 1972. *Forests and Floods in the Eastern United States*. Forest Service Research Paper NE-226. Upper Darby, Pa.: U.S. Department of Agriculture.

Soil Conservation Service, 1969. *Engineering Field Manual for Conservation Practices*. Washington, D.C.: U.S. Department of Agriculture.

Spencer, B. A. 1975. Current management practices on metropolitan Boston's municipal watersheds. In *Municipal Watershed Management*, Forest Service Technical Report NE-13. Upper Darby, Pa.: U.S. Department of Agriculture.

Van Haveren, B. P. and R. W. Brown. 1975. Soil-plant water relations of revegetation. In *Watershed Management*. New York: American Society of Civil Engineers.

**SELECTED READINGS**

Bruce, J. P. and R. H. Clark, 1966. *Introduction to Hydrometeorology*. New York: Pergamon Press.

Garstka, W. U. 1964. Snow and snow survey. In V. T. Chow, ed., *Handbook of Applied Hydrology*, New York: McGraw-Hill.

Miller, D. H. 1977. *Water at the Surface of the Earth*. New York: Academic Press.

Pereira, H. C. 1973. *Land Use and Water Resources in Temperate and Tropical Climates*. London: Cambridge University Press.

# 10 HYDROLOGIC OBSERVATIONS

## 10.1. Climate Stations

Climate stations are generally intended to provide long-term data that characterize local atmospheric phenomena; measurements of precipitation and air temperature are most common, but humidity, wind, radiation, evaporation, and other data are also frequently in demand for hydrologic purposes. At forest climate stations the raw data must be viewed primarily as indices, or as a general reference base for comparison with, or extrapolation to, surrounding sites. In some instances it is possible to adjust the observational data to account for instrumental inaccuracies and local influences on the measured quantity.

### 10.1.a. Precipitation Measurement

The most widely used precipitation gage is a cylindrical open-topped vessel in which rainfall depth is magnified 10-fold by funneling the catch into a smaller internal cylinder (see fig. 10.1). In these *standard nonrecording* gages, the depth of rainfall (or melted snow) is measured by noting the water line on a calibrated stick; the gages are read once daily, at the same time of day, so the data are 24-hour precipitation totals. Gage sizes and installation criteria vary among countries; in the United States gage diameter is 20 cm and the orifice is located at about 1 m above the surface.

Numerous mechanisms have been devised for recording the time-distribution of rainfall; most common in the United States is the *weight-type recording* gage illustrated in figure 10.2. In this type,

Figure 10.1. Standard nonrecording rain gage (courtesy of Science Associates, Princeton, N.J.).

Figure 10.2. Recording rain gage, weighing type (courtesy of Science
  Associates, Princeton, N.J.).

precipitation falls through the orifice into a collector that is mounted on a weighing mechanism; the weight of the catch is transmitted mechanically to a pen arm that records equivalent depth on a calibrated clock-driven chart. Other common types include the *tipping-bucket* gage that records precipitation in discrete increments of depth (usually 0.25-mm increments), and the *punched-tape* (Fischer-Porter) gage that records 2.5-mm increments of depth on paper tape designed for use in machine data processing.

Despite mechanical improvements that make it less cumbersome, the basic technique of rain gaging has not changed appreciably for hundreds of years; and despite numerous investigations, the problem of measurement accuracy is a matter of continuing concern in quantitative hydrology. Rain-gaging errors of minor importance (usually <1% of catch) may result from any of several instrumental and observational inadequacies, but major errors are associated with the exposure of the gage to wind. Falling raindrops and snowflakes tend to move with air currents, and the rain gage is an obstruction that modifies the windfield in its immediate vicinity; following the treatment of section 3.3.b, the orifice of the gage becomes a "blow-over" zone of deficient precipitation.

It is known that the deficiency in catch of a common rain gage increases with windspeed, but the precise relationship is difficult to define because it also depends on the buoyancy, or terminal (fall) velocity, of precipitation particles. Fall velocity is a function of raindrop mass (or equivalent diameter) and, in the case of snowflakes, particle shape is also important; in general, catch deficiency is greater for smaller raindrops, and much greater for snow than for rain. The experimental problem is further complicated by the extreme variability of windspeed during precipitation periods, and by the fact that precipitation particles come in a range of sizes that varies with storm type and atmospheric conditions.

Raindrop diameters vary in size from about 0.5 to 5.0 mm (smaller and larger drops are relatively rare), but the distribution of sizes varies with rainfall intensity; larger drops are associated with more intense storms. Table 10.1 lists the percentages of rain that occur in various drop-size categories at different intensities as determined by Laws and Parsons (1943); ordinarily from 50 to

Table 10.1. Percentage of Rainfall by Drop Diameter
Classes and Rainfall Intensities (adapted from
Laws and Parsons, 1943)

| Diameter | Intensity (mm/hr) | | | | | | |
|---|---|---|---|---|---|---|---|
| (mm) | 1 | 2 | 5 | 10 | 20 | 50 | 100 |
| <1 | 32 | 22 | 14 | 9 | 6 | 4 | 3 |
| 1–3 | 67 | 76 | 79 | 80 | 76 | 66 | 55 |
| >3 | 1 | 2 | 7 | 11 | 18 | 30 | 42 |

80% of precipitation occurs in the 1 to 3 mm drop-size range. The
median drop size ($d$) increases with rainfall intensity ($i$) according
to the rule

$$d = 1.238\ i^{0.182} \tag{10.1}$$

or

$$i = 0.31\ d^{5.5} \tag{10.2}$$

where $d$ is in mm, and $i$ in mm/hr (modified after Laws and
Parsons, 1943); solutions to these equations are given in table 10.2
along with the terminal velocities of median drop sizes as determined by Gunn and Kinzer (1949).

Table 10.2. Median Rainfall Drop Diameter, Terminal Velocity, and Rainfall
Intensity

| Diameter (mm) | Intensity (mm/hr) | Velocity (cm/sec) | Diameter (mm) | Intensity (mm/hr) | Velocity (cm/sec) |
|---|---|---|---|---|---|
| 1.09 | 0.5 | 430 | 0.5 | 0.01 | 206 |
| 1.24 | 1 | 475 | 1.0 | 0.31 | 403 |
| 1.40 | 2 | 517 | 1.5 | 3 | 541 |
| 1.66 | 5 | 578 | 2.0 | 14 | 649 |
| 1.88 | 10 | 625 | 2.5 | 48 | 742 |
| 2.14 | 20 | 678 | 3.0 | 130 | 806 |
| 2.52 | 50 | 745 | 3.5 | 305 | 852 |
| 2.86 | 100 | 789 | 4.0 | 635 | 883 |
| 3.25 | 200 | 831 | 4.5 | 1213 | 901 |
| 3.84 | 500 | 874 | 5.0 | 2166 | 909 |

Since it is known that rainfall catch deficiency is greater for smaller drops and greater windspeeds, it must also be related to the angle of inclination ($I$) of the falling drops (which depends primarily on the same variables); from equation 3.24 (section 3.3.b),

$$I = \text{arc tan } \frac{u}{v} \tag{10.3}$$

where $u$ and $v$ are the horizontal (windspeed) and vertical (terminal velocity) components of the raindrop fall velocity, respectively. It has been suggested (Lee, 1978) that the deficiency in catch ($C_d$) of a standard rain gage might be estimated as

$$C_d = 100(1 - \cos I) \tag{10.4}$$

where $C_d$ is in percent of true rainfall; the physical meaning is that $C_d$ is the deficiency of a normal gage (with horizontal orifice) as compared with a gage directed so that the plane of the orifice is normal to the trajectory of the falling rain. The inclination angle ($I$) must be estimated for a given raindrop size (or given $v$), but since each storm consists of a range of drop sizes, it is necessary to select an appropriate average size to characterize the storm.

In an assemblage composed of various drop sizes, the mean angle of inclination ($\bar{I}$) must be a compromise between that which would be assumed by individual drops in isolation. As a first approximation $\bar{I}$ can be obtained as a function of median drop size ($d$) as defined by equation 10.1; but $d$ is simply the size above and below which 50% of rainfall volume occurs, and in an assemblage the mean inclination must be influenced disproportionately by larger drops (since drop mass is proportional to $d^3$). Drops falling at different velocities collide frequently, but with conserved total momentum (the product of mass and velocity); the drop size with mean momentum ($d_m$) can be determined by weighting individual drop momenta according to their relative frequencies as given in table 10.1, and

$$d_m = 1.6 \, i^{0.15} \tag{10.5}$$

is obtained from the relationship between $\ln d_m$ and $\ln i$ which plots as a straight line.

Using equation 10.5 to define the appropriate drop size, the estimated rainfall inclination angle $(\bar{I})$ is given by

$$\bar{I} = \text{arc tan } \frac{u}{v_m} \qquad (10.6)$$

where $v_m$ is the terminal velocity corresponding to $d_m$ ; and from equation 10.4

$$C_d = 100(1 - \cos \bar{I}) \qquad (10.7)$$

is an estimate of the catch deficiency in a standard gage. Adjusting for the deficiency, an estimate of true rainfall depth $(P_t)$ is

$$P_t = \frac{P_o}{\cos \bar{I}} \qquad (10.8)$$

Table 10.3. Estimated and Observed Rainfall Catch Deficiencies (%)

| Rainfall intensity (mm/hr) | Effective drop diameter (mm) | Terminal velocity (cm/sec) | Windspeed (m/sec) | | | | |
|---|---|---|---|---|---|---|---|
| | | | 2 | 4 | 6 | 8 | 10 |
| 1 | 1.60 | 565 | 6 | 18 | 31 | 42 | 51 |
| 2 | 1.78 | 605 | 5 | 17 | 29 | 40 | 48 |
| 5 | 2.04 | 657 | 4 | 15 | 26 | 37 | 45 |
| 10 | 2.26 | 701 | 4 | 13 | 24 | 34 | 43 |
| 20 | 2.51 | 744 | 3 | 12 | 22 | 32 | 40 |
| 50 | 2.88 | 792 | 3 | 11 | 20 | 30 | 38 |
| 100 | 3.19 | 825 | 3 | 10 | 19 | 28 | 36 |
| *Mean for all intensities* | | | 4 | 14 | 24 | 35 | 43 |
| *Mean for all authors (below)* | | | 7 | 14 | 23 | 32 | 42 |
| *Observed averages* | | | | | | | |
| Koschmieder (1934), gage height 1.1 m | | | 4 | 11 | 21 | 41 | 64 |
| Wilson (1954), 11 studies, 1884–1954 | | | 5 | 13 | 26 | 33 | 39 |
| Bratzev (1963), 5% per m/sec | | | 10 | 20 | 30 | 40 | 50 |
| Struzer et al. (1965), $i < 2$ mm/hr | | | 8 | 15 | 23 | 30 | 38 |
| Larson and Peck (1974), shielded gages | | | 6 | 11 | 15 | 18 | 20 |
| *Range (listed authors)* | | | 4–10 | 11–20 | 15–30 | 18–41 | 20–64 |
| *Range (estimated, equation 10.7)* | | | 3–6 | 10–18 | 19–31 | 28–42 | 36–51 |

where $P_o$ is the observed depth. Solutions to equations 10.5 through 10.7 are given in table 10.3 for rainfall intensities between 1 and 100 mm/hr and windspeeds from 2 to 10 m/sec; the estimated catch deficiencies are plotted in figure 10.3.

Rainfall catch deficiencies are obtained empirically by comparing the catch in a standard gage with that in a *ground-level* or *pit* gage; with the orifice at ground level, and the collector in a pit below, there is little disruption of the windfield and the catch is assumed to be true. Observations of this sort have been reported by numerous investigators, and from diverse climatic regions; the

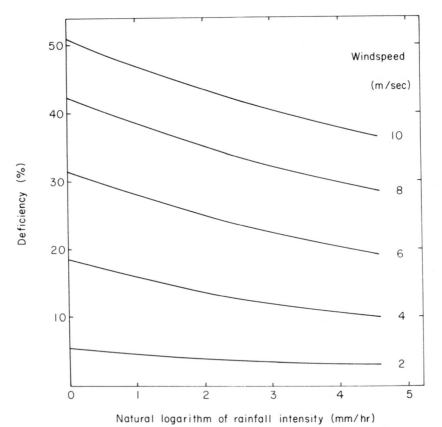

Figure 10.3. **Rainfall catch deficiency as a function of rainfall intensity and windspeed.**

deficiencies are usually given simply as a function of mean wind-speed, and the results vary considerably as shown in table 10.3. The means and ranges of the empirical estimates are comparable to those based on equation 10.7, which suggests the usefulness of the latter as an hypothesis in more definitive studies.

The precipitation gaging error can be reduced to some extent by the use of a wind shield around the gage orifice; the *Alter-type shield* shown in figure 10.4 is common in regions of the United States where snow constitutes a major part of the annual water input. The standard rain gage, with funnel removed, can be used to measure snow-water equivalent (the snow is melted and measured the same as rain), but catch deficiencies are usually several times greater than for rain. The daily accumulation (depth) of snow is measured on *snow boards* or other cleared areas, and

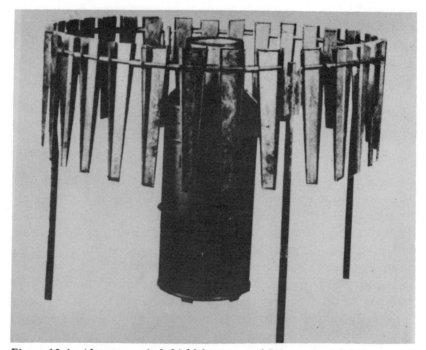

Figure 10.4. Alter-type wind shield (courtesy of Science Associates, Princeton, N.J.).

converted to equivalent liquid-water depth by melting a known volume and determining its density; the total accumulation at any time is determined by sampling at numerous points along an established *snow course* where permanent depth markers, *snow stakes*, may be installed to facilitate depth measurements.

### 10.1.b. Screen Data

Climate station instruments that must be protected from condensation, precipitation, and radiation are housed in *climate shelters* or *screens*. The typical shelter (fig. 10.5) is white, double-topped, with louvered sides to permit free circulation of air; it is mounted rigidly, to minimize vibrations, at a height of about 1.5 m over a natural surface. Screen air temperature and humidity are important hydrologically as indices of local air mass properties.

*Maximum* and *minimum thermometers* of the liquid-in-glass type (fig. 10.6) are commonly used to measure screen temperature extremes; these are read once daily, at the same time each day, and the daily mean temperature is taken as the arithmetic average of the extremes. Hydrologists frequently use monthly and annual temperature means computed from the daily observations; at representative sites the long-term average, or *normal temperature* $(T_n)$, can be estimated with acceptable accuracy using an equation of the form

$$T_n = a + bZ + c\phi \tag{10.9}$$

where $Z$ is elevation and $\phi$ is latitude. The coefficients in equation 10.9, as determined for the northeastern United States, are given in table 10.4 (Lee, 1969); relationships of this sort are useful in estimating temperatures at sites where observations are lacking, but deviations occur locally in response to the influences of land form, large water bodies, and cultural developments.

Deformation thermometers, with bimetal or Bourdon-type sensors, are used in the common *thermograph* to obtain a continuous recording of screen temperature; these sensors magnify temperature-related expansions and contractions which are transferred mechanically to a pen arm and inscribed on a rotating clock-driven drum chart. The thermograph is combined with an

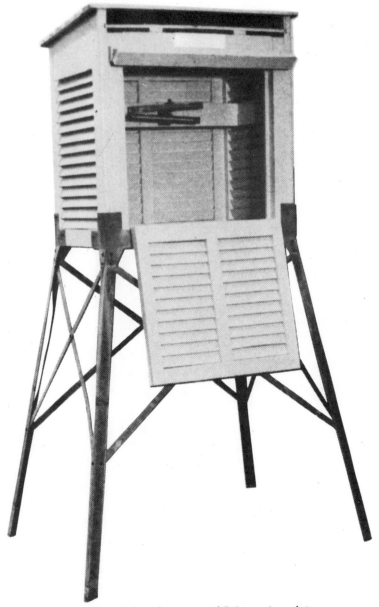

Figure 10.5. Instrument shelter (courtesy of Science Associates, Princeton, N.J.).

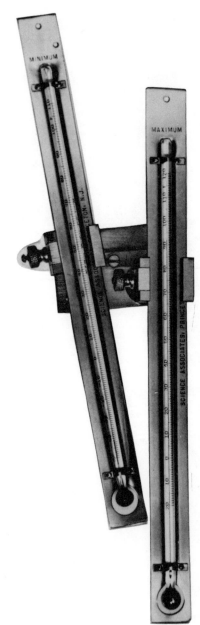

Figure 10.6. Liquid-in-glass maximum and minimum thermometers (courtesy of Science Associates, Princeton, N.J.).

**Table 10.4. Coefficients Relating Normal Temperature (°C) to Elevation ($10^2$ m) and Latitude (degrees) in Northeastern United States**

| Period | Coefficient | | | Standard error (°C) |
|---|---|---|---|---|
| | $a$ | $b$ | $c$ | |
| January | 68.3 | -0.482 | -1.684 | 0.75 |
| April | 58.2 | -0.436 | -1.171 | 0.66 |
| July | 52.6 | -0.604 | -0.702 | 0.66 |
| October | 49.4 | -0.517 | -0.891 | 0.65 |
| Year | 56.5 | -0.523 | -1.101 | 0.58 |

*hygrometer* (humidity instrument) in the common *hygrothermograph* shown in figure 10.7; in the standard *hair hygrometer*, changes in the dimensions of human hair strands with ambient humidity changes are magnified and transmitted to a recording chart that is calibrated in units of relative humidity. Relative humidity varies inversely with temperature (as illustrated in fig. 3.2, section 3.1.a), so extrapolations to adjacent forest sites must be accomplished in terms of absolute humidity or actual vapor pressure.

More accurate measurements by ambient humidity are obtained with a *psychrometer*; the common *sling psychrometer* shown in figure 10.8 is used periodically to check the accuracy of the hair hygrometer. Psychrometer measurements consist simply of paired temperature measurements, one with an ordinary "dry-bulb" thermometer that indicates air temperature ($T$), and one with a "wet-bulb" (an ordinary bulb covered with wet muslin); the wet bulb, cooled by evaporation, indicates the wet-bulb temperature ($T_w$), and the ambient vapor pressure ($e$) is given by

$$e = e_w - \gamma \, \frac{p}{1000} \, (T - T_w) \qquad (10.10)$$

where $e_w$ is saturation vapor pressure at $T_w$, $p$ is barometeric pressure, and

$$\gamma = 0.66 \, (1 + 0.00115 T_w) \qquad (10.11)$$

Figure 10.7. Hygrothermograph (courtesy of Science Associates, Princeton, N.J.).

for pressure in mb and temperature in °C. Tables based on solutions to equation 10.10, and the relationships given in section 3.1.a, are commonly used to obtain the desired measure of humidity; table A.5 is an example.

Figure 10.8. Sling psychrometer (courtesy of Science Associates, Princeton, N.J.).

## 10.1.c. Other Data

Other climate station data that are useful as hydrologic indices include soil and water (evaporation pan) temperatures, evaporation, wind, and observations of mean cloudiness and the duration of "bright sunshine" to index solar radiation for a day. Soil temperatures can be recorded continuously using a variety of electrical (thermocouple or resistance) or other *distance thermometers*, or extreme values can be read daily from a *dial type maximum-minimum thermometer* (fig. 10.9). Water temperatures in an evaporation pan are commonly measured with a submerged *Six's maximum-minimum thermometer* (fig. 10.10).

An index to catchment evaporation can be obtained at a local climate station using the standard evaporation pan (fig. 10.11); in the United States the standard pan is 122 cm in diameter and 25 cm deep. Water depth in the pan is measured to the nearest 0.25 mm and, in the absence of precipitation, the change in water level

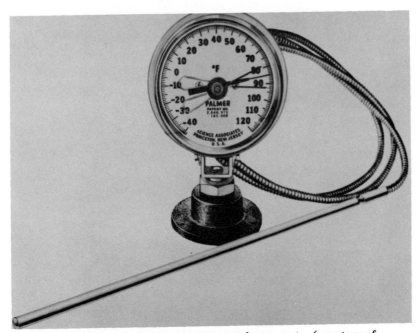

Figure 10.9. Dial type maximum-minimum thermometer (courtesy of Science Associates, Princeton, N.J.).

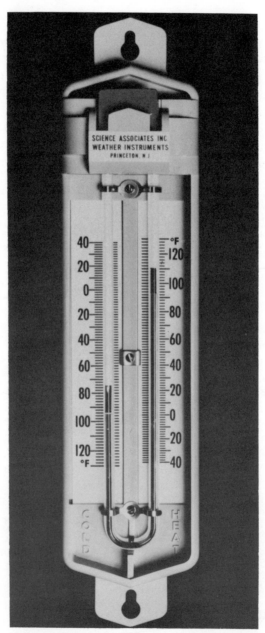

Figure 10.10. U-shaped (Six's) maximum-minimum thermometer (courtesy of Science Associates, Princeton, N.J.).

Figure 10.11. Standard evaporation pan with cup anemometer
(courtesy of Science Associates, Princeton, N.J.).

from one day to the next is a measure of evaporation depth. Since
the rate of evaporation is strongly influenced by wind and water
temperature, the pan is usually operated with a *totaling anemometer*
near the water surface and a maximum-minimum thermometer in
the water.

*Wind vanes* and *anemometers* are used to measure the components (direction and speed) of air velocity; ordinarily only the
horizontal components are observed, and wind direction is taken
as the direction upwind. Windspeed tends to fluctuate rapidly in a
natural environment, so the mean value for a desired interval is
obtained either by averaging instantaneous speeds from a *recording anemometer*, or by dividing the accumulated wind run by
elapsed time; the *cup anemometer* pictured in figure 10.11 is
equipped with an odometer that is read once daily to obtain the
average speed in km/day. Since windspeed tends to increase
logarithmically with height, and is much subdued in forest openings, it is important to assess the general applicability of data in

Figure 10.12.  Campbell-Stokes sunshine recorder (courtesy of Science
Associates, Princeton, N.J.).

terms of instrument exposure; measurements at 2 m height are common in microclimatology, but at airport stations data are collected at greater heights (6–10 m is common).

Observations of mean cloudiness and the duration of bright sunshine are useful as indices of global radiation. The former are judgmental, based on the observer's ocular estimates of sky cover in tenths. Sunshine duration is measured with the Campbell-Stokes *sunshine recorder* which utilizes a glass sphere to concentrate the sun's rays and burn a trace on a prepared paper chart; this instrument, adopted as standard by the World Meteorological Organization, is shown in figure 10.12.

## 10.2. Energy Flow

Energy-flow measurements are used in hydrology primarily to quantify water phase changes in terms of equivalent energy transfers as outlined in section 2.2.c. But, in a broader context, energy parameters are also useful in characterizing watershed climate and the influences of forest cover, and cover type changes, on the heat transfer processes. Instruments and observational techniques used exclusively in studies of evaporation and transpiration are treated separately in section 10.6.

*Radiometer* is a general name for instruments used to measure shortwave and longwave radiation; more specific names are given to those designed to measure particular components of radiative exchange. *Pyrheliometers* measure direct solar radiation only (not the diffusive component), but the term was formerly used for instruments designed to measure total incoming shortwave radiation (global radiation); the accepted name for the latter is *pyranometer* (World Meteorological Organization, 1965). The *Eppley pyranometer* (fig.10.13), the official standard in the United States, can be used to record electronically or to totalize global radiation over any selected interval; the less expensive *pyranograph* (fig. 10.14) records mechanically and is used in remote areas where electrical power is not available.

Figure 10.13. Eppley pyranometer (courtesy of Science Associates,
Princeton, N.J.).

If global radiation is measured in a forest opening, the observed
values are grossly in error during periods when the solar beam is
excluded (i.e., when the instrument is shaded by surrounding trees);
a minor error occurs throughout the day because a part of diffuse
sky radiation is excluded, but there is partial compensation (or
overcompensation) for this effect by shortwave reflection to the
instrument from surrounding trees. An approximate correction for
the major error can be attained by finding the percentage of daily
total radiation that normally occurs during the period of shading;
the theoretical values for hourly intervals are given in table 10.5.
Table 10.5 shows, for example, that during a 14-hour day about
80% of the total occurs within ±4 hours of noon, so if shading
occurs during the remaining hours the instrument records only
80% of the daily total; these theoretical values have been con-

Figure 10.14. Pyranograph (courtesy of Science Associates, Princeton, N.J.).

Table 10.5. Normal Hourly Percentages of Daily Total Solar Radiation

| Day length (hrs) | Interval (hrs from noon) | | | | | | | |
|---|---|---|---|---|---|---|---|---|
| | 0–1 | 1–2 | 2–3 | 3–4 | 4–5 | 5–6 | 6–7 | 7–8 |
| 8 | 18.7 | 16.1 | 11.1 | 4.1 | — | — | — | — |
| 9 | 16.8 | 14.9 | 11.3 | 6.2 | 0.8 | — | — | — |
| 10 | 15.2 | 13.8 | 11.1 | 7.3 | 2.6 | — | — | — |
| 11 | 14.0 | 12.9 | 10.7 | 7.8 | 4.1 | 0.5 | — | — |
| 12 | 12.9 | 12.1 | 10.4 | 7.9 | 5.0 | 1.7 | — | — |
| 13 | 12.1 | 11.3 | 9.9 | 8.0 | 5.5 | 2.8 | 0.4 | — |
| 14 | 11.3 | 10.7 | 9.6 | 7.9 | 5.8 | 3.5 | 1.2 | — |
| 15 | 10.7 | 10.2 | 9.2 | 7.7 | 6.0 | 4.0 | 2.0 | 0.2 |
| 16 | 10.2 | 9.7 | 8.8 | 7.6 | 6.1 | 4.3 | 2.5 | 0.8 |

firmed by Whillier (1956), Lee et al. (1979), and others in diverse climatological regions.

The glass domes over the sensing elements of pyranometers (figs. 10.13 and 10.14) protect against condensation, precipitation, and wind in order to isolate the radiation effect. But since glass is opaque to longwave radiation, *longwave radiometers* (or, somewhat ambiguously, *infrared radiometers*) are shielded with plastic or other materials that transmit long wavelengths. Usually the difference between incoming and outgoing longwave radiation (the net longwave flux) is of primary concern, and the appropriate instrument is called a *pyrgeometer*.

An instrument that measures both shortwave and longwave radiation is the *pyrradiometer*, and that used to measure net all-wave radiation is the net pyrradiometer, radiation balance meter, or simply *net radiometer*. The Fritschen net radiometer (fig. 10.15), and others by Funk and Gier-Dunkle are in common use in the United States. The so-called *economical radiometer* designed by Tanner et al. (1969) can be equipped with four sensing heads to measure incoming and outgoing components of both shortwave and longwave radiation.

For adequate evaluation of other energy flows between the atmosphere and the forest, or atmosphere and the soil, it is usually necessary to measure vertical profiles of the critical parameters. The conduction and heat-storage equations (equations 2.27 and 2.28) require measurements of soil temperature at various depths either to describe the vertical profile or to determine the change

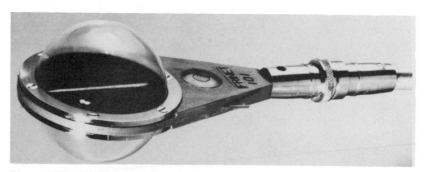

Figure 10.15. **Fritschen miniature net radiometer (courtesy of Science Associates, Princeton, N.J.).**

in mean temperature; ordinarily electronic sensors, *thermocouples* (junctions of dissimilar metals that generate a temperature-dependent electrical current), *thermistors* (metallic oxides with temperature-dependent electrical resistance), or other electrical resistance thermometers are used for this purpose. Alternatively, the flux of heat into and out of soils can be measured directly using *heat flux plates*, which measure the temperature drop across a thin body of low thermal capacity and known thermal impedance.

Evaluating convective exchanges in terms of equations 2.33 and 2.34 requires measurements of both temperature and windspeed at several levels above the surface or forest canopy. Ordinarily small electrical thermometers are used for this purpose, and these are shielded and ventilated to prevent radiation errors; windspeed is usually measured with sensitive cup anemometers of low mass. In evaluating latent heat exchanges over the surface or canopy (equations 6.10 and 6.11), humidity measurements are an added requirement; psychrometers, with thermocouples or electrical resistance temperature sensors, are often used for this purpose, as are "dewcell" sensors in which the electrical resistance of a moisture-sensitive film electrolyte is calibrated to indicate ambient humidity.

Energy-flow measurements within and above a forest canopy usually require the construction of observation towers for instrument support; lightweight metal towers are preferred because they can be constructed in sections with minimum disturbance of the canopy environment. The exposed instruments can be wired to ground-level indicators or recorders, but the difficulty of routine inspection and maintenance is a major problem. Ladders or stairs add to the bulk of the installation, and to the possible artificiality of canopy microclimate; sometimes retractable towers are used, or elevator systems are installed for raising and lowering instrument assemblies.

## 10.3. Forest Precipitation

Point rainfall measurements are inherently inaccurate, as discussed in section 10.1.a; *gage errors* result because the measurement process itself introduces a change in the spatial distribution of rainfall in the immediate vicinity of the gage. A similar phenomenon occurs when openings in a forest canopy are created for the purpose of establishing a gaging station at the surface; in this case rainfall distribution at ground level is not the same as it would have been over the same area at canopy level in the absence of an opening. Consequently rainfall catch near the ground in a forest opening is subject to an additional *site error* of unknown magnitude.

Numerous studies have been conducted to determine the optimum size of a circular forest opening—the implicit assumption being that true (above-canopy) rainfall will occur at the center of an opening of *some* unknown size; this assumption has not been verified (and is necessarily true only in the trivial case of extensive clearcut areas). It is known that canopy interception causes an area of relatively low rainfall near the windward edge of an opening, and that there is a rain-rich zone near the leeward edge, but it would be naive to suppose that true rainfall occurs at some intermediate or central position. Forest opening size is usually chosen so that, in the judgment of the observer, it is large enough to preclude the interception effect and small enough to minimize wind-induced gage errors.

Weiss (1963) developed a theoretical expression for the trajectories of raindrops as they fall into the relatively calm air of a forest opening; in the form used by Repa (1977), the horizontal distance $X$ (in m) traversed by a drop with initial horizontal speed $u$ (in m/sec) and fall velocity $v$ (in m/sec) is

$$X = \frac{v^2}{g} \ln \frac{\tanh \left[ (Mv^2 + hg)/2v^2 \right]}{\tanh (M/2)} \tag{10.12}$$

where

$$M = \ln \frac{v + (v^2 + u^2)^{0.5}}{u} \tag{10.13}$$

$g$ is the acceleration of gravity (9.81 m/sec), and $h$ (in m) is forest height. Solutions to equation 10.12 are given in table 10.6 for a range of forest heights and rainfall characteristics. The distance $X$,

**Table 10.6. Interception Zone Width (in meters) at the Windward Edge of a Forest Opening**

| Forest height (m) | Rainfall type[a] | Windspeed (m/sec) | | | | |
|---|---|---|---|---|---|---|
| | | 2 | 4 | 6 | 8 | 10 |
| 10 | L | 1.1 | 2.1 | 2.9 | 3.6 | 4.2 |
| | M | 1.2 | 2.4 | 3.4 | 4.3 | 5.1 |
| | H | 1.3 | 2.5 | 3.6 | 4.6 | 5.6 |
| 20 | L | 1.1 | 2.1 | 3.0 | 3.7 | 4.3 |
| | M | 1.4 | 2.7 | 3.8 | 4.8 | 5.7 |
| | H | 1.6 | 3.1 | 4.4 | 5.7 | 6.7 |
| 30 | L | 1.1 | 2.2 | 3.0 | 3.7 | 4.4 |
| | M | 1.5 | 2.7 | 3.9 | 4.9 | 5.8 |
| | H | 1.6 | 3.2 | 4.6 | 5.9 | 7.0 |

[a]Symbols refer to rainfall intensities, drop sizes, and terminal velocities given in table 10.3; intensities are (in mm/hr): L = 1, M = 10, and H = 100.

which is a measure of the interception zone width at the windward edge of an opening, varies between about 1 and 7 m under the given conditions; it increases with increases in windspeed, raindrop size, and forest height.

Equation 10.12 (or the data of table 10.6) can be used to define maximum height-diameter ratios for circular forest clearings such that, if the ratios are not exceeded, a rain gage exposed at the clearing center will be unaffected by canopy interception. The ratios given in table 10.7 vary between 0.9 and 3.4; these are based on a 10-m/sec windspeed and will be smaller at greater windspeeds. The critical size of a forest opening, insofar as the interception effect is concerned, is obviously a function of forest height, windspeed, and rainfall characteristics; this means that any rule of thumb with regard to a *single* optimum size is unwarranted.

The aerodynamic properties of forest openings are poorly understood, undoubtedly in part because of their variability and the consequent difficulty involved in giving meaningful physical descriptions: "circular" openings are not truly circular, of course, "tree height" is at best an average value, canopy density is highly

Table 10.7. Critical Height-Diameter
Ratios for Forest Openings
Used as Rain Gage Sites
(Windspeed = 10 m/sec)

| Rainfall type[a] | Forest height (m) | | |
|---|---|---|---|
| | 10 | 20 | 30 |
| L | 1.2 | 2.3 | 3.4 |
| M | 1.0 | 1.8 | 2.6 |
| H | 0.9 | 1.5 | 2.1 |

[a]See footnote in table 10.6.

variable and subject to seasonal changes, and the windfield above the canopy may be modified considerably by local undulations in topography. As a consequence, accurate precipitation measurement in forested areas is one of the major unsolved problems in quantitative hydrology. No solution is in sight; current station and network design criteria are useful primarily in reducing the uncertainty as much as possible, and in maintaining the relative consistency of catchment precipitation records.

The numbers of stations and types of instruments used in precipitation networks vary with catchment size, heterogeneity of precipitation climate, and network objectives or expected applications of the recorded data. Once a network has been established the number of gages required to estimate mean catchment precipitation with a given level of accuracy can be determined statistically; in this context, however, "mean catchment precipitation" refers to the mean of a large (infinite) number of randomly located gages, *not* to the true unknown catchment mean (statistical analysis is no substitute for gage accuracy). If a large number of gages is used initially in the establishment of a network, it may be possible later to reduce the number with little loss of accuracy by selecting a subgroup of stations such that the precipitation mean of the subgroup is approximately equal to the network mean.

Standard rain gages (fig. 10.1) are used on catchments to obtain daily, monthly, or annual totals, but recording types (fig. 10.2) are required to characterize hydrologic responses to short-term precipitation events. *Storage* gages, with capacity for several months or more of precipitation, are used in remote forest areas where routine measurements are difficult; *tilted* gages, with orifice parallel to the ground surface, are not much used but have been recommended by some investigators for measurements on steeply sloping land. *Miniature* or *small-orifice* gages are an economical alternative when a network of greater density is required, and these are sometimes preferred on the basis of an alleged superior accuracy.

## 10.4. Precipitation Disposal

The flow and attenuation of precipitation as it moves from above the forest canopy to the mineral soil are described quantitatively by measuring individual fluxes. Above-canopy precipitation is usually assumed to be the same as that observed near the ground in a forest clearing or adjacent open area, but sometimes it is measured near the tree tops. Above-canopy measurements are difficult logistically for obvious reasons, even though the catch may be funneled into a tube leading to a collector at ground level; miniature gages with shielding devices attached have been used in attempts to minimize wind-induced gage deficiencies, but their accuracy is questionable.

The fraction of precipitation that is intercepted, transiently stored, and eventually evaporated from the forest canopy cannot be measured directly under normal circumstances, but small trees grown in pots or lysimeters (see section 10.6) can be weighed during natural or simulated storms to obtain analogous information. The results of such studies, expressed in terms of unit leaf area, can be extrapolated to natural forest stands; such extrapolations are precarious, however, because there is no assurance that forest trees are comparable in this respect to isolated saplings. More commonly canopy interception is taken as the difference between precipitation and the sum of throughfall and stemflow.

Throughfall is measured with a variety of rain-gage types, but since its variability is much greater than that of precipitation the sampling problem is also greater. The variability of throughfall is a function of both forest and rainfall characteristics, so the number of gages needed to estimate the mean with a given level of accuracy must be determined statistically for each stand. Measurement accuracy per se is not a significant problem, except in open forests and with deciduous types in winter, because windspeeds are greatly reduced under a closed canopy.

Throughfall gages are called *interceptometers*, evidently because of their function in estimating canopy interception; a superior type of interceptometer is the *trough* gage. The orifice of the trough gage may be long (several meters) and narrow in plan view; it is superior in the sense that, because of its size and shape, it samples a range of throughfall conditions. The catch in a trough gage may be channeled to a storage tank, or diverted to a weighing or tipping-bucket recording gage.

Stemflow is also highly variable, even among individual trees of the same species; but stemflow quantity relative to total precipitation is small, so sampling criteria can be relaxed. Water running along the stem of a tree can be channeled into a collector or recording raingage by attaching a curled collar to the trunk; collars of metals, rubber, or plastic are incised in the bark to divert the normal flow. Stemflow for any particular tree can be expressed in terms of volume or depth for the projected area of the crown.

The fraction of precipitation that eventually reaches the mineral soil is also diminished by litter interception at the forest floor. Litter interception can be determined by sampling, but again the quantity is small relative to precipitation (except, of course, in the case of snow), so measurement accuracy is not a critical factor in the overall water budget. The amount of litter interception during any particular storm can be measured gravimetrically as the difference in litter moisture content before and after the storm.

## 10.5. Subsurface Water

The infiltration capacity of mineral soil can be estimated directly using *infiltrometers*, or indirectly through hydrograph analysis. The latter method embodies a special definition of infiltration (see section 5.1.a), and its application in connection with catchment discharge was discussed in section 7.1.b. The direct method employs either *rainfall simulators* or *flooding-type* infiltrometers.

An infiltrometer is essentially a plot of isolated soil to which water can be applied at a known rate. In the flooding type, small metal tubes or concentric cyclinders (rings) are driven into the soil, and water is applied to the isolated section at a rate sufficient to maintain constant water depth over the surface; since there is no surface discharge, the rate of water application is a measure of the infiltration capacity of the plot. In the rainfall simulation method, water is sprinkled over the surface of a larger plot (and of a boundary strip to impede lateral flow), surface discharge is measured, and the infiltration capacity is estimated as the difference between the rates of sprinkling and surface discharge.

Infiltration capacity estimates are useful in catchment hydrology simply as relative values or indices. Infiltrometer data vary greatly depending on local site conditions and infiltrometer type; it is difficult to obtain an adequate statistical sample for a catchment and, in general, the smaller the infiltrometer the greater the estimated capacity. Hydrograph analysis has the apparent advantage that the "infiltrometer" is an entire catchment, but in this case it is impossible to obtain close experimental control: the water application rate (rainfall) is highly variable, and the discharge (streamflow) may consist largely of infiltrated water that reaches the stream as subsurface flow.

There are four common methods of measuring soil moisture in the forest, but *gravimetric sampling* is the only direct one, and it is required for calibrating equipment used in *electrical-resistance*, *radioactive*, and *tensiometric* methods. In the gravimetric method a sample of soil is extracted from a given stratum and weighed before and after drying; the difference in weight is expressed as a percentage of dry weight. Since the hydrologist usually prefers to express soil moisture in units of depth, it is also necessary to measure the volume of the sample, or to determine the bulk density of the stratum.

The gravimetric method is time-consuming, but not only because of the laboratory work involved; soil moisture samples are difficult to obtain, especially in stony soils, and a great number are needed to adequately describe the variability over a catchment area. Cylindrical sampling augers of various types have been developed, some of which facilitate the work of obtaining an undisturbed core of known volume. The field work can also be reduced by rational selection of sampling points; indiscriminate or random sampling is a valid statistical concept, but there are numerous instances when it should be violated without compunction (it makes no sense to sample obvious local extremes, e.g., stream bottoms).

Indirect methods of soil moisture sampling are much used because, once the equipment has been calibrated, repeated measurements can be obtained quickly at the same place without disturbing the soil. The electrical-resistance method utilizes sensing elements (blocks) of nylon, fiberglass, or plaster of Paris in which the resistance between embedded electrodes is affected by moisture content; when the blocks are placed in close contact with mineral soil, the observed resistance is a measure of soil moisture content. Electrical-resistance sensing units are difficult to calibrate accurately, tend to deteriorate with age, and are especially unreliable at high soil moisture levels.

The most common equipment used in the radioactive sensing of soil moisture includes a source of fast neutrons that are slowed by collisions with the hydrogen nuclei in water. In practice the source is lowered into the soil through a permanent access tube along with a slow neutron detector, and the responses of the detector are transmitted to a battery-powered counter at the surface; the displayed count is a measure of soil moisture at the level of the probe. Radioactive sensing is fast, can be repeated indefinitely at the same site without disturbing the soil, and measures the moisture content in a volume of soil around the access tube; disadvantages are that the equipment is relatively expensive and requires calibration, and its use involves some radioactive hazard.

Tensiometers are inexpensive devices used to measure soil moisture suction, or tension (negative pressure), at higher moisture levels; they can also be calibrated to measure soil moisture content. A common tensiometer consists of a porous ceramic cup connected to a manometer or vacuum gauge by a water-filled tube;

Figure 10.16. Water-level recorder, float type (courtesy of Science
Associates, Princeton, N.J.).

when the cup is buried water in the tensiometer comes to equilibrium with that in the soil, and any changes in soil moisture tension are indicated by the manometer. At negative pressures less than about -800 mb (pF $\simeq$ 3) the system fails as air enters the cup; this means that the instrument's use is restricted to the range from slightly below field capacity to saturation.

Groundwater levels are measured in wells with any of several types of *water-level recorders*; the most common instrument records changes in the level of a counter-balanced float (figure 10.16). The float is attached to a perforated steel tape that moves a floatwheel in response to water-level changes; the floatwheel is geared to a pen arm that records on a clock-driven drum chart. The same instrument is used to record water stage in connection with streamflow measurements (see section 10.7).

## 10.6. Vaporization Processes

Techniques used to measure evaporation and transpiration are based on four general approaches; water budgeting, energy budgeting, vapor flow, and correlation methods. The only direct methods are those included under water budgeting (e.g., the use of evaporation pans, section 10.1.c), but these are also most artificial. Most measurements of evaporation and transpiration are point samples; the only methods that are directly applicable to land areas are those described formally in sections 2.2.b and 6.3.a for catchments and small plots.

In catchment and plot studies, vaporization losses are taken as the difference between liquid water inflows and outflows; other water-budgeting methods measure the loss as a change in water depth, or as the change in weight of a discrete evaporating system. The *Piche evaporimeter* (fig. 10.17), much used by ecologists in former times, permits water to seep from a small upright graduated cylinder onto a disc of porous paper from which it evaporates; total evaporation for any period is the observed difference in the level of the meniscus in the cylinder. Other common types of evaporimeters that measure evaporation from free water surfaces are the *evaporation recorder* (fig. 10.18), which continuously re-

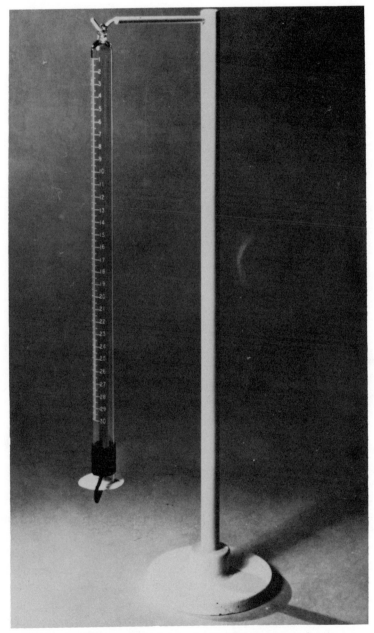

Figure 10.17. Piche evaporimeter (courtesy of Science Associates, Princeton, N.J.).

**Figure 10.18.** Evaporation recorder (courtesy of Science Associates, Princeton, N.J.).

cords the weight of a small evaporation pan, and the Livingston *atmometer*, which consists of a porous porcelain bulb that draws water from a calibrated tube or flask.

*Phytometers* and *potometers* are small vessels from which evaporation and transpiration are measured by periodic weighing. The typical phytometer is simply a small potted plant sealed to prevent evaporation from all save the aerial portions of the plant; the observed difference in weight during any drying period is an accurate measure of transpiration, but the results are specific with regard to plant type and age and microclimatological conditions, and therefore cannot be extrapolated to areas of forest land. If the phytometer soil surface is also exposed, permitting direct evaporation, the instrument is called an *evapotranspirometer*.

A large container filled with soil, resting on a weighing device, and installed with the upper surface at ground level, is called a *lysimeter*; excess water that percolates through the container is drained to a storage tank. Lysimeters may be used to measure normal evaporation rates from bare soil, or evapotranspiration from low crops or trees, or "potential" rates if water is added as necessary to maintain the soil at field capacity; the installations are usually placed within areas of soil and vegetation similar to that of the lysimeter. Lysimeters have been used mostly with low crops and small trees, but Fritschen, Cox, and Kinerson (1973) described an installation containing a 28-m tall Douglas fir tree and weighing 29 metric tons.

All of the water-budget methods yield results that are useful as indices for special purposes, but none provide the absolute data that are needed in quantitative hydrology. Catchment water budgeting does not provide rigorous results because precipitation data are generally unreliable and subsurface flows are largely unmeasurable; the other methods provide point samples, usually for artificial or atypical conditions, that can not be extrapolated to entire catchment areas. Energy-budget methods, based on the formal relations of section 2.2.c and chapter 6, and the measurements described in section 10.2, are potentially more rigorous, but estimating the required parameters for catchment areas introduces considerable uncertainty.

Vapor-flow methods, as applied under natural conditions, involve the formal relationships reviewed in chapter 6; temperature, humidity, and wind profile data are usually required, and in the combination method (equation 6.12) some additional energy-flow data are needed. The vapor-flow method may be applied under controlled conditions where greater precision can be attained—but with the risk of artificiality. A tree branch (or an entire tree) may be enclosed in a cuvette or other chamber through which air is forced at a measured rate (fig. 10.19); the absolute humidity at the

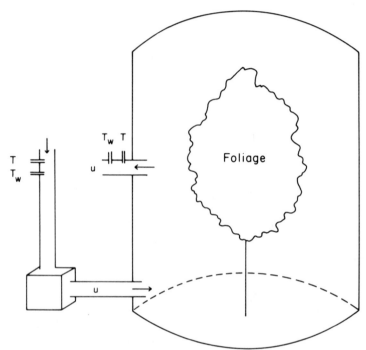

**Figure 10.19. Enclosure used to measure vaporization rates.**

entrance ($\rho_i$) and exit ($\rho_o$) are measured, and the vaporization rate ($V$) is found as

$$V = Au(\rho_o - \rho_i) \qquad (10.14)$$

where $A$ is the cross-sectional area of the inlet tube in which $u$ is the mean windspeed.

Correlation methods are an outgrowth of other methods, being based on historical records; some of the empirical relationships were given in section 6.3.c. In the simplest case, for example, it is possible to estimate daily, monthly, or annual evaporation from a standard evaporation pan with a high degree of accuracy from existing correlations with air and dew-point temperatures, solar radiation, and wind data. Unfortunately the same degree of accuracy is unattainable for catchments because no satisfactory method has ever been found to obtain the required data.

## 10.7. Streamflow Measurement

The flow of water in a natural channel may be described in terms of its stage (height of the surface above some arbitrary level), velocity (speed with respect to channel direction), or discharge rate. These properties are interrelated in that, for any particular stream segment, stage is a measure of cross-sectional area and, according to the continuity equation (equation 7.6), discharge is the product of area and velocity. Stage and velocity data are independently useful for other purposes, but more frequently they are used to determine the discharge rate.

Stream stage at any particular cross-section may be read directly from a graduated vertical scale, or *staff gage*, that is immersed in the stream at its deepest point. Usually, however, a continuous measurement of stage is required, and a water-level recorder is used; the float-type recorder (fig. 10.16) is operated in a shelter erected near the stream bank, and water is diverted from the stream through intake pipes to a *stilling well* beneath the shelter. Water in the stilling well is at the same level as that in the stream, but the float is protected from debris and waves.

Stream velocity in a natural channel is usually measured with a *current meter* in which the flowing water acts against a bucket wheel or propeller, causing it to rotate, break an electrical circuit, and activate an acoustical device or digital counting mechanism; the *pygmy current meter* (fig. 10.20) is preferred for measurements in shallow headwater streams. Approximate velocities may be obtained by timing the movement of some visible object carried by the stream; any small float, or a water-soluble dye that is easily observed, may be used for this purpose. Since stream current velocity is greatest just beneath the surface, and near stream center, a float will generally travel about 20% faster than the current average.

Stream discharge computations based on stage and velocity are complicated because stage must first be related to cross-sectional area. The practical solution is to measure depth at regular intervals across the stream, to compute the cross-sectional area ($a$) for each interval, and to obtain the average velocity ($v$) for each interval by

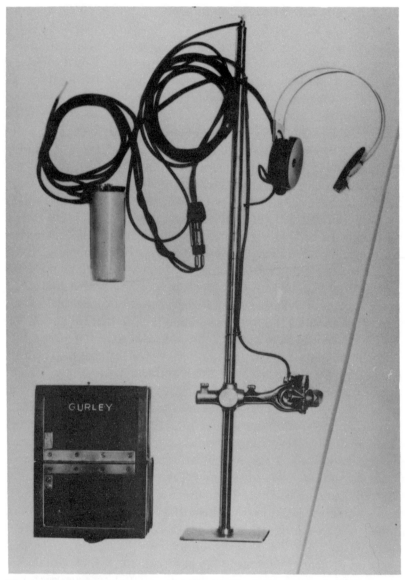

Figure 10.20. Pygmy current meter (courtesy of Science Associates, Princeton, N.J.).

taking measurements at various depths (usually at 0.2 and 0.8 of total depth); then

$$q_i = a_i v_i \qquad (10.15)$$

is the discharge rate for any interval, and

$$Q = \sum_{i=1}^{n} q_i \qquad (10.16)$$

is the discharge rate for the entire stream consisting of $n$ intervals. Once these measurements have been repeated to obtain a wide range of values, $Q$ can be related directly to stage in the form of a *stage-discharge relation* or *rating curve*; subsequently, if stream channel characteristics do not change appreciably, the rating curve can be used in lieu of other observations to obtain $Q$ as a function of stage alone.

The accuracy of a rating curve can be improved significantly if an artificial control section is placed in the stream. A *weir* is a physical obstruction that forces the flow to pass through an overflow section of precise dimensions where $Q$ is a known function of stage; sharp-crested weirs with triangular (V-notch) sections are preferred for accuracy in small streams where flow rates may be as low as 1 m$^3$/hr. The flow rate ($Q$, in m$^3$/sec) through sharp-crested V-notch weirs is

$$Q = Ch^{2.5} \qquad (10.17)$$

where $h$ (in m) is water stage above the point of zero flow, and $C$ is a coefficient that depends on the angle of the weir blade ($C = 1.38$ in the common 90° V-notch weir).

The capacity of all stream-gaging equipment may be exceeded when exceptional flooding occurs. In this case a measure of peak flow may be obtained by application of Manning's formula (equation 7.21). The water surface slope at the time of the peak can be determined from high-water marks along a reach of channel, and measurements of cross-sections are used to estimate the area and hydraulic radius.

## LITERATURE CITED

Bratzev, A. P. 1963. The influence of wind speed on the quantity of measured precipitation. *Soviet Hydrology, Selected Papers* 4:414–17.

Fritschen, L. J., L. Cox, and R. Kinerson. 1973. A 28-meter Douglas-fir tree in a weighing lysimeter. *Forest Science* 19:256–61.

Gunn, R. and G. D. Kinzer. 1949. The terminal velocity of fall for water droplets in stagnant air. *Journal of Meteorology* 6:243–48.

Koschmieder, H. 1934. Methods and results of definite rain measurements. *Monthly Weather Review* 65:5–7.

Larson, L. W. and E. L. Peck. 1974. Accuracy of precipitation measurements for hydrologic modeling. *Water Resources Research* 10:857–63.

Laws, J. O. and D. A. Parsons. 1943. The relation of raindrop size to intensity. *Transactions American Geophysical Union* 24:452–60.

Lee, R. 1969. Latitude, elevation, and mean temperature in the Northeast. *The Professional Geographer* 21:227–31.

Lee, R. 1978. *Forest Microclimatology.* New York: Columbia University Press.

Lee, R., D. G. Boyer, V. J. Valli, and W. H. Dickerson. 1979. *Global Radiation in West Virginia.* Morgantown: West Virginia University.

Repa, E. W. 1977. *The effect of circular obstructions on rainfall catch.* Master's thesis, West Virginia University, Morgantown.

Struzer, L. R., I. N. Nechayev, and E. G. Bogdanova. 1965. Systematic errors of measurements of atmospheric precipitation. *Soviet Hydrology, Selected Papers* 5:500–4.

Tanner, C. B., C. A. Federer, T. A. Black, and J. B. Swan. 1969. *Economical Radiometer Theory, Performance and Construction.* Research Report 40. Madison: University of Wisconsin.

Weiss, L. L. 1963. Securing more nearly true precipitation measurements. *Journal of Hydraulics Division, American Society Civil Engineers* HY 2:11–18.

Whillier, A. 1956. The determination of hourly values of total radiation from daily summations. *Archives of Meteorology, Geophysics, and Bioclimatology* 7:197–206.

World Meteorological Organization. 1965. Measurement of radiation and sunshine. In *Guide to Meteorological Instruments and Observing Practices.* Geneva: World Meteorological Organization.

## SELECTED READINGS

Chow, V. T., ed. 1964. *Handbook of Applied Hydrology.* New York: McGraw-Hill.

Linsley, R. K., M. A. Kohler, and J. L. H. Paulhus. 1975. *Hydrology for Engineers.* New York: McGraw-Hill.
Rodda, J. C., R. A. Downing, and F. M. Law. 1976. *Systematic Hydrology.* Boston: Butterworth.
Wadsworth, R. M. 1968. *The Measurement of Environmental Factors in Terrestrial Ecology.* Oxford: Blackwell Scientific Publications.

# APPENDIX TABLES

**Table A.1. Some Common Units and Conversions**

| Quantity | Units | Equivalent values | |
|---|---|---|---|
| Length | 1 meter (m) | 39.37 inches (in.) | 3.281 feet (ft) |
| | 1 kilometer (km) | | 3281 ft | 0.6214 miles (mi) |
| Area | 1 m$^2$ | 1550 in.$^2$ | 10.76 ft$^2$ |
| | 1 hectare (ha) | $10^4$ m$^2$ | 2.471 acres (ac) |
| | 1 km$^2$ | | 247.1 ac | 0.3861 mi$^2$ |
| Volume | 1 m$^3$ | 264.2 gallons (gal) | 35.31 ft$^3$ |
| | 1 ha-m | $10^4$ m$^3$ | 8.107 ac-ft |
| | 1 km$^3$ | | 8.107 ($10^5$) ac-ft | 0.2399 mi$^3$ |
| Mass | 1 kilogram (kg) | 35.27 ounces (oz) | 2.205 pounds (lbs) |
| | 1 metric ton | | 2205 lbs | 1.102 tons |
| Time | 1 day | 8.64 ($10^4$) seconds (sec) | 1440 minutes (min) |
| | 1 year | | 5.26 ($10^5$) min | 8766 hours (hrs) |
| Speed | 1 m/sec | 3.281 ft/sec | 196.9 ft/min | 2.237 mi/hr |
| Density | 1 g/cm$^3$ | 999 oz/ft$^3$ | 62.43 lbs/ft$^3$ | 113.3 tons/ac-in. |
| Pressure | 1 millibar (mb) | 0.7501 mm Hg | 0.0295 in. Hg | 0.0145 lbs/in.$^2$ |
| Energy | 1 calorie (cal) | 4.187 joules (J) | 3.087 ft-lbs | 3.968 ($10^{-3}$) BTU |
| Power | 1 cal/min | 4.187 J/min | 0.0698 watts (W) | |
| Energy/area | 1 langley (ly) | 1.000 cal/cm$^2$ | 0.0116 kW-hr/m$^2$ | 3.686 BTU/ft$^2$ |
| Power/area | 1 ly/min | 69.76 mW/cm$^2$ | 697.6 W/m$^2$ | 221.1 BTU/ft$^2 \cdot$ hr |
| Discharge | 1 liter/sec | 127.1 ft$^3$/hr | 2.282 ($10^4$) gal/day | 0.8406 ac-in./day |
| | 1 m$^3$/sec | 35.31 ft$^3$/sec | 22.82 ($10^6$) gal/day | 70.04 ac-ft/day |

Table A.2. Blackbody Function, $\sigma T^4$ (ly/min)

| $T(^{\circ}\text{C})$ | $\sigma T^4$ | $T(^{\circ}\text{C})$ | $\sigma T^4$ | $T(^{\circ}\text{C})$ | $\sigma T^4$ |
|---|---|---|---|---|---|
| −40 | 0.242 | −5 | 0.423 | 30 | 0.691 |
| −39 | 0.246 | −4 | 0.429 | 31 | 0.700 |
| −38 | 0.250 | −3 | 0.436 | 32 | 0.709 |
| −37 | 0.254 | −2 | 0.442 | 33 | 0.718 |
| −36 | 0.259 | −1 | 0.449 | 34 | 0.728 |
| −35 | 0.263 | 0 | 0.455 | 35 | 0.737 |
| −34 | 0.268 | 1 | 0.462 | 36 | 0.747 |
| −33 | 0.272 | 2 | 0.469 | 37 | 0.757 |
| −32 | 0.277 | 3 | 0.476 | 38 | 0.766 |
| −31 | 0.281 | 4 | 0.482 | 39 | 0.776 |
| −30 | 0.286 | 5 | 0.489 | 40 | 0.786 |
| −29 | 0.291 | 6 | 0.497 | 41 | 0.796 |
| −28 | 0.295 | 7 | 0.504 | 42 | 0.806 |
| −27 | 0.300 | 8 | 0.511 | 43 | 0.817 |
| −26 | 0.305 | 9 | 0.518 | 44 | 0.827 |
| −25 | 0.310 | 10 | 0.526 | 45 | 0.838 |
| −24 | 0.315 | 11 | 0.533 | 46 | 0.848 |
| −23 | 0.320 | 12 | 0.541 | 47 | 0.859 |
| −22 | 0.325 | 13 | 0.548 | 48 | 0.870 |
| −21 | 0.331 | 14 | 0.556 | 49 | 0.881 |
| −20 | 0.336 | 15 | 0.564 | 50 | 0.892 |
| −19 | 0.341 | 16 | 0.572 | 51 | 0.903 |
| −18 | 0.347 | 17 | 0.579 | 52 | 0.914 |
| −17 | 0.352 | 18 | 0.588 | 53 | 0.925 |
| −16 | 0.358 | 19 | 0.596 | 54 | 0.936 |
| −15 | 0.363 | 20 | 0.604 | 55 | 0.948 |
| −14 | 0.369 | 21 | 0.612 | 56 | 0.960 |
| −13 | 0.375 | 22 | 0.620 | 57 | 0.971 |
| −12 | 0.380 | 23 | 0.629 | 58 | 0.983 |
| −11 | 0.386 | 24 | 0.637 | 59 | 0.995 |
| −10 | 0.392 | 25 | 0.646 | 60 | 1.007 |
| −9 | 0.398 | 26 | 0.655 | 70 | 1.134 |
| −8 | 0.404 | 27 | 0.664 | 80 | 1.272 |
| −7 | 0.410 | 28 | 0.672 | 90 | 1.422 |
| −6 | 0.417 | 29 | 0.681 | 100 | 1.585 |

Table A.3. Daily, Seasonal, and Annual Totals of Potential Solar Radiation, ly

| Latitude (degrees) | Vernal equinox | Summer solstice | Autumnal equinox | Winter solstice | Summer half-year | Winter half-year | Annual total |
|---|---|---|---|---|---|---|---|
| 90 N | – | 1110 | – | – | 133,300 | – | 133,300 |
| 80 | 160 | 1093 | 158 | – | 134,520 | 3,240 | 137,760 |
| 70 | 316 | 1043 | 312 | – | 138,700 | 13,440 | 152,140 |
| 60 | 461 | 1009 | 456 | 51 | 149,080 | 33,620 | 182,700 |
| 50 | 593 | 1020 | 586 | 181 | 160,860 | 58,740 | 219,600 |
| 40 | 707 | 1022 | 698 | 327 | 169,710 | 84,030 | 253,740 |
| 30 | 799 | 1005 | 789 | 480 | 174,450 | 107,800 | 282,250 |
| 20 | 867 | 964 | 857 | 624 | 174,570 | 128,980 | 303,550 |
| 10 | 909 | 900 | 898 | 756 | 169,950 | 146,800 | 316,750 |
| Equator | 923 | 814 | 912 | 869 | 160,580 | 160,580 | 321,160 |
| 10 | 909 | 708 | 898 | 962 | 146,800 | 169,950 | 316,750 |
| 20 | 867 | 585 | 857 | 1030 | 128,980 | 174,570 | 303,550 |
| 30 | 799 | 449 | 789 | 1073 | 107,800 | 174,450 | 282,250 |
| 40 | 707 | 306 | 698 | 1092 | 84,030 | 169,710 | 253,740 |
| 50 | 593 | 170 | 586 | 1089 | 58,740 | 160,860 | 219,600 |
| 60 | 461 | 48 | 456 | 1078 | 33,620 | 149,080 | 182,700 |
| 70 | 316 | – | 312 | 1114 | 13,440 | 138,700 | 152,140 |
| 80 | 160 | – | 158 | 1167 | 3,240 | 134,520 | 137,760 |
| 90 S | – | – | – | 1185 | – | 133,300 | 133,300 |

NOTE: The solar constant is assumed to be 2.00 ly/min.

Table A.4. Annual Totals of Potential Solar Radiation on Slopes in the Middle Latitudes, kly

| Inclination (%) | Aspect | | | | |
|---|---|---|---|---|---|
| | N | NE–NW | E–W | SE–SW | S |
| *Latitude 30°N* | | | | | |
| 10 | 266.5 | 271.1 | 281.6 | 291.3 | 295.1 |
| 20 | 248.9 | 258.9 | 280.2 | 298.4 | 305.2 |
| 30 | 230.1 | 245.9 | 277.9 | 303.3 | 312.3 |
| 40 | 210.8 | 232.8 | 274.9 | 306.2 | 316.6 |
| 50 | 191.8 | 220.1 | 271.3 | 307.1 | 318.5 |
| 60 | 173.6 | 208.1 | 267.4 | 306.6 | 318.3 |
| 70 | 157.0 | 197.0 | 263.3 | 304.9 | 316.6 |
| 80 | 142.9 | 187.1 | 259.1 | 302.3 | 313.8 |
| 90 | 131.1 | 178.2 | 254.9 | 299.2 | 310.2 |
| 100 | 120.8 | 170.2 | 250.8 | 295.7 | 306.0 |
| *Latitude 40°N* | | | | | |
| 10 | 234.5 | 240.3 | 253.4 | 265.7 | 270.6 |
| 20 | 214.0 | 226.2 | 252.6 | 275.9 | 284.8 |
| 30 | 192.9 | 212.0 | 251.4 | 284.1 | 296.1 |
| 40 | 172.3 | 198.4 | 249.7 | 290.1 | 304.6 |
| 50 | 153.2 | 185.8 | 247.7 | 294.3 | 310.4 |
| 60 | 137.4 | 174.4 | 245.3 | 296.7 | 314.0 |
| 70 | 123.8 | 164.4 | 242.7 | 297.6 | 315.7 |
| 80 | 112.0 | 155.6 | 239.9 | 297.5 | 316.0 |
| 90 | 101.9 | 148.1 | 237.1 | 296.6 | 315.2 |
| 100 | 92.9 | 141.5 | 234.3 | 295.0 | 313.6 |
| *Latitude 50°N* | | | | | |
| 10 | 198.2 | 204.7 | 219.7 | 233.8 | 239.4 |
| 20 | 176.4 | 189.9 | 219.8 | 246.5 | 256.8 |
| 30 | 155.5 | 175.9 | 220.0 | 257.5 | 271.6 |
| 40 | 138.0 | 163.2 | 220.0 | 266.5 | 283.6 |
| 50 | 122.8 | 152.1 | 219.8 | 273.5 | 293.0 |
| 60 | 109.5 | 142.6 | 219.3 | 278.6 | 299.9 |
| 70 | 97.9 | 134.6 | 218.6 | 282.2 | 304.8 |
| 80 | 87.8 | 128.0 | 217.6 | 284.6 | 308.0 |
| 90 | 79.2 | 122.5 | 216.4 | 285.8 | 309.9 |
| 100 | 71.8 | 117.9 | 215.1 | 286.3 | 310.7 |

NOTES: Values for other latitudes and aspects were given by Frank and Lee (1966). See reference in chapter 7.
The solar constant is assumed to be 2.00 ly/min.

Table A.5. Relative Humidity (%) as a Function of Wet-Bulb Temperature ($T_w$) and Wet-Bulb Depression ($T - T_w$) at Standard Pressure

| $T - T_w$ ($^{\circ}$C) | Wet-bulb temperature ($^{\circ}$C) | | | | |
|---|---|---|---|---|---|
| | 0 | 10 | 20 | 30 | 40 |
| 0 | 100 | 100 | 100 | 100 | 100 |
| 1 | 83 | 89 | 91 | 93 | 94 |
| 2 | 68 | 78 | 83 | 86 | 88 |
| 3 | 55 | 69 | 76 | 80 | 83 |
| 4 | 43 | 60 | 69 | 75 | 78 |
| 5 | 32 | 52 | 63 | 69 | 73 |
| 6 | 23 | 46 | 58 | 65 | 69 |
| 7 | 15 | 39 | 52 | 60 | 65 |
| 8 | 8 | 34 | 48 | 56 | 61 |
| 9 | 2 | 29 | 43 | 52 | 58 |
| 10 | — | 24 | 39 | 48 | 54 |
| 11 | — | 20 | 36 | 45 | 51 |
| 12 | — | 16 | 32 | 42 | 48 |
| 13 | — | 13 | 29 | 39 | 45 |
| 14 | — | 10 | 26 | 36 | 43 |
| 15 | — | 7 | 24 | 34 | 40 |
| 16 | — | 5 | 21 | 31 | 38 |
| 17 | — | 3 | 19 | 29 | 36 |
| 18 | — | 1 | 17 | 27 | 34 |
| 19 | — | — | 15 | 25 | 32 |
| 20 | — | — | 13 | 23 | 30 |

# SUBJECT INDEX

161-64; freezing, 27, 62, 133, 136;
hydraulic conductivity, 147-53; porosity, 138-39; thermal properties, 48-49
Soil moisture: available, 139, 158-59,
179; depletion, 143-44, 161-64; field
capacity, 139; global amount, 1-2; measurement, 319-20, 322; movement,
145-50, 152-53; potential, 140, 145-
50, 164; recharge, 143-44; storage,
137-41; terminology, 137-41; wilting
point, 139
Soil moisture, related to: evaporation,
160-64; forest cover, 143-44, 161-64;
infiltration rate, 132-37; interception,
115-16, 122, 144; potential evaporation, 176, 179; stemflow, 124-25;
throughfall, 116, 122; transpiration,
161-66
Solar radiation, see Radiation, shortwave
Specific heat: air, 48-49; common materials, 48-49; ice (snow), 26-27, 48-49;
liquid water, 29, 48-49; water vapor,
31
Specific retention, 141-42
Specific yield, 142, 174
Stage: discharge relation, 192, 329; flood,
277; measurement, 321-22, 327
Stefan-Boltzmann constant, 42
Stemflow, 36, 124-25; chemical quality
of, 231; measurement, 318; and soil
moisture, 124-25
Stomata, 156, 160-62, 165-68
Storage, 38; canopy, 111-14; depth of,
190; equation, 38; groundwater, 140-
42; soil moisture, 138-41
Stormflow, see Direct runoff
Storm wind analysis, 96
Stream: bifurcation ratio, 67; classifications, 60-61; drainage density, 67,
185; laws, 64, 67; length-discharge
relation, 200; orders, 59-60; temperature, 82, 232, 235-39, 248-49; turbidity, 233; velocity measurement, 327-29
Streamflow (discharge): atmospheric influences on, 194-97; buffering capacity,
226-27; catchment influences on, 60-
68, 197-200; components, 182-86;

determinants, 194-204; effects of natural disturbances on, 269-73; forest
influences on, 15-16, 143-44, 173-74,
200-204; formal relations, 190-94;
hydrograph, 182, 186-90; interception
effect on, 115, 211-12; land use effects
on, 267-70; management influences on,
204-14; 284-86; measurement, 321-22,
327-29; natural quality of, 223-32;
processes, 182-94; quality, see Water
quality; recession, 186-90, 213-14;
regime, 196, 210-12, 284-86; storage
influence on, 143; terminology, 37;
units, 182; in water budgeting, 37-40;
see also Base flow; Direct runoff; Peak
flow; Water yield
Sublimation, 36-37, 79, 283
Subsurface flow, 37, 145-53; capillary
movement, 145-47; catchment leakage,
57-58, 205; plant influences on, 145,
173-74; to plant roots, 149-50; in
saturation zone, 150-53; in soils, 145-
50; topographic influences on, 151-53,
198; of vapor, 145, 149; in water budgeting, 38-40, 171-72; see also Interflow; Underflow
Subsurface water, 130-53; see also Groundwater; Soil moisture
Sunshine recorder, 308-9
Surface tension, 29-30, 83, 145-46

Temperature: dew-point, 74-75, 77; function, 158, 160; measurement, 300-306,
313; normal, 300, 303; wet-bulb, 75,
77, 303, 339; see also Stream, temperature; Water temperature
Temperature, related to: air density, 31-
33, 49; atmospheric water, 6, 73;
blackbody radiation, 42-45, 336; conduction, 47-49; convection, 50-52;
evaporation, 155-60; forest cover,
14, 74, 76, 232; humidity terms,
73-78; infiltration, 133, 136; latent
heats, 52; latitude and elevation, 300,
303; mining spoil rehabilitation, 274-
75; potential evaporation, 178-79;
saturation vapor density, 32-33, 179;